Interventions into Modernist Cultures

PERVERSE MODERNITIES
A series edited by Judith Halberstam and Lisa Lowe

Amie Elizabeth Parry

# Interventions into Modernist Cultures

*Poetry from Beyond the Empty Screen*

DUKE UNIVERSITY PRESS
Durham & London 2007

© 2007 Duke University Press
All rights reserved

Designed by Jennifer Hill
Typeset in Adobe Garamond by Tseng Information Systems, Inc.

Library of Congress Cataloging-in-Publication Data appear
on the last printed page of this book.

Hsia Yü: Amie Parry's English translation of Hsia Yü's poem
"Leaving on a Jet Plane" and of parts of her poem "Making Sentences"
are used by permission of the poet; Hsia Yü, "Ventriloquy": English translation
by Steve Bradbury is reprinted by permission of the translator; Yü Kwang-chung,
"Hsilo Bridge": English translation by the poet is reprinted by his permission.

# Contents

vii *Acknowledgments*

Introduction
1 Canonical Modernisms, Minor Modernisms, and the Cultural Politics of Fragmentation

One
21 The Historicity of the Fragment: Toward a Critical Comparativism

Two
44 "Completely Painted Over but Painted Full of Empty Spaces": Stein's American Allegories and the End of Progress

Three
80 "Learning a Lesson in the Superficial Song Lyrics": Hsia Yü's "Underground" Poetry

Four
113 "For the Other Overlapping Time": Pound's Ideogramic Universalism and Cha's Countermodernist Translation

Conclusion
148 The Cultural Uses of an Interventionary Poetics

153 *Notes*

171 *Works Cited*

181 *Index*

# Acknowledgments

AS I HOPE TO SUGGEST by its title, *Interventions into Modernist Cultures* foregrounds texts that make historical and epistemological interventions, and it groups together texts that are not usually seen as constituting a coherent body of literature, whether the latter is nationally, aesthetically, or thematically defined. In the long process of writing this book, I found myself faced with a wide range of challenges coming from many different directions. Dialogue with scholars in diverse fields has, therefore, been even more essential to the overall writing process than it generally is. As I worked on this project, many friends, colleagues, and former teachers offered helpful responses, too many to acknowledge adequately here. However, because of the challenges inherent in a project such as this, I would like to begin by acknowledging my own responsibility for any remaining shortcomings of this book.

I received exceptionally generous mentorship at the University of California, San Diego, that will always be invaluable to me intellectually, personally, and politically; in this regard, I would like to express my enduring gratitude to Wai-lim Yip and Michael Davidson. Page DuBois, Rosemary George, and Christena Turner provided immeasurably helpful direction on early drafts. Judith Halberstam introduced me to a more synthetic methodology for queer critique that transformed my sense of what constitutes the politics of sexuality. I continue to appreciate the unsettling difficulty of Masao Miyoshi's intellectual challenges; his responses have shaped many of the arguments in these chapters. Lisa Lowe provided uniquely astute guidance and generous encouragement that continued into this project's later stages. I would like to especially thank her for this and for compelling me to take up the ongoing task of unraveling the many subtleties of the larger social vision that directs intellectual work. Mentorship happens among peers as well as with professors, and in this regard I am deeply grateful to Helen Jun and Chandan Reddy for profoundly illuminating discussions, for their willingness to keep engaging with this project over a long course of its development, and for a truly rare quality of friendship. Finally, I would like to acknowledge the many good friends who were important interlocutors as some of the ideas developed here were first taking shape, including Kim Dillon, Kulvinder Aurora, Natalia Chan, Leo Ching, Grace Hong, Eleanor Jaluague, Berta Jottar, Michael Lin, Tracey Walker, and Randy Williams.

The initial research that eventually led me to this comparative project was funded by a Fulbright grant. I would like to thank Dr. Wu and the entire staff at the Taipei Fulbright office for kindly direction and assistance that well exceeded the call of duty and Ko Ching-ming for generously guiding my early forays into the aesthetic and social complexities of Taiwan modernism. Part of my early research was supported by the University of California Humanities Research Institute. I would like to thank Theodore Huters for organizing and leading the research group "Nationalism, Colonialism, and Modernity in East Asia: The Cases of Korea, Japan, and China." I am grateful to the members of this in-residence group—Yoko Arisaka, Chungmoo Choi, Tak Fujitani, James Fujii, Gail Hershatter, Lisa Rofel, Shu-mei Shih, Miriam Silverberg, and Lisa Yoneyama—for their helpful comments on my work and overall research direction. The National Science Council, Taiwan, funded much of the subsequent research on theories of modernity and aesthetics as well as making it possible for me to present some of the material from these chapters at international conferences. And, for providing a truly congenial space for reading and intellectual discussion, I would like to thank the owner and staff of Norwegian Wood.

My teaching and research environment in Taiwan has fostered intellectual exchange of the highest quality. I would like to thank all my colleagues at the Foreign Languages and Literatures Department of National Chiao Tung University, especially Ying-hsiung Chou and Pin-chia Feng. The sections of chapter 4 on Ezra Pound were largely written during a research leave at Academia Sinica's Institute of European and American Studies. I would like to thank that institution for its support and Yuan Wen Chi, Wen-ching Ho, Yu-Cheng Lee, and Te-Hsing Shan for feedback and friendly lunchtime discussions. At the English Department at National Central University, I thank David Barton and Dave Stuart for enlightening conversation about the Western philosophical canon and public cultures of reading, respectively; and I thank Steven Bradbury and Susanna Kuan for enlivening conversation that made commuting pleasurable and educational. At Central and beyond, I am grateful to all those involved with the interdisciplinary and interinstitutional Center for the Study of Sexualities and the Cultural Studies Center. In addition to Josephine Ho and Kuan-hsing Chen, I can offer only an abbreviated list of those members and affiliates to whom I am intellectually indebted: Asha Achuthan, Antonia Chao, Spencer Lin, Fran Martin, Jiazhen Ni, Karl Yin-Bin Ning, Cindy Patton, Wang Ping and all those involved with G/S RAT, Rob Wilson, and Jonathan Yeh. I would like to offer special words of gratitude to Naifei Ding and Jen-peng Liu; their brilliance has brightened my work and my life, as it has for so many other scholars around the globe. I also appreciate the intellectual community provided by Teri Silvio and her media studies reading group. I feel uniquely grateful to Ru-Hong Lin for a contribution to this manuscript that was simultaneously intellectual and of another more rare quality that cannot be adequately described here. Conversations with Lucifer Hung have left their baroque mark on my argument's queerer moments. I thank Chen Ting for her translation of part of chapter 4, which made it possible for me to publish an article in Chinese, and for her clarifying comments on the manuscript. I also thank Hsia Yü for her insistence that my translations of her poetry capture, as much as is possible, the subtlety of her language. Finally, for valuable research assistance and for thoughtful questions that have influenced my thinking on these matters, I thank the graduate students Jaren Lin, Emma Liu, David Tsai, and especially Richard Hsu, who also helped edit the manuscript.

I acknowledge Perseus Books and Chiao Tung University Press for permission to reprint early versions of sections from chapter 2 and chapter 4. I am deeply grateful to my editors at Duke University Press. Ken Wissoker recognized the potential of this project at its earliest stage and saw it through to maturity; his foresight and his suggestions have been invaluable. At the later stages, Anitra Grisales and Pam Morrison provided helpful and patient direction, while Joseph Brown's meticulous copyediting greatly improved the quality of the manuscript. I would also like to thank the two anonymous reviewers, whose engaged and detailed commentaries helped tremendously in fleshing out the ramifications of argument.

I would like to conclude by acknowledging those who influenced and encouraged me at personally formative stages. First, I thank Mr. Taylor for being the first to bravely suggest an unlikely course of intellectual development for me and William Cheek for permanently transforming my understanding of U.S. history and culture. I am grateful to Maureen Wang for her steadfast support during a vital and challenging time. For enduring friendship I thank Eva Caraher and Glenda Hsu. For his always-inspiring intelligence during the final years of writing this book, I thank Jim Chou. I thank my sister, Melissa, for always challenging me to ask the difficult questions and for our shared attempts to answer them. Finally, I dedicate this book to the memory of my father, whose delight would have been unparalleled if he had seen its publication, and to my mother, whose continuing support has been unfaltering on every level, for which I am forever grateful.

Introduction

Canonical Modernisms, Minor Modernisms, and the Cultural Politics of Fragmentation

GERTRUDE STEIN'S *The Geographical History of America* employs many paradoxical statements about the time and space of modernity, such as: "Progress is just that, it has come to go away and so here we are now . . ." (129). Such statements can be read as critical in their parodic appropriation of a masculinist nationalist historiographic voice, or, because the modern is, for Stein, most paradigmatically American, they can be read as an uncritical restatement of American exceptionalism. My concern in this study, however, is not to discover any author's intentionality, for example, whether Stein bought into the nationalist ideologies of her time (nor do I think that, if it could ever be known by literary critics, this kind of intentionality determines the critical possibilities and limitations of any literary text). Instead, I find the question of the cultural politics of modernism important for contemporary readers precisely because these texts make explicit how, before the intellectual community at large had to scrutinize fascistic strains in populist sentiments as well as those in elitist (and "mythological") aesthetic theories, being critical of modernity was as often taken up in a reactionary mode as in a progressive one. I take up the formal term *modernism* in this book because it registers this form as a critical response to modernity, and it is just such a response that, although its content varies greatly, is shared by the wide range of poetic texts that constitute the subject of this study.

In taking up modernism as a critical project, my intent in this book is to theorize the exclusionary cultural politics of U.S. literary modernism by situating that canon in a historicized comparative context that allows it to be analyzed alongside alternative representations of the modern in experimental writing from Taiwan and U.S. minority writing. In other words, I do not use the term *modernism* to refer to a literary movement in and of itself. In fact, no such movement existed in the U.S. context. Rather, there were many different movements, all of which were later placed under the umbrella term *modernism* because to a certain extent they shared some formal characteristics: a difficult, experimental, and fragmented form, combined with a highly subjective response to perceived breakdowns in realism's developmental narrative, its underlying sense of progress, its unified subject, and its faith in objective knowledge. Literary critics have pointed out that this formal difficulty reflects a representational crisis. In previous readings of modernism, this formal difficulty has been seen as registering a turn toward the abstruse, subjective realities of the psyche and, consequently, as a turn away from historical context. More recently, such a clear-cut distinction between subjective representation and objective history has been called into question in studies of modernism. What this debate has illuminated is that in certain contexts the temporality of historical knowledge and historical memory itself takes the form of juxtaposition rather than development. What this debate has glossed over, however, is the range of types of cultural politics that such a formal structure can accommodate.

These previous studies form an important inquiry into the psychic effects of industrialization, especially those that read the content *through* the literary form.[1] This content includes such themes as alienated man, meaningless work, changing sexual identifications and self-understandings, unsolvable ethical dilemmas, and the loss of any sense of "progress." The form typically is that of temporal rupture and fragmentation narrated in such a way as to call attention to the loss of objectivity or the questioning of objective knowledge. This form creates an aesthetic of emptiness that is often contrasted with the fullness of the developmental, realist novel: since literary fragments are, by definition, images taken out of context, their presence evokes the *absence* of context. This aesthetic emptiness is read as addressing a modernist sense of loss related to the experience of alienation, the meaninglessness of work or social conditions, new forms of sexual anxiety accompanying changing gender roles that make self-knowledge an impossible task, etc. The more critical contributions of inquiries into the link between aesthetic fragmentation and psychological conditions include a theorization of reversals and endings. Specifically, there is what I would call the *reversal of the subject/object binary* (usually referred to as the *loss of unified subjectivity*) and the perceived breakdown of Western developmental narratives. In this kind of modernist criticism, the form itself is seen as inherently subversive because it is believed either to reflect the breakdowns in or to challenge dominant cultural narratives (the latter being based on the assumption of the enlightened progress of Western culture toward a more perfect civilization). This reading of the aesthetics of fragmentation thus repeats the modernist critical stance, as literary criticism takes up a project similar to that of the modernist literary texts.

Recently, critics like Fredric Jameson have more broadly historicized the modernist representational crisis by arguing that it is brought about through necessarily incomplete imperialist structures of knowledge—that a significant part of Western history, the history of imperialism and colonialism, was unknown, or could not come into representation as such, in "high culture" (although it did in other kinds of cultural narratives, such as the sea voyage novel). These arguments are based on British texts and usually do not include any sustained examination of minority or non–First World texts, not to mention texts that are not written in English. This book takes up what has been left out of the arguments that intend to read modernism in its global context of production and circulation, not by including more sites of cultural production per se, but, on the contrary, by specifying one possible critical comparative context for understanding its avowedly internationalist cultural politics. In response to recent readings of modernism in relation to imperialism, one of my points of departure is that imperialist structures of knowledge circulate differently in the modernism of U.S. writers, considering that the U.S. imperialistic histories are quite distinct from those of the British Empire and that the political and popular discourses on U.S. imperialism were characterized by exceptionalism until after World War II (with the United States framed as a fundamentally anticolonial nation, as opposed to the British Empire, even after its expansion into the Pacific). My more central concern, however, is to demonstrate that reading U.S. canonical modernism in critical juxtaposition to that of Cold War U.S. minority immigrant writing and avant-garde writing from Taiwan illuminates how the very formation and signification of the modern exceeds the geopolitical grounds of its own self-referentiality; the modern is made meaningful from more than one site and, thus, has more than one relation to the norms that it creates and upholds, paradoxically denying the hybridity of its own formation. This book is an attempt to address one context for that formation.

This study differs from a more traditionally comparative one in that it does not anchor its comparison in thematic parallels or in literary influences. It does account for these, but by reading both as deriving from historical sources. I argue that both are symptomatic of a suppressed history linking these two sites of modernity. This is the history of U.S. imperialist expansions and colonial formations in Asia, which were beginning to form by the time the earliest U.S. modernists were writing, and that of the U.S. Cold War neocolonial military presence and economic and political influence in East Asia such as in post-1949 Taiwan. U.S. neocolonialism has been overlooked as a context for Taiwan's modernism of the 1960s and after. This neglect is part of a larger historiographic one: in his recent *Parallax Visions*, the Korea scholar Bruce Cumings has documented the history of the historiographic blind spots that have characterized understandings of the United States in East Asia in the twentieth century. My study pursues questions that historical research in itself cannot explore, however, by arguing that these suppressed histories are, in fact, known but that they are known in an obscured and fragmented mode rather than through more immediately legible cultural narrations that are developmental, realist, or *triumphalist* (I borrow the latter term from Edward Said's description of narrations of the British Empire). Such fragmented knowledge formations of U.S. imperialist and neocolonial modernity, and their implicit critiques (whether progressive or reactionary), come into representation in cultural forms now labeled *modernist* (rather than *realist, historical, factual,* etc.).

Unlike previous scholars who have also seen modernism as a critical project, I argue, not that modernist form's challenge to developmental narratives is unconditionally or inherently subversive, but that it can be put to interventionary ends in minor modernisms. One goal of my inquiries into the already much-studied canon, then, is to explore the more neglected question not only of how the breakdown of developmental form registers the fragmentation of the subject in universalist terms but also of how the very universalism of that breakdown performs a dominant function in managing and erasing the heterogeneity of less recognized imperialist histories that are formative of its own status as the voice of modernity. Exploring this latter function of nondevelopmental form makes it possible to understand how an elite internationalist modernist culture can define itself as such in explicitly historical terms while performing historical erasures. Most important, this study aims to distinguish adequately the distinct forms of emptiness and repetition that constitute different types of modernist or avant-garde writing in order to understand how apparently similar aesthetic forms can be put to vastly different ends in cultural politics. The national contexts of the United States and Taiwan and their historical, political, and social realities are constitutive of the spheres of cultural politics that these texts participate in. However, I want to begin by acknowledging that some of the texts, most notably those that can be labeled *minor*, complicate and raise questions about what constitutes a national culture, or a modernist movement, or a formation of modernity.

Although far from being contained to the field of modernist literary criticism, work on the subject of *minor literature* and *minority discourse* has provided an important paradigm for reading nondevelopmental texts. This area of research itself is very differentiated, but one crucial difference that can be posited between it and modernist criticism is that, for minority discourse, the critique of modernity contains no lament for modernity's lost Enlightenment project. In their influential essay "What Is a Minor Literature?" Gilles Deleuze and Félix Guattari warn that literary movements often aspire "to assume a major function in language, to offer themselves as a sort of state language, an official language (for example, psychoanalysis today which would like to be master of the signifier, of metaphor, of wordplay)" (27). This major function is also referred to as a *canonical function*. In contrast to the major or canonical function of literature, Deleuze and Guattari famously define a minor literature as one that is *deterritorialized*. In his essay "Genet's Genealogy," David Lloyd helpfully schematizes Deleuze and Guattari's definition of a minor literature as "the questioning or destruction of the concepts of identity and identification, the rejection of representations of developing autonomy and authenticity, if not the very concept of development itself, and accordingly a profound suspicion of narratives of reconciliation and unification" (381). Lloyd's and Abdul JanMohamed's theorization of minority discourse in the introduction to *The Nature and Context of Minority Discourse*, in which "Genet's Genealogy" appeared, builds on this critique of the ways in which the canonical function of developmentalism supports the unseen representational violences of liberal humanism. Also helpful as a theorization of minority discourse in this sense is Paul Gilroy's discussion of a black modernism in *The Black Atlantic*, including his chapters on the transnational intellectual formation and contributions of Richard Wright and W. E. B. Du Bois as well as his attention to how Toni Morrison's historiographic intervention in *Beloved* is carried out in a highly experimental form. Although these approaches are usually seen as disparate, my method in this book involves combining them because they all foreground in different ways the critical potential of experimental aesthetics; however, I do this in order to understand the neglected issue of how nondevelopmental forms can also perform a canonical function. I therefore use *minor* and *canonical* to distinguish the different kinds of cultural politics carried out in texts that use a similar experimental and fragmented literary form. In this study, I use the term *canonical* not to refer to a text's status within an established literary canon but according to Lloyd and JanMohamed's definition of the canonical function and how it can be countered in minority discourse.

This book analyzes the cultural politics of canonical modernism, especially that of the United States, as a first step in the larger project of attempting to understand how modernist formal structures have been taken up and differently elaborated in writing from Taiwan and in immigrant Asian American writing. For this reason, methodologically it is not exactly a comparative study of the poetry of two national contexts. My intention is to upset that paradigm in the interest of pursuing other lines of epistemological inquiry that follow the trajectories of nonnormative sexuality and what in *Siting Translation* Tejaswini Niranjana has termed *interventionary translation*, both discussed later in this introduction and the latter at greater length in chapter 4. On the one hand, my readings thus highlight the extent to which the international modernism of expatriate writers is also importantly grounded in specifically U.S. discourses of empire and their material histories. On the other, they foreground the hybridity addressed by the modernist aesthetics of Hsia Yü and Theresa Hak Kyung Cha rather than, for example, reading Hsia Yü's emphasis on sexuality as transparently representative of a Taiwanese feminism.[2] My goal here is to counter the tendency toward maintaining a fundamentally First World designation of international modernist culture, however "expanded," and instead to account for the complex particularities of hybrid writing that such a tendency renders illegible.

The hybridity registered in texts such as Cha's and Hsia Yü's is formed out of the layered temporality of what, by adapting Néstor García Canclini's definition of *hybrid cultures* to different contexts (see his *Hybrid Cultures*), I will refer to as *neocolonial modernities*. The term *modernity* is understood throughout this book as a condition of society with political structures and economic systems formed through specific colonial and imperialist histories. Chapter 1 outlines how the imperialist histories of the pre–World War II United States, which have been designated as taking on the forms of *internal colonialism* and *imperial anticolonialism*, and the experience in Taiwan of Western imperialism, Japanese colonialism, Kuomintang (KMT, the Kuomintang, or the Nationalist Party) occupation, and U.S. neocolonialism cannot be entirely accounted for from within the inside-outside model of metropolis and colony developed for the nineteenth-century peak of the British Empire and for similar colonial ventures by European nations.[3] New models are needed, and in recent years have begun to be developed, for these sites, especially the former. As mentioned in chapter 1, my project is not one of developing a historiographic model as such. Rather, partly by drawing on these new models, I mean to examine the importance of nondevelopmental representational problematics to the epistemological frameworks of these formations of modernity.

Previous studies that have foregrounded the relation between modernism and modernity are important because they allow a modernist position to be distinguished from a modern one by way of the former's critical stance toward modern society; in this way, these studies posit the subversive potential of modernism.[4] However, in contrast to most previous work on modernism, my analysis follows a broadened conceptualization of the material conditions of modernity by always conceiving of modernity as formed through ongoing transformations in and legacies of imperialism and colonialism. It also further specifies *Western modernism* to account for the distinct historical formations of modernist writings discussed in the following chapters. When Western modernism is approached from this understanding of its contexts, it becomes apparent that even the more general subversive critical stance of Anglo-American canonical modernism also erases alternative historical meanings and trajectories other than the narratives of history—narratives based on progress and increasing enlightenment—that it subversively marks the "end" of. I argue that, in carrying out this kind of historical erasure, the emptiness and repetition of a modernist text can be critical (by marking the end of the progress of Western civilization, etc.) while performing the canonical function of asserting a nondevelopmental universalism (by representing its own end as a universal condition or excluding other representational possibilities in asserting its own self-containment). As discussed above with regard to modernist scholarship, many critics have taken up the difficult task of offering definitions of *modernism* as a movement within the Western canon with aesthetically distinguishable features or philosophical groundings.[5] In distinction to that approach, I consider this nondevelopmental universalism to be the designation of canonical *modernist culture*, which can be understood as a feature of the ongoing self-construction of Western culture as such.

Bruno Latour has referred to one aspect of the limits of what I'm calling *canonical modernism* by theorizing a modern critical stance as one that includes a critical response to modernity based on a singular ("one-dimensional") dialectic that brings about a reversal of terms without challenging the overall structure that produces the terms and their oppositions. Latour's formulation sheds light on the limits of modernism's critical project. For example, Pound's modernist reversals and a related strategy of the displacement of reversal into a nondevelopmental (and nondialectical) universalism will be considered in this light in chapter 4. In chapter 2, I examine how Stein seems to evade the logic of reversal by a refusal of the value of what is felt to have been lost in modern society, yet inadvertently retains part of that value in the redeployment of a revised but still importantly self-contained domesticity. Latour's model, however, does not address how noncanonical modernist writing includes that critique and its reversals but also brings in other dialectical fields, otherwise obfuscated by, yet also indicated in, the flatness, emptiness, and absences that characterize modernist culture (although his concept of the *hybrids* may be leading in this direction). The texts that I discuss are similarly modernist only in the sense of calling into question an underlying narrative of progress and development (although that narrative is not necessarily identified as a temporality of modernity per se in Hsia Yü's work) and in using an aesthetic of repetition, emptiness, or apparent nonsense in order to do so. Yet Cha's and Hsia Yü's encompass *and* go beyond that modernist critique, by which I mean indicating or entering the dimensions, micro- or macrostructural, that are erased in its canonical forms of emptiness and repetition. These dimensions are not those of a lost, more integrated modern (or premodern) tradition and its values but those of displaced histories and knowledges that have been suppressed by dominant or emergent universalist discursive systems. In the case of the United States, these suppressive discursive systems include canonical developmentalism *and* the modernist culture that believes itself to have superceded the modern.[6] In Hsia Yü's experimental poetry, on the other hand, the lack of a critique of modernity per se (an explicit component in Stein, Pound, and Cha) indicates the limits of that critique as it has been developed in Anglo-American and European critical traditions and leads us to another understanding of modernity as less transparent and fully established—one that may, indeed, prove the exception that reveals the rule. Chapter 4 distinguishes Cha's explicit presentation of modernity from that found in canonical modernism by critically juxtaposing Cha's modernist translation with Pound's. This unlikely comparison brings out the interventionary contributions of Cha's historiographic project with relation to modernist culture.

One goal of drawing these distinct projects together in one book is to discern some sense of the range of ways in which modernist form can be mobilized in the difficult project of rendering legible otherwise disavowed histories, knowledges, and differences and to account for how that range is no accident but determined by historical relations among the sites of cultural production and circulation. Unlike the pluralist definition, *difference* as I am defining it marks the failures and breakdowns in nationalist and imperialist structures of meaning; therefore, it arises out of what can be termed the *temporal disjunctures* of a given formation of modernity. With the term *disjuncture* I am suggesting that the breakdown in meaning is both temporal and representational. Disjuncture marks the point at which developmental narratives of history as progressive, forward movement cannot be maintained. Additionally, the representational fullness of subjecthood cannot be as effectively maintained within faltering developmental narratives, and, instead, it becomes something else; for example, it can become the paradoxical, modernist self-containment that I discuss with regard to Stein's "characters," portraits, and objects. The temporal aspect of difference is marked both within the modernist culture that registers an end to developmental narratives and within those narratives' less seamless, but perhaps, therefore, all the more urgent, deployment in the more layered and strained temporality of the modern in minor texts. Importantly for this project, Homi Bhabha has in *The Location of Culture* termed temporal breakdown *postcolonial time lag* (see esp. 236–56). Bhabha defines *time lag* as the disruptive temporality of the colonial site, a temporality that interrupts the teleological structure of progress and the homogeneous space of the present, both of which underlie the narrations of nations. He argues that it is from the time lag of postcolonial sites that modernity and its ways of understanding itself (based on spatial metaphor) must be reformulated. In the following chapters, I will suggest that time lag opens up the possibility for a Benjaminian type of allegory, one that is premised on a nondevelopmental temporality, to be mobilized as a strategy that brings the ruinous histories and other knowledges of this time lag into articulation. Instead of reading the texts as being fully contained by the temporal crisis that marks them, however, I look at the ways in which their temporal structures and spatial categories produce new knowledge by rescripting time as well as space. In some instances, the rescripting of time is achieved by spatializing it in order to replace a modernist lament for the lost vertical, teleological colonial time with a horizontal conceptualization of alternative modernities. This spatialization is not a pluralist one, however, because the alternative modernities are not positioned as formally equivalent; rather, it is their inequivalences and unequal relations that are articulated in these representations. Bhabha's formulation, however, lacks the kind of specification that would account for, or at least open up discussion toward an account of, how time lag might take on different forms and signify differently depending on its context.[7] To account for how this rescripting works, my concern with time difference in each chapter is based on a consideration of the specificities of each historical context.

Kumkum Sangari has developed a formulation of temporal breakdown that distinguishes between its significance in postcolonial and Western locations and theorized it in relation to literary techniques. In "The Politics of the Possible," Sangari uses the term *cultural simultaneity* to indicate a "historical sedimentation" that is "the restless product of a long history of miscegenation, assimilation, and syncretization *as well as* of conflict, contradiction and cultural violence" (217). She demonstrates how, in contradistinction to simultaneity, "the synchronic time of the modern and postmodern in the West is an *end* product of the now discredited linear time of modernity and progress" that "takes shape through the conglomerative modality of collage" (219). This distinction between simultaneous and synchronic time begins to unravel the different ends to which modernist form is put in the texts that come under consideration in the following chapters. The notion of synchronic time is also helpful for interrogating the project of self-definition inherent to modernist cultures. As Sangari writes, with reference to the representational effects of empire in British and, perhaps, European contexts:

> Modernism is a major act of self-definition, made at a time when colonial territories are being reparceled and emergent nationalisms are beginning to present the early outlines of decolonization. As a cultural ensemble, modernism is assembled, in part, through the internalization of jeopardized geographical territory—which is now incorporated either as "primitive" image/metaphor or as mobile nonlinear structure. Though intended as a critique, such incorporation often becomes a means for the renovation of bourgeois ideology, especially with the institutionalization of modernism. (241)

Sangari thus suggests that, however obscure, subjective, and psychological the canonical modernism of synchronic time may be, its aestheticism is precisely a way to manage a historically derived predicament. For the purposes of my study, a part of this predicament is the way in which it is necessarily caught up in the problematic of attempting to construct an East/West binary and only somewhat escapes falling under the shadows of the violent histories that it must disavow when it participates in, rescues, or helps construct that elite terrain called *Western culture*. The historically reductive East/West binary, however, is not simply false; rather it is emblematic of the discursive system that twentieth-century writers and intellectuals on both sides of the symptomatic East/West divide have had to work with, and the extent to which my project is a comparative one is a result of the importance that I place on addressing precisely this problem, which persists into the present.[8] As Kuan-hsing Chen has recently stated: "The imaginary 'the West and the Rest' problematic still occupies our psychic-cultural space. The West has to be dealt with not so much as a geographical entity but as emotionally charged imaginary" ("The Decolonization Question," 31).[9]

I see these modernisms' appropriation of their respective "others" (in the attempt to make sense of what are considered new experiences that can no longer be put into language according to conventional literary methods) as symptomatic of this divide's prevalence as an epistemological structure. One way of expressing something emphatically new is to appropriate a space long considered other in order to redefine the parameters and environs of the self. Although this is not the focus of my discussion throughout these chapters, during the literary period known as *modernism*, influential U.S. modernists from the 1910s on, often writing as expatriates, did turn to "China" to develop what some considered to be a significantly American poetic language.[10] After World War II, and into the 1960s (most often considered the decade of modernism in Taiwan) and 1970s, influential Taiwan-based poets, some of whom would participate in establishing modernist schools of poetry, turned to "America" to develop a Chinese modernism that would be ideologically distinct from mainland literature (but not necessarily culturally distinct from a Chinese literary tradition). However, this kind of influence in itself is not central to my analyses in this book. This is because I believe that it should not be taken as the source of modernist cultural production. Rather, it should be understood as a symptom or effect of one manifestation of the East/West binary within a larger field of historical determinants. The use of an unhistoricized paradigm of literary influence would actually *mask* the historical concerns that motivate this study by reifying an East/West binary as *cultural difference* rather than exploring the heterogeneity of cultural forms and their social and political meanings produced in imperialistically formed modernities. It is the latter task that the following chapters take up. Further, none of the texts considered here is fully described by the project of national or geopolitical self-definition. For this reason, my readings explore the ways in which some writings—especially those that address the alternative knowledge formations that emerge out of sexual alterity and what I'm calling *translation*—grapple for language within a given system and create new meanings that challenge the erasures accomplished by the East/West binary structure in both its developmental and its modernist expression. In fact, one reason for analyzing the cultural politics of experimental literary form is precisely to gauge the range (from directly challenging to noncritical) of responses that nondevelopmental forms can accommodate to the discursive violences of the East/West epistemological structure.

Sangari's distinction between postcolonial simultaneity and imperialist synchronicity acknowledges distinct types of temporal disjuncture without attributing them to essential qualities according to a binary model of difference. Moreover, by grounding this argument in historical conditions, Sangari also points toward an understanding of how, like any epistemological construct, an East/West binary grows out of material conditions and, equally, shapes subjects' understandings of reality and affects historical events. Therefore, although that binary—which Latour refers to as the *second great divide* after nature/culture—should not be reified as a reality in itself, I believe that it must be addressed in a project such as this one in order for its erasures to be adequately critiqued and to understand the more complex uses to which its apparently simple formula is put. One salient reason for its importance is that, ironically, when historical conditions have produced exceptionally layered and simultaneous cultural formations such as Taiwan's, it can be just such a binary that provides a clarifying framework, one that can make tenable necessary oppositional positions that otherwise might be largely obscured and difficult.[11] This may be the case because, in Taiwan, opposition to the West as such is not as readily produced as it is in postcolonial locations where colonialism consisted of a single, formal administrative colonialism by a Western nation.[12] In post–World War II Taiwan, whether that opposition is produced ultimately depends on the positioning of a given movement within the internal, complex organization of society. However, generally, the West as a target of critique may not be so immediately recognizable in the more distant aftermath of layered imperialist conquests and less formal occupation by Western powers, just after fifty years of Japanese colonialism, during KMT martial law, and at the beginning of the implementation of a strikingly successful U.S. neocolonialism.[13] Unlike formal colonialism, it is the nature of neocolonialism that, the more effective it is, the more invisible. Taiwan is, thus, a singularly important site in any study of U.S. neocolonialism because of the notable difficulty in waging effective intellectual critique of U.S. imperialism; a difficulty resulting, as Kuan-hsing Chen has shown, from Taiwan's Cold War formation and its pervasive anticommunism, which has been kept very much alive because of the ongoing perceived threat from the mainland (see "Missile Internationalism," 184).

A central thesis of the following chapters is that the relative invisibility of neocolonialism and the erased narration of U.S. imperialism can be traced in cultural texts through the combined axis of sexuality and translation (the latter understood in the broader theoretical sense as the site of disparate and even incommensurate yet overlapping structures of knowledge formed through imperialist histories). My project takes up sexuality and translation as the loci of complex and conflicting epistemes that, when figured through a minor modernism, can displace and challenge the erasures of U.S. neocolonialism in modernist cultures. This is accomplished not only by naming the United States as the agent of neocolonialism but also by shifting epistemological frames in the attempt to account for "impossible" knowledges and practices that are, nevertheless, made possible in particular formations of modernity. The minor texts that I analyze take up the difficult task of addressing histories, conditions, practices, and identity formations that, although produced in relation to modernist cultures, are derived out of social formations alterior to those that are recognized as knowledge producing and culturally legible. Specifically, I examine to what extent nonnormative sexuality might be positioned as alterior to the epistemological frameworks of a universalizing normative sexuality (inclusive of but not limited to heterosexuality) in a given context.[14] Likewise, I argue that interventionary translation as a form of minor modernist writing can be taken up to shift epistemological structures and, thus, address knowledges that exceed both developmental historiographies and a more recent nondevelopmental universalism. In chapters 2 and 3, I analyze how certain formations of nonnormative sexuality can generate interventions in the cultural logics that they exceed, including critical modernist ones. In chapter 4, I turn to the hard-to-discern knowledges that constitute *translative writing*, which I define as writing that intervenes in the historiographic normativity of nondevelopmental universalism. Further, however unexpected this convergence might appear to be, the distinct foci of translation and sexuality have significant interconnections. Sexual alterity operates in some of the following texts as a kind of translative hybridity bringing together "impossible" frameworks for identity and practices. Translation, in turn, provides a complex mapping of modernist universalism that foregrounds the role of sexuality and gender within it.

The range of literary forms that can carry out this highly synthetic intervention I refer to as *allegorical writing*, following Walter Benjamin's definition of *allegory* from "Trauerspiel and Tragedy" in *The Origin of German Tragic Drama*. Benjamin describes allegory as being nondevelopmental and, perhaps most famously (and most allegorically), as a form in which words in texts function as ruins do in history. Part of Benjamin's definition of *allegory* is his formulation of the allegorical image, which works in a counter-representational way to defy the fullness of meaning in literary symbolics. We might now say that the allegorical image signifies the slippages (what Benjamin refers to as *loss*) in signification. Benjamin was not concerned with the question of sexuality; however, Chandan Reddy, drawing on Benjamin, has theorized sexuality allegorically as a narrative repository of the contradictions of colonial histories—a formulation that I will take up especially in my reading of Hsia Yü's poetry. The centrality of allegorical, nondevelopmental forms in my project accounts for its focus on poetry: in its formal elements, poetry resists development and replaces it with juxtaposition and association, presenting paradox, contradiction, or conflicting epistemes without the demand to resolve them in a developmental logic. Taken out of that metanarrative, poetic images thus have the potential to counter, in this allegorical sense, the meaningfulness of the symbol and the representational logics that prop up its meaningfulness. One possible reason for the neglect of poetry in critical postcolonial studies is its lack of popularity, especially compared to novels and film, which makes it difficult to read as broadly representative of its context. In this project, however, I am especially interested in texts that are not typical of their times and that are representative not of existing dominant knowledge structures but of critical alternative or emerging universalist ones.[15] Accordingly, this is not to argue the completely insupportable claim that all poetry is critical of dominant knowledge structures. Rather, it is to argue that, both aesthetically (in not requiring narrative development and resolution) and materially (in the sense that it is relatively cheap to produce and not expected to sell widely), poetry is particularly well suited to facilitating a critique of the long-standing discourses of progress that buttress these formations of modernity.

One salient effect of poetry's use of juxtaposition rather than narrative is that it can represent contradiction without resolving it through development; it thus can become a vehicle for representing contradictions that are glossed over or resolved by existing dominant narratives of modernity.[16] In the present study, I explore, on the one hand, how poetic cultural texts are particularly capable of bringing contradictions denied in other discursive arenas (including realist and novelistic cultural production) into representation and, on the other, how fragmentation can work not only to represent contradiction but also to sublate it, depending on the type of cultural politics at work in the text in question.

However, by focusing on poetry, I am not suggesting that only poetry operates in this way. The highly experimental prose passages that constitute most of *Dictee* are an example of allegorical prose (although this novel does contain sections and chapters that are clearly written as poems and, indeed, is sometimes referred to as a poem or a poetic text). By emphasizing the formal qualities of poetry, I am not so much interested in contributing to scholarly debates on what precise distinction, if any, can be made between it and prose. Rather, my concerns lie in trying to account for the possibilities opened up by nondevelopmental form that juxtaposes, rather than concluding or resolving, its contents, and this kind of form is found often in poetic texts. Nevertheless, poetry has been overwhelmingly absent in recent studies of politics and aesthetics in the various fields influenced by postcolonialism. This study's primary focus on poetry is intended as a corrective to this oversight. A second qualification to my thesis on poetry is the recognition, explained above, that not all poetic or nondevelopmental texts are allegorical according to our definition, even though their nondevelopmentalism may be formed as such precisely in response to the impingement of allegorical knowledges on them. On the contrary, I argue that, not entirely unlike the developmental narratives it seems to replace, a canonical modernist poetics presents new paradoxical forms of self-containment and universalism with which the minor modernist texts that can be called *allegorical* are inherently at odds; it is the latter problematic that is central to the following chapters.

Chapter 1, "The Historicity of the Fragment: Toward a Critical Comparativism," begins with a reading of the poem "Hsilo Bridge" by the Taiwan-based Chinese modernist poet Yü Kwang-chung in order to sketch out how, and to what distinguishable ends, the very irresolution and discontinuity of modernist form perform the historiographically significant task of opening up representational possibilities for fragmented knowledge, memory, and experience suppressed by the formal structures of other representational means and more dominant discourses of progress in the context of rapid industrialism under U.S. neocolonialism. This is followed by a consideration of Ezra Pound's "Hugh Selwyn Mauberley" to show how knowledge of U.S. imperialism in Asia becomes obscured and fragmented as this imperialism is discursively denied. I argue that canonical modernism like Pound's is not a complete break from realism to the extent that it reasserts a new form of nondevelopmental universalism in its fragmented representation, in this case, of the "oblivion" of some South Pacific islands. Pound's persona's critical relation to narratives of modernity still asserts a privileged claim as the voice of that critique, attempting to relegate to the realm of the provincial other possibilities, such as the one put forward in Yü's poem from another Pacific island some forty years later. U.S. canonical modernism attempts to overcome the modernist sense of knowledge as hidden and obscured by asserting the concrete, solid forms of its new universalism; ironically, however, its abstruseness is what is actually heightened by its attempts at exclusivity. This is because its universalizing tactics render other knowledges obscure but cannot fully exclude them from its own representational terrains, where they circulate phantasmagorically as the suppressed histories of an imperialism that inhabits both the interiority and the exteriority of the nation. There are, however, texts that provide representational possibilities for knowledges that are doubly suppressed, first by the U.S.-based, self-designated internationalist modernist narratives, and then by modernist narratives circulating in other national contexts that have an imperialist or neocolonial relation to the United States. These texts intervene from behind what I term the *empty screen* of those modernist cultures and their historical erasures.

The term *empty screen* is taken from Gertrude Stein's description of an "American" movie screen as an empty space filled with movement, a screen that, for Stein, is evocative of the epistemological contours of U.S. modernist culture. This description is from her book of essays *Lectures in America*, which was written for a U.S. lecture tour after she had permanently relocated to Paris (as with Pound, the expatriate condition determining an interest in defining and analyzing U.S. cultural forms—popular ones for Stein, high-cultural ones for Pound). Chapter 2, "'Completely Painted Over but Painted Full of Empty Spaces': Stein's American Allegories and the End of Progress," sets up the discussion of Stein with a brief reading of Joseph Conrad's novel *Lord Jim* in order to map out the distinct cultural effects of the different imperialist histories in the United States and England. Unlike Jameson, who reads modernism as a narrative of British imperialism, I argue that it is U.S. imperialism, not British, that is narrated in a fragmented form while that same inconclusive literary form in the British context marks the breakdown of imperialist cultural narratives and corresponds historically to the breakup of empire. My discussion of *Tender Buttons* as an emblematic text of U.S. modernism identifies the extremely experimental reconstruction of domestic space, pleasure, and desire as the most interventionary element of Stein's modernism. I argue that, although this reconstruction entails a radical critique of developmental teleology (in narrative structure) and unity (of character), the latter is at the same time redeployed in a new, fragmented form as her texts retain and celebrate bourgeois domesticity as a self-contained sphere. In a final section on *The Geographical History of America*, I argue that this kind of self-containment in Stein's texts is, ultimately, haunted (and challenged) by allegories of the nondevelopmental histories of U.S. imperialism, histories that have shaped the racialization of U.S. domesticity since its beginnings.

Chapter 3, "'Learning a Lesson in the Superficial Song Lyrics': Hsia Yü's 'Underground' Poetry," examines the work of a contemporary woman poet who had, until recently, relocated from Taiwan to Paris and whose experimental, difficult poetry creates new representational possibilities for sexuality. In terms of content, these possibilities are created both in the poetry's outspoken stance on nonmarital and other types of "perverse" sexuality and in its ironic references to the institutions and standards of normative sexuality. This chapter continues the allegorical readings of poetry on sexuality in relation to narratives of modernity begun in the previous chapter. However, I argue that, unlike Stein's, Hsia Yü's poetry consistently refuses to sublate the failures of macrostructural narratives of modernity into promises of fulfillment in the domestic sphere. I show that, in the context of 1980s martial law and "liberalization" into the 1990s in a neocolonial economy and political structure, where such macrostructural promises of development are beset with internal contradictions, this refusal is all the more significant. This is not to say that U.S. macrostructural narratives are not contradictory but simply to recognize that another layer of contradiction is involved when discourses of modernity cannot attain the transparency that would allow modernity as a concept to function as a given, since, unlike even that of the early-twentieth-century United States, the modernity of Taiwan is discursively constructed as indefinitely postponed, "behind"—behind that of the United States, the West in general, Japan, etc. Hsia Yü's nondevelopmentalism and fragmentation are not the result of an explicit critique of modernity per se (as is Pound's, Stein's, and Cha's). I argue, however, that this is not a symptom of a neocolonial ahistoricity. On the contrary, it signals a less transparent and assumed understanding of modernity, the study of which can benefit contemporary critical discourses that persist in positing it as a given.

Chapter 4, "'For the Other Overlapping Time': Pound's Ideogramic Universalism and Cha's Countermodernist Translation," reads Theresa Hak Kyung Cha's "interventionary translation" (Niranjana) as a response to the kind of canonical modernist translation epitomized by Pound's "ideogramic method" in the *Cantos*. The *Cantos* include translations or quotations from an impressive range of languages and even have Chinese characters written directly into the English lines. However, I argue that Pound's method remains universalist because it incorporates such a variety of referents in an attempt to have them all resonate as examples of a single, transhistorical truth. Ironically, because their images are radically decontextualized, the *Cantos* read more like an incoherent collection of fragments—a formal structure that epitomizes the fragmented mode in which U.S. histories of imperialism and neocolonialism are known and represented. This method is then juxtaposed with Cha's translative writing in her poetic, experimental novel *Dictee*, where several languages and innumerable ruinous fragments signify precisely through their embeddedness in the specific, nondevelopmental, incomplete, and overlapping imperialist and neocolonial histories that shape the lives of her Korean and Korean immigrant characters. This reading of Cha begins with an analysis of her "empty theater," which evokes Stein's empty screen. Unlike the latter, however, Cha's "oblivion" blocks out historical memories of other settings and other times, and, at the same time, its very blankness recalls the processes of historical erasure in canonical modernism. This chapter's comparative structure is based on the larger goal behind drawing these distinct writings together in one book. This goal is to outline the ways in which modernist form can be mobilized in the difficult, interventionary project of rendering legible otherwise disavowed imperialist and neocolonial histories, knowledges, and differences in a way that neither forces them into a linear narrative, nor reasserts a new universalism, but, instead, can represent the historicity of the fragment.

# 1

## The Historicity of the Fragment: Toward a Critical Comparativism

I BEGIN THIS STUDY of modernism with a comparative analysis of modernity-troped poems by Ezra Pound and Yü Kwang-chung, two poets who are widely influential in their own contexts. My intent in doing so is not to name these poets as patriarchs of any poetic movement or school; rather, I want to flesh out a problematic for which their poems can stand as emblems, one canonical and universalist, the other combining canonical and minor functions. I begin with Yü's poem, then move back in time to Pound's, in order to allow the historical hindsight gleaned from the reading of "Hsilo Bridge" to frame an understanding of "Hugh Selwyn Mauberley" and, thereby, illuminate how the often-unseen historical trajectory of twentieth-century U.S. imperialist expansion and "remote control" (Chen, "Missile Internationalism") in the Pacific surfaces in modernist writings as oblique references, aporial temporalities, or dispersed fragments. Specifically, my initial concern in this chapter is to show how an ambivalent illustration of some of the effects of postwar U.S. neocolonialism (with this agent never identified as such) are drawn in Yü's representation of one of the first steel suspension bridges in East Asia as a metaphor for industrial modernization. Second, by way of critical contrast, I illustrate how, in "Hugh Selwyn Mauberley," which as Pound's "farewell to London" is purportedly not about "America," the early stages of U.S. imperialism in the Pacific are, nevertheless, narrated in a modernist poetics of erasure and displacement.

## Thresholds of Modernity

The unsettling circumstance of existing in the moment of an impending crossing is represented in Yü Kwang-chung's "Hsilo Bridge" vis-à-vis the bridge it describes and the sensations it provokes, and, as do many poetic texts, this one ends where it begins, that is, before the crossing takes place:

> Loomingly, the soul of steel remains awake.
> Serious silence clangs.
>
> Over the Hsilo plain sea winds wildly shake
> This design of strength, this scheme of beauty; they shake
> Every nerve of this tower of will,
> Howling and yelling desperately.
> Still the teeth of nails bite, the claws of iron rails clench,
> A serious silence.
>
> Then my soul awakes; I know
> I shall be different once across
> From what on this side I am; I know
> The man across can never come back
> To the man before the crossing.
> Yet fate from a mysterious center radiates
> A thousand arms to greet me; I must cross the bridge.
>
> Facing the corridor to another world,
> I tremble a little.
> But the raw wind over the Hsilo plain
> Blows against me with the tidings
> That on the other side is the sea.
> I tremble a little, but I
> Must cross the bridge.
>
> And tall looms the massive silence,
> And awake is the soul of steel.
>
> (Chi et al., *Anthology of Contemporary Chinese Literature*, 101–2; Yü Kwang-chung's translation)

Probably written in the 1960s, the poem is about a real structure: a suspension bridge located in the rural county of Yunlin on the First Provincial Highway, which, before the construction of the north-south superhighway, used to be a main thoroughfare for cross-island traffic. Completed in 1952, it is the first of its kind in Taiwan and is reputed to be the largest suspension bridge in East Asia. Whether or not this is the case, it remains well-known locally for its impressive size and length and is, therefore, an immediately recognizable marker of modernity. The reference to this real bridge in Yü's poem addresses a complicated "time lag" because the bridge serves as a marker *of* modernity while at the same time representing a mysterious but inevitable and high-speed passage *to* it. The poem thus suggests that modernity is neither taken for granted nor seamlessly in place; yet it has arrived in a concrete form, even in Hsilo, the home of the timeless legends of martial arts practitioners.

At one level, the Hsilo Bridge in this poem could be taken for a Bakhtinian chronotope as it draws out the temporal and spatial significance of the highway connecting the northern and southern parts of the island.[1] For this period in Taiwan, possible clusters of discursive associations that the chronotope of the highway or road might trigger include the radical newness of mobility; rapid industrialization; all changes considered or experienced as part of a larger movement toward technological Westernization and a break with tradition;[2] the mainlanders' passage or crossing from the mainland to Taiwan after 1949; and, alternatively for Taiwanese, Hakka, or indigenous peoples, the move into expanding urban centers. The imperative to cross the bridge also resonates with some of Yü's biographical crossings: one of Taiwan's most well-known poets, with a career spanning from the 1960s to the present, Yü, like other "mainlanders" of his generation, crossed from mainland China to Taiwan around 1950. Then, as have other intellectuals of his generation, he traveled from Taiwan to the United States as a new and foreign mainland and from the United States back to Taiwan as a home that is still removed from the motherland.[3] This reading emerges especially as the other side is described as "another world" whose alien quality is underscored by a physical response: "Facing the corridor to another world, I tremble a little." As the bridge spatially embodies the future and the past in the emphatically new present, then, *this* road chronotope is complicated by a necessarily aporial desire for a return to a home [*hui gui*] that is both spatially (removal from the mainland) and temporally (irreversible processes of industrialization, of displacement, etc.) distanced. Further, in Yü's poem, the chronotope takes the form of a particular kind of road. As a bridge, it also suggests a crossing, a threshold, a point or junction that marks another stage, both spatially and temporally. Yet, as the bridge to and simultaneously the arrival of that new stage, it complicates the condition of juncture or threshold, and, as a result, this chronotope embodies temporal contradictions in its frightful strength and inevitability. To this extent, it can be a figure for the temporal narrative of modernity as a point or junction of temporal crisis per se and, thereby, provide a discursive space in which the crisis can be addressed as such, without demand for its resolution. The lack of resolution is significant because it can open up a possibility for the critique of the conditions that have produced the crisis in the modernist (as critically antimodern) sense. The progress heralded by modernity is not seamlessly in place but "before" this occurs; it is called into question as such.

This is a provisional before because it is significant and appropriate that the time frame is not a straightforward one; rather, it is aporial: the poem is about the inevitability not only of the crossing but also of having already crossed. The possibility for critique brought out in the multivalenced temporality of the poem, however, can also obscure the simultaneous sublation of another critical possibility into precisely the irresolvability of the poem's modernist thematics and form. This would be the possibility for critiquing the way this poem, albeit subtly, positions Taiwan itself, emblematized in the industrial transformation of the symbolics of the Hsilo legends, as that unknowable, mysterious, and darkly anticipated future. As unknowable and irresolvable in form and content, this modernist depiction supports the post-removal Kuomintang (KMT) rhetoric that presented Taiwan not as a location of culture in itself but only as a periphery that is being used as a stop on the way back to full recovery of the mainland, which is seen as the legitimate site of Han culture.

That said, the poem's aporial temporality bears further comment: "I know / The man across can never come back / To the man before the crossing." To know this, one must already be across, if only in the sense that the bridge as crossing and as threshold is itself a state of modernity, an impending one that nevertheless has already transformed its historical and geographic context. At this level, if the bridge is a chronotope, it is an aporial one: you can know you have crossed only after you have crossed and entered the threshold and its oscillations. Further, such an aporia might also be another way to address an exilic temporality characterized, as another mainlander poet has put it, by the impossibility of retracing one's steps.[4] The temporality of this threshold that is also a forced forward movement with no way back can also be understood as an appropriation of a modernist discontinuity that is used here to mark, however obliquely, the historical circumstances that have brought about this sense of discontinuity. Wai-lim Yip has argued that Chinese modernism appropriates the aesthetic structures of Western modernism to formulate a response to the histories of invasion that largely contributed to bringing about the kinds of displacements that it narrates:

> Their works must not be read . . . by putting them against the stylistic markers as we understand them in the West, but rather, we must see them in light of their *perception* and their *appropriation* of Western aesthetic strategies as a function of their anxiety. . . . [T]he intensities—anxieties, solitudes, hesitations, doubts, nostalgia, expectancy, exile and dreams—of the Chinese writers rarely come from an insulated private space; they are at once intensely inward-personal and outward-historical, because they cannot help but be dialectical transfigurations from tensions and agonies of acculturation under visible and invisible forms of colonizing activities. ("Language Strategies," 19)[5]

With Yip's definition of modernism in mind, we might understand Yü's aporial temporality as a distinct type of formal discontinuity partly based on enforced displacement. This is not to argue that discontinuity is a new form in Chinese writing, especially poetry.[6] Rather, it is to point out that, given the historical contexts of the intensity of *this* discontinuity, including its expectancy and its hesitation, it constitutes an aesthetic strategy that "asks some unanswerable questions of Progress, and offers some answers of its own."[7] Like Yü's oblique reference to a "mysterious center" that directs the crossing, these questions and answers put forward, in the formal hesitations that they constitute, a critical modernist stance with regard to these imperialistically derived histories of crossings and displacements while nevertheless sublating, into the poem's spatial aporia, another critical possibility concerning the representation of Taiwan as a location of culture.

This brings us again to the concern of this chapter, which is, by way of two case studies, to introduce how the disjunctions, gaps, and absences of what is often referred to as *modernist* aesthetic form (nondevelopmental, fragmented writing) address suppressed knowledges, both macro- and microstructural, that point to a shared historical formation connecting two locations of modernity (the United States and Taiwan). These distinct and geopolitically nonequivalent modernities, far from having nothing to do with one another, have formed out of a larger imperialist history that connects them and that does not conform to the inside/outside model of Anglo-European metropolis versus Third World colony that forms the basis of much postcolonial theory. This is the history of the building up of U.S. world hegemony over the course of the twentieth century (see, e.g., Miyoshi, "A Borderless World?"). This buildup culminated in the establishment of neocolonial sites such as Taiwan in the last half of the century, where U.S. "remote control . . . can be even more effective, less imposing, more acceptable" than previous forms of colonialism (Chen, "Missile Internationalism," 178). As I have outlined briefly in the introduction, the fact that, in the United States, these sites are often taken as not having a shared history attests to a particular type of historical blind spot, one that Bruce Cumings has termed *parallax vision*, that characterizes the production of knowledge concerning the United States and East Asia. This larger history is itself a suppressed knowledge; yet, in this book, I demonstrate that it is "known" in the necessarily fragmented sense produced by layered historical erasures and disavowals. It is one form of suppressed knowledge that, even when it does not appear as the content, constitutes a fragmented epistemological structure derived from the text's unspoken historical contexts. Such contexts are addressed by the experimental form of modernist texts like Yü's to very different and sometimes mixed ends, however, depending on the cultural politics of the text in question. The aporial temporality of this poem that is tied to the sense of not being able to retrace one's steps, for example, registers a historical context that includes not only the diplomatic relationship (or lack of one) between China and Taiwan but also the more invisible agency of U.S. Cold War containment policies. This fragmented way of knowing and producing meaning constitutes a representational arena within which a politically varied range of understandings of otherwise invisible macro- and microstructures are formed; it can do so, moreover, precisely to the extent that these writings are safely framed as poetic, fictional, and nonrealist.

    The complexity of Taiwan's modern history may have contributed to the relative neglect of academic studies on it as compared to other East Asian sites, the vexed issue of sovereignty in Taiwan causing it, in East Asian studies, to fall between categories—it cannot be studied as a part of China, and at the same time it is has not been recognized by the United Nations as an independent nation since 1971.[8] However, it is precisely this complexity that makes it an important site in extending and revising current understandings of the effects of colonial histories on culture. Taiwan's modernity has been formed out of multiple imperialist occupations, beginning with the partial occupation of the Dutch, who were finally driven out by anti-Manchu forces in 1662. According to Jonathan Spence in *The Search for Modern China*, the several indigenous populations, on the one hand, and the smugglers and pirates who had long had footholds in Taiwan, on the other, were then joined by an increasing number of anti-Qing, pro-Ming factions (53–55). Although the island was soon recovered by the Qing, over the next two centuries it continued to attract political dissenters because geographic remoteness helped prevent the central government from maintaining a strong hold on the island until it was ceded to Japan in 1895, beginning a fifty-year period of Japanese colonialism. Spence maintains that Taiwan's historically marginal and ambiguous relation to the mainland had its roots in the Qing's badly conceived emigration policy: "By forbidding emigration to Taiwan but failing to enforce order adequately, the Qing ensured Taiwan's development as a rough-and-tumble frontier society, only peripherally bound to the administrative structure of the Qing state" (58).[9] The post-1949 Nationalist removal to Taiwan (after the loss of the mainland) is the most recent of these crossings of the Strait. KMT nationalism—presenting the Republic of China, as opposed to the People's Republic of China, as the last reserve of Chinese culture (especially after the Cultural Revolution)—had to disassociate the KMT's own flight and "settlement" from those of its "rough-and-tumble" predecessors and the indigenous inhabitants. Part of this attempt included maintaining that, because "We are all Chinese," KMT occupation and martial law were justified, even as the "temporary" period of martial law lasted almost forty years (until 1987), making it one of the longest in world history. During the martial law period, all forms of media were strictly controlled, travel to and from the island was restricted, Mandarin was enforced as the official language in schools and other public arenas even though Taiwanese and Japanese were the most prevalent languages at the time, and intellectually led resistance from the Left was almost completely suppressed by means of tactics that have come to be known as the White Terror, culminating in the February Twenty-eighth Incident.[10]

This occupation and its rhetoric implicitly define Chinese cultural modernity as that of the mainland in the early days of the Republic, and Taiwan, that "rough-and-tumble frontier society," is positioned as a stop on the way back to recovering the mainland. Such a stop is not a destination in itself and is seen as lacking a legitimate culture of its own. In "Making Time," Marshall Johnson argues that KMT nation constructing in Taiwan is caught up in a temporal state of betweenness, with KMT rule of a unified China posited as both the past and the future of the nation. Johnson shows further how this is a particularly difficult stance considering that, prior to the KMT removal from the mainland, the Republic of China never existed on Taiwan since the island was under Japanese colonial rule until 1945. He points out that such a vexed temporality could actually be put to use in KMT ideological rationalization of its ongoing martial law rule: "The KMT ran the world's longest-lived martial law regime as China's delegate. Another armed group temporarily usurped the space of China, and so elections were matters of other past and future times, past and future space" (111). This focus on Chinese national identity, combined with the violence and suppression of the martial law regime, incited the development of contending Taiwanese identities and a Taiwan independence movement. This situation, moreover, is further complicated by the histories of the indigenous peoples who have been continually forced off their land, first by the Fukinese, who began to emigrate to Taiwan in the seventeenth century, then by the Japanese colonists, and, finally, by the KMT in the latter half of the twentieth century.[11] By the 1980s, the division of labor had played out in a complex manner along ethnic lines: government positions and many positions of the highest intellectual and cultural capital were held by elite mainlanders; many businessmen, scientists and doctors, and wealthy entrepreneurs were Taiwanese; and agricultural, industrial, and domestic labor forces were and are constituted by indigenous people, working-class Taiwanese, and migrant and undocumented workers from the Philippines, Thailand, and other Southeast Asian locations. The aging, low-ranking KMT soldiers who also made the crossing, many with no relatives in Taiwan, were provided with poor-quality, high-density housing and little monetary compensation.[12]

Within such historical conditions, if discourses of modernity are necessarily defined by that modernity's contradictory relation to its past, then one temporality over and against which modernity gains significational force is the larger one of the nostalgic framing of a past prior to imperialism and the invasion and economic exploitation of much of China as well as Taiwan. At the same time, another important past is that which is prior to the resulting industrialization. These two temporalities can work together to produce possibilities for resistance to the persisting effects of Western imperialism, even if that imperialism is not named as such. However, they are also complicated by a simultaneous interest in, not to mention the necessity for, certain aspects of what is experienced as Westernization. Potentially, both these temporalities can function in literature as counterhegemonic discourses aimed at the conditions produced by the dominance of the West and the KMT, respectively. The latter is evidenced in the rural settings of much *hsiang-t'u* or nativist literature, which critiques the elite cosmopolitanism of 1960s modernism and its primarily mainlander constituency.[13] However, these temporalities and their functions are further complicated by their interconnectedness to a third "prior" temporality of the *primitive* as non-Han. This category can include indigenous peoples, Southeast Asians, and the other, "primitive" West—South Asia, Africa, and Latin America. This third temporality presents an obvious complication for the East/West binary, yet it is reinforced by the cultural effects of the layered imperialist histories described above, which dovetail with the racialized motivation that it provides for nonidentification with postcolonial nationalisms in those locations. It therefore complicates as well the political effects of the other senses of the past because it indicates that there is not one West but two, one of the present and future and one of the past, creating a hegemonic but contradictory discourse of modernity that positions Taiwan on a temporal threshold of sorts, but facing, or moving toward, a U.S.-style modernity.[14] Kuan-hsing Chen has demonstrated how, in postwar Taiwan, *the United States* has come to be synonymous with *the West* and to operate as a standard in all things from forms of governance to English pronunciation: "In short, 'America' has been the model with which to 'catch up'" ("Missile Internationalism," 179). This condition is also necessarily caught up with the trajectory of Japanese modernity. However, exactly how caught up is a difficult question since Japan represents a post–World War II model of modernization under U.S.

world hegemony, a former colonial regime, and at the same time the history of Japanese colonialism presents evidence of a past that is alternative to that of KMT rule, evidence that is important to the oppositional sentiment.[15]

It is beyond the scope of this study to comprehensively account for the historical complexity of Taiwan's formation of modernity. What I would like to submit in this regard is, rather, that, if this complexity is atypical, it is as such an exception that illuminates a rule the operations of which are not always clearly discernible in more "typical" places. One aspect of this is the general constructedness of the taken for grantedness of national space and time, as Johnson has shown: "Cut off from Taiwan for generations, absent China's space could only exist for the great majority by a 're'cognizing of what had not been experienced directly, an allegation, a Past. That alone seems to set Taiwan apart, yet insofar as we adopt the standpoint of the living, nationalism's territorial imperative in every nation-state is the institutional production of its pastness" ("Making Time," 106). Another rule that Taiwan may help bring to light by virtue of its apparent atypicality is what Bruce Cumings has called the *web* of U.S. hegemony in East Asia. According to Cumings, this hegemony began around the turn of the century and, until 1941, was trilateral with Britain and a subordinated Japan, with only (the still-subordinated) Japan after 1945, and then with Europe and (subordinated) Japan after 1970 (*Parallax Visions*, 27, 209): "Shortly after World War I ended, in 1922 to be overly exact, America came to be the major partner in the trilateral hegemony in Northeast Asia. This was the period when American banks became dominant in the world economy, the Anglo-Japanese alliance had become tattered, and the United States became more important than England in Japanese diplomacy. The Washington conference was the occasion for this transfer of the baton [from Britain to the United States], a 'locking in' with the critical element of global military reach, the American Navy" (29).

Typically, the operation of this hegemony is obscured by paradigms developed by First World scholars who see international relations with East Asian sites as competition among autonomous nation-states (*Parallax Visions*, 16, 94, 225) or see what Cumings identifies as differences in temporal stages of capitalist production and geopolitical situatedness within a globalizing economy instead as the "clash of civilizations" (2–3, 15). By arguing, for example, that not only Taiwan but other East Asian sites are semisovereign states and that even Japan has been number two and not number one over the course of the twentieth century in East Asian hegemony, with the exception of the years between 1941 and 1945 (16, 26–27), Cumings maintains that, on the contrary, those international relations must be understood as operating within a hegemonic web whose main players (the United States, Britain, and Japan) have shifted positions of relative power over the course of the last century but within which East Asian nations have never held sustained sway equal to that of the United States. This argument offers a significant historiographic intervention because, to offer just one example, starting with the understanding that U.S. hegemony manifested itself in the form of military and economic support of the Nationalists on the loss of the mainland makes discernible how the establishment of Taiwan's martial law regime had everything to do with U.S. interests and interventions in the area. In light of the paradigm according to which autonomous nation-states compete on a neutral terrain, on the other hand, that regime has too often been presumed to be another example of Asian despotism. This presumption in turn seems to assume a cultural, essentialist understanding of non-Western regimes as based on force, in contrast to an enlightened and rational West—an assumption that, as Cumings points out, somehow allows the increasing pathology of U.S. society to be suddenly forgotten (97).

The importance of work by historians like Cumings and his predecessors in U.S. historiography William Appleman Williams, V. G. Keirnan, and Howard Zinn to this study is that it reveals U.S. history to be imperialist from the beginning and expansion into East Asia at the turn of the twentieth century to be an extension of an imperialist movement that began with the conquest of the continent. Although discourses of exceptionalism claim that the United States did not exert its force in much imperialism during the first half of the twentieth century, not to mention earlier than that, its history is implicitly one of imperialistic conquest. This is evidenced in how its colonial and early national economic stability was dependent on a large population of African slaves, who provided the plantations of the South with free labor. Also fundamentally, initial growth and expansion was founded on massive appropriation of land and the near genocide of the various Native American peoples in an imperialistic movement across the continent. It is important to keep in mind that these are just two examples of the long traditions of exertions of racialized force all of which have occurred, in comparison with Anglo-European forms of empire, to a larger extent on the same continent as the "metropolis." And, by the turn of the century, this force was extended when the United States moved into the Pacific and annexed Hawaii, Guam, Samoa, and the Philippines. Even so, with the exception of the short-lived Progressive Era, the United States did not recognize its own imperial expansion into Asia until after World War II—and then amid great controversy—even though its military force was exerted quite brutally in the Philippines. At the same time, U.S. hegemony was also forcefully exerted in Latin America. This was especially true during the first three decades of the twentieth century, when the United States annexed Puerto Rico (in 1898) and exerted economic hegemony in much of Latin America. However, U.S. hegemony in Latin America was not admitted to be a kind of imperialist formation, perhaps because there were fewer formal colonies, and perhaps, less obviously, because Latin America had long been considered "America's backyard," a conceptualization made possible by the combination of its geographic proximity and the long history of justifying annexations of land from indigenous peoples across the continent as a natural consequence of Manifest Destiny (see Zinn, *A People's History of the United States*, 147–66).

Because they include significant imperialist ventures taking place within national borders or in the violent work of extending them in the conquest of an already inhabited continent, the different geographic boundaries of the U.S. empire determine that the discursive displacement of imperial violence must work differently than it does in Anglo-European colonial discourses. To recognize this difference is not to reaffirm U.S. exceptionalism but to begin to consider how the discursive effects (including those of exceptionalism) of the historical formation of U.S. empire constitute a distinct discourse of modernity. It is distinct in the sense that, if the "colonial sites" are in part within the boundaries of the nation, as expansionism is at the same time downplayed with the rhetoric of anticolonialism and exceptionalism, then U.S. imperialist discourses must circulate in complex and highly strained ways in culture prior to World War II because one of their primary functions is to erase not just the violence of imperialist histories but imperialist histories per se.

Precisely as the United States was firmly establishing this overseas empire in the Pacific, the long-standing post-Enlightenment rationalization of Anglo-European colonial expansion as progress was being discredited in a broadly international intellectual development that influenced the writers who would develop the tenets of what is now referred to as *modernist poetics*. One of the goals of this book is to contextualize the historiographic impulse of modernist cultures within this historical problematic by analyzing some U.S. variations of the attempt to represent "the thing itself" as a self-contained entity and the tendency to view this kind of image as the crowning achievement of "American letters." Of course, although set forth explicitly by Pound (after conversations in 1912 with H.D. and Richard Aldington), this was and is by no means only a U.S. poetic project.[16] However, in the case of expatriate U.S. writers who exhibit an abiding concern for finding definitions of American letters (Pound) or America itself (Stein), as some of these modernists themselves have suggested (as we will see below and in chapter 2), the representational challenge proffered by the thing itself, when mobilized toward a representation of "America" or the "American" thing, object, space, or poetics, speaks to the larger discursive problematic of national self-containment versus empire. This began to happen, moreover, when the United States had been exerting its presence across the Pacific for a decade or longer, and it was still happening in 1922, now considered the peak moment of "high modernism," by which time the United States had already achieved hegemony in East Asia (Cumings, *Parallax Visions*, 29). Because of its focus on national self-definition through the representation of self-contained objects, such modernist writing—although this is far from its intent—necessarily puts some "strain" (more on this word presently) on the larger ideological insistence on contradicting the facts of expansion by allowing denied contradictions to surface in culture. To explore how this happens, for the remainder of this chapter and in chapter 2 I will analyze some canonical modernist texts that reveal how the formal possibilities of poetic discourse can facilitate the surfacing of the deep contradictions of the political when these contradictions are systematically obscured, or excluded from being explicitly expressed with adequate coherence and complexity, in the political and other discursive arenas (Lowe, *Immigrant Acts*, 22) by the pervasive rhetoric that posits the United States as fundamentally anticolonial, established in an anticolonial revolution, etc.

## How Mauberley Leaves Modernity

About sixty years before the writing of "Hsilo Bridge" and the occurrence of the historical displacements that it registers, "E.P.," another poetic persona, self-designated as such, was "born in a half-savage country" (the United States at the end of the nineteenth century). Two decades or so later, "the chopped seas held him," "out of date" with the new century, and later "he passed from men's memory." In effect, E.P. is lost from the progress of history; he has somehow exited modernity, which is attached to other temporalities in spite of itself, at least enough to allow for the "synchronic" sense of having unwittingly but irrevocably moved from one into another. There, "unaffected by 'the march of events,'" his poetry fails: "The case presents no adjunct to the Muses' diadem" ("Hugh Selwyn Mauberley" [hereafter "HSM"], 185). In spite of the reference to the contrary in "Hugh Selwyn Mauberley," Pound's overall historiographic project suggests that it is a more fragmented, faltering march of history that has given E.P. up as lost. The threat of this fate—the fate of becoming lost to a history that itself is beginning to lose its direction, a fate that is also embodied by the poem's other major persona (Mauberley)—is described in phantasmagoric imagery that darkens and obscures the poem's would-be clear, bright images (i.e., the Neoplatonic poetic ideal of the virtu), the creation of which is the goal of Pound's modernist poetics.[17] As many critics have noted, the fate of E.P. and his poetry—a fate that I am also calling *phantasmagoric*—is an allegory of the larger modernist crisis of representation. Below, I argue that, in this case, this crisis registers how, precisely in its internationalist intentions, Pound's U.S. modernism must attempt to overcome or sublate suppressed neocolonial histories in order to become the new (but antimodern) voice of modernity (precisely in its narration of the faltering history of modernity). Becoming such a voice entails, by definition, the implementation of a canonical logic that is exclusive of the other knowledges of these histories and of alternative formations of modernity coming from colonial or neocolonial sites, including when such knowledges are fragmented and ambivalent. In a moment, we will see how this is true even when it is precisely these other knowledges that Pound's internationalism seems to embrace most warmly (if least often). The knowledge formations from the neocolonial sites in particular reveal the processes of erasure in U.S. canonical modernism; they operate according to a distinct mode of fragmentation, which I have introduced in the preceding discussion of "Hsilo Bridge," and which will be further explored in later chapters.

Although not necessarily placing it in the context of modern discourses or, conversely, modernist critiques like Pound's, many recent studies have focused on the influence of the specific forms of U.S. imperialism on U.S. literature.[18] Others have considered the influence of colonial histories on modernism in particular, but these are usually discussions of British or European modernisms. In his chapter on modernism in *Culture and Imperialism*, Edward Said describes the early appearances of a modernist aesthetic in novels not usually categorized as modernist (e.g., those of Forster that Jameson discusses in "Modernism and Imperialism") as marking the moment when "the triumphalist experience of imperialism" is no longer tenable. Said explains this shift as a cultural response to a new sense of the vulnerability of Europe:

> I would like to suggest that many of the most prominent characteristics of modernist culture, which we have tended to derive from purely internal dynamics in Western society and culture, include a response to the external pressures on culture from the *imperium*. Certainly this is true of Conrad's entire *oeuvre* and it is also true of Forster's, T.E. Lawrence's, Malraux's; in different ways, the impingements of empire on an Irish sensibility are registered in Yeats and Joyce, those on American expatriates in the work of Eliot and Pound. (188)

Because the *we* in this passage refers to critics of modernism, not the writers themselves, before going into Said's argument I would like first to point out that modernists have also made direct connections between the decline of empire (British) and new literary forms. In chapter 2, I examine in some detail Stein's analysis of the relation between Victorian and modernist literary form and the boundaries between colony and metropolis for Britain and "self-contained" U.S. national boundaries. Here, I would like to submit a passage from Pound's essay "Losses" that makes a point similar to Said's, but by drawing a more direct connection and in a rather less generous tone: "Never in all my twelve years in Gomorrah on Thames did I find any Englishman who knew anything, save those who had come back from the edges of Empire where the effect of the central decay was showing, where the strain of the great lies and rascalities was beginning to tell" (*Guide to Kulchur*, 228). As to the influence of this "strain" on culture, Pound has more to say:

> Let me set it down as a matter of record, in case this book lasts fifty years, that men of my generation in the occident have witnessed the belly-flop or collapse of kingdoms and empires, all of them rotten, none of them deserving any pity or two words of regret. Among the putridities it is difficult to make a just estimate....
>
> Their flop did however for a few years enrich bohemia or la vie humaine des litterateurs by a dispersal of fragments. (81–82)

These passages by Said and Pound share a similar historical thesis on the advent of fragmented or modernist writing. Said's main point is to demonstrate how a nineteenth- and early-twentieth-century "triumphalism" is itself a celebratory rendering of the experience of imperialism, even, and perhaps especially, when the content of literature does not include it in any explicit sense. This is so because, in that case, it records only the internal results—the domestic prosperity—of the colonial conquests, often in a domestic and, apparently, apolitical narrative. In this way, the "promise" of colonialist prosperity can be "triumphantly" represented and simultaneously depoliticized. Said then argues that narrative triumphalism should be understood as structured by the developmental, teleological temporality that breaks down with the advent of modernism. In this sense, the temporal breakdown that generates the modernist crisis of representation as, in Pound's words, "a dispersal of fragments" can, in part, be attributed to what Pound terms *the strain of the great lies* or what Said has described as a sense of cultural vulnerability as new pressures are exerted on that culture "from the *imperium*." Pound's use of typically highly descriptive terms like *belly-flop* allows his statement, like Said's, to register not only the "collapse" of Anglo-European empires but also the breakdown of the Enlightenment structures of knowledge that rationalized them. In the readings that follow, I also take up an account of how the condition of empire and the breakdown of its previous rationalizing narratives produce structures of knowledge that both threaten (with "vulnerability") and "enrich" (with fragments) Anglo-American modernist texts. However, I find that both Pound and Said are too brief in their accounts to explore how such fragments signify differently according to the national context and political investments of a given text. I would like to suggest that this breakdown in narratives of progress requires modernism to narrate, in part, the anticipated end of empire and its expansive projects in the British case while in the U.S. case registering this "end" and at the same time also becoming a new mode of imperialistic representation. This means that, as representing historical knowledge, fragmented form both marks and erases the history of U.S. imperialism. This is a representational phenomenon I will refer to as *empire under erasure*. For U.S. writers, as expansion and its cultural narrative of "progress" is beginning to be rendered irrational, self-containment is taken up in its stead and rationalized as a new nondevelopmental form of universality. However, as self-containment, it operates in direct contradiction to another tendency: the attempt to *externalize* both imperialism in general (by projecting it entirely into the Anglo-European context) and the partly internal histories of U.S. imperialism that contaminate the purity of the self-containment. The reading of "Mauberley" offered below explores an example of this modernist problematic by arguing that the cultural effects of U.S. imperialistic histories are registered in this poem, but under erasure according to a thematics and a logic that are *phantasmagoric* (the term is Pound's).

Pound, in his strong internationalist mode, sees empire as knowledge producing for colonists, but that knowledge goes unrecognized in the metropolis: "Douglas had been in India. Nobody wanted to hear about THAT" (*Guide to Kulchur*, 228). The colonial sites instill knowledge in those (European) subjects, like Douglas, who visit them because the corruption of the colonial enterprise, which stems from a domestic one, is more obvious in the nation's outposts. Pound's sense of the importance of the production of meaning from colonial sites is also clearly indicated in the passage quoted earlier that refers to the cultural effects of the empire's corruption. Pound maintains that the empire's corruption makes its mark despite the suppression of the knowledge of it, by placing "strains" on culture and providing "a dispersal of fragments" that influenced all the arts. Most significant in Pound's formulation of the colonial production of knowledge, however, is that the subject of knowledge is Clifford Hugh Douglas (whose economic theories Pound applied to poetics) and unnamed modernist artists and writers.[19] Pound's pointing out that the most important knowledge is produced in the colonies but overlooked in the metropolis thus still has the effect of resituating the metropolitan intellectual, broadly conceived, as the source and voice, even if unheeded, of that colonially derived knowledge, obscuring the possibility of the colonial subject's knowledge. Further, we should note that, as a U.S. national in London, Pound occupies a position similar to Douglas's on the latter's return from India. Like E.P., Pound was born and raised in the "half-savage" nation derived from an English settler colony where what he considered to be a debased social order that did not grant appreciation or status to its artists drove him to England and then to Italy, where he lived most of his life; he would labor at making his outsider's knowledge and reactionary critique of modernity known in metropolitan cultural centers such as London at a time when American literature did not have institutional status. Douglas functions here as another persona for a modernist predicament whose internationalism, even in using Douglas as its vehicle, masks its specific formation in U.S. histories. To recognize "Douglas" as a persona is to provincialize the poem's internationalism in order to unravel the particular conditions out of which it constructs itself as the voice of modernity, as the internationalist subjectivity that can produce the necessary critique, and how as such it attempts to construct authority for its own critique and exclude or provincialize other subjects and other critiques.

Unlike the rest of the poems collected in *Personae*, "Hugh Selwyn Mauberley" is made explicitly internationalist by the note that, in the 1926 edition, precedes and introduces it: "This sequence is so distinctly a farewell to London that the reader who chooses to regard this as an exclusively American edition may as well omit it and turn at once to page 205" (*Personae*, 274). This comment rather urgently instructs the reader to understand the "Mauberley" series as "distinctly" about London and, therefore, not as an example of American letters. In what follows, I would like to take the urgent tone of this note as a symptom of anxiety rather than a simple description. Therefore, I will turn this directive around and read the modernist form and imperialistically troped content of this sequence of poems as not simply appropriate to the English setting but also deeply informed by U.S. modernity's imperialism and its discourses of exceptionalism, even as this history is erased, ironically, by the poem's historically knowledgeable and critical internationalism.

In poem 2 of the second section, Pound uses the term *phantasmagoria* to describe the dilemma of a minor poet, the persona "Mauberley," whose proclivity for yielding to distracting, feminized temptations renders his verse ineffectual:

> He had moved amid her phantasmagoria
> Amid her galaxies
> NUKTOS 'AGALMA
>
> . . . . .
> Drifted . . . drifted precipitate,
> Asking time to be rid of . . .
> Of his bewilderment; to designate
> His new found orchid. . . . ("HSM," 197)

In this passage, the poet Mauberley is placed in a metaphorically cosmic setting within which his adventures and travels are described in disjointed, stutteringly hesitant lines as a kind of drifting in a dark and disorienting cosmos. The capital letters used in the line containing the poem's only light imagery, "NUKTOS 'AGALMA," suggest an emphatic attempt in the image of a "night jewel" to overcome the darkness and vagueness of this setting and its allegorical qualities, while this image itself remains overshadowed by surrounding references to a phantasmagoric night.[20] In other words, the theme of the "Mauberley" series is echoed in this poem's failure to produce the virtu, Pound's poetic ideal of the direct presentation of the thing itself (and its true, transhistorical value), as it describes Mauberley's failure to produce a masterpiece.

The historical erasures involved in the pre–World War II discursive construction of "America" inform the conundrum of this poetic process in producing what could be called the *historical emptiness* of poem 4. This happens as Mauberley's "drifting" in a darkened phantasmagoric cosmos from poem 2 is reconfigured as shipwreck:

> Scattered Moluccas
> Not knowing, day to day
> The first day's end, in the next noon;
> The placid water
> Unbroken by the Simoon;
>
> Thick foliage
> Placid beneath warm suns,
> Tawn fore-shores
> Washed in the cobalt of oblivions

Or through dawn-mist
The grey and rose
Of the juridical
Flamingoes;

A conscious disjunct,
Being but this overblotted
Series
Of intermittences

Coracle of Pacific voyages
The unforecasted beach
Then on an oar
Read this:

"I was
and I no more exist:
Here drifted
An hedonist." ("HSM," 201)

This poem is characterized by an extreme form of disjuncture: very short, truncated lines with a strong use of caesura. The content as well centers on this idea: disjuncture is geographically embodied in the "scattered" islands among which the poet "drift[s]," and the islands are juxtaposed with "not knowing" the passage of time. The opening lines thus suggest an equation between an epistemological emptiness and a historical-temporal emptiness that is premised on the condition of being lost in equally unknowable geographic sites, or washed ashore on an "unforecasted beach." The poet Mauberley is completely immersed in the loss of coherent knowledge that this disjuncture has produced: he is, in fact, "washed in the cobalt of oblivion" (a line that recalls the "phantasmal sea-surge" ["HSM," 200] of the preceding poem). This utilization of the sea voyage trope renders Pacific islands, implicitly identified here in opposition to Anglo-European modernity, as the site of a "scattered" and phantasmagoric oblivion that functions as a generalized figure of the colonial landscape. That the beach is "unforecasted," moreover, suggests the anxiety derived from a condition of being "vulnerable"—to use Said's term—to unforeseeable and unknown "landings." This is the case because, as we will see in chapter 2, in an inside/outside discursive model of colonialism like the one being explicitly constructed here, the imperialist subject is always subjected to the possibility of finding himself adrift on the colonial road. The final irony, moreover, further emphasizes the vulnerability of culture in relation to the colonies at the level of artistic subjectivity. It does this by suggesting that such landings would require the *disappearance* of the poetic persona, the subject of culture per se, into an exteriorized oblivion: "I was / And I no more exist: / Here drifted / An hedonist."

Throughout "Mauberley," Pound suggests that the modern poet's task is to rescue coherence, light, and distinct form from within a modernity threatened by and permeated with ambiguity and the hovering presence of phantasmagoric terrains. The phantasmagoric presence arises, however, as the histories of the "Moluccas" are erased in the designation of their shores as "unforecasted" and, by implication, as unknowable. In other words, the phantasmagoric ambience of the tropical seas operates, despite the poem's explicit historiographic desires to the contrary, as a residue of a historical erasure: the obtuseness of the islands' phantasmagoria itself is a representation of a specific history that has been obscured, made unclear, while at the same time a nondevelopmental, fragmented knowledge of the larger history of imperialism comes through in the formal disjunctions of modernist culture. I suggest this because, on the one hand, Pound's use of the familiar, European-derived sea voyage trope supports the narrative of exceptionalism by reasserting a binary, inside/outside model of metropolis and colony (characteristic of English colonialism) that was considered non-American even as the United States was expanding its imperialist enterprises across the Pacific. In other words, if imperialism is repeatedly represented in cultural narratives like sea voyage novels according to a familiar, British inside/outside model of formal colonialism, then the U.S. formation remains harder to recognize as imperialistic because it includes both internal forms and a new form of expansion that is not identical to the British model. On the other hand, at the same time, the inside/outside model of this literary trope can also attempt to *externalize* a phantasmagoric presence of histories that are partly internal to the nation—histories, in other words, whose overall formation cannot be mapped onto an exterior position vis-à-vis an already "half-savage" metropolis. The passages from Said and Pound quoted above have already suggested that, to the extent that colonial locations exert pressure on the imperium from its self-designated "margins" and threaten to break the logic of the triumphalism of colonial narratives, the task of the modern poet is to grapple with (and, in Pound's case, to attempt to overcome) the ensuing epistemological and historical emptiness. In the larger Anglo-European-U.S. formation of imperialism, whether or not the margins can be defined according to an inside/outside model, this historical emptiness becomes threatening when its phantasmagoric traces reveal themselves as an integral part of Western modernity and history. In the case of U.S. histories in particular, the threat becomes harder to negotiate for at least two reasons: (1) because these phantasmagoric traces are the mark of a "past" that also informs the internal geographic landscape of the modern nation and (2) because, rather than only marking the end of a triumphalist narrative of empire, they also mark the beginning of an Asia-Pacific imperialism that cannot explicitly attempt to justify itself as imperialist expansion and development per se and must, paradoxically, represent itself in highly strained modes of erasure only partly facilitated by exceptionalism.

In its urgency to locate this poem and its sea voyage trope firmly in a London literary context, Pound's prefacing note suggests that the predicament of empire has not been fully projected onto other national contexts outside the United States and that there is a pressing discursive need to externalize it. Pound's personae and their "stranded" predicaments illustrate how, in the U.S. context, a canonical modernist poetics does not only represent the breakdown of empire's "triumphal" narratives. It also problematically "narrates" twentieth-century U.S. imperialism. As a U.S. modernist text, "Mauberley" specifies and adds to Said's and Pound's statements in literary criticism by illustrating how its fragmented modernist present does not only reflect the cultural effects of the British Empire as it begins to sense its own vulnerability and anticipate its own end. It also attempts to erase the marks of U.S. imperialistic histories in the Pacific by constructing a concrete, transhistorical image as the thing itself (the virtu; the night jewel) that can overcome the phantasmagoric traces of the histories it suppresses. This attempt is far from successful. Ironically, instead of concrete universal truths, what is more often produced is the kind of aesthetic hesitation and emptiness that we have just observed. This lack of significational fullness in turn becomes the vehicle for precisely that phantasmagoric historical presence that haunts the under-erasure narration of U.S. imperialism as a threat not only from afar but also from within its own national boundaries. Ironically, the very historical erasures of its universalism make phantasmagoric the self-containment of Pound's modernist image. Instead of being finally accomplished, the attempt to overcome the phantasmagoric traces of empire is repeatedly exerted in the demand—which ultimately cannot be met—for the virtu to embody the distinct form of the known.

# 2

# "Completely Painted Over but Painted Full of Empty Spaces": Stein's American Allegories and the End of Progress

> It is natural that a woman should be one to do the literary thinking of this epoch.
> Gertrude Stein, *The Geographical History of America*

IF SOME INTERNATIONALIST modernist personae express fears about aesthetic predicaments such as that of Mauberley, who is set adrift from modernity and culture, other modernist literary subjects have purportedly purposeful tasks to accomplish in those outpost locations, and some can avoid these issues altogether by staying at home, or so it seems. Moving from the sea voyage trope to the domestic sphere, this chapter examines how Gertrude Stein's texts explicitly remind the reader of modernism about important connections between home and nation, imperialism and writing. This chapter also takes up some of the same epistemological inquiries that Stein does with regard to these interconnections. However, in doing so, it follows the conceptual threads that are apparent in other questions that are not uttered, but are nonetheless suggested, in Stein's inquiries. These other questions are about the problematics of representing pre–World War II U.S. imperialism and, therefore, contradict Stein's more apparent thesis on America.[1] Before turning to Stein's texts, however, we will return to the sea voyage trope, this time following a narrative road in British colonial fiction in order to outline a few of the distinct ways in which the British and U.S. formations of empire are given modernist narrative form. In this way, a contrast will become apparent between Joseph Conrad's inconclusively structured novel *Lord Jim*, which reads as a kind of narrative road that marks the impossibility of its own ending (which was formerly provided by the heroic narration of imperialism), and the way in which U.S. modernism's poetic object functions as an emblem of American exceptionalism by both erasing expansion in this object's self-containment and displacing into an aesthetic of emptiness the imperialist violence that takes place within national boundaries. Although, in both cases, the space of the nation is often represented in literature through the metaphor of the home, the possible forms that the figuration of the nation can take on and the fraught sites of intersection between nation and empire are significantly different. This difference is, moreover, a historically derived one; to recognize it is not to capitulate to the notion of American exceptionalism, which would be to deny that the United States has an imperialistic history. On the contrary, recognizing the historical difference allows us to understand exceptionalism itself as a response to this historical difference in the formation of empire, a response that takes the form of a symptomatic disguise. On the other hand, Stein's argument that there is an important distinction between American and English literature is a form of American exceptionalism to the extent that it asserts that English culture threatens to lose itself in its definitional outside because of its empire, while the United States is culturally and geographically self-contained. If we further historicize Stein's literary history by calling into question the belief in U.S. self-containment versus the English imperialist expansion on which it is based, we will find that, in both national contexts, even while making possible a critique of ideologies of "progress," the nondevelopmental structures of modernist writing are redirected into a canonical function with regard to the very colonial and imperialist histories that ideologies of progress rationalize by narrating new, nondevelopmental forms of universalized knowledge. And, beyond this commonality, we will find that their respective forms of nondevelopmental writing are responses to different significational demands produced out of distinct histories of imperialism. I will argue that, as a result, the apparently similar aesthetic forms signify differently in each national context, a difference that can be summarized in the contrast between an emphasis on inconclusiveness in the British case and on self-containment in the U.S. case. This is not to argue, however, that British modernism can never emphasize self-containment or vice versa. Rather, it is to point out that inconclusiveness and self-containment are the forms of nondevelopmental writing that best facilitate the representation of the sense of the insecure future and breakdown of the British Empire, on the one hand, and the emergence of a new form of imperialism that includes but is less thoroughly based on formal colonialism and that presents itself as nonimperialistic, on the other. Identifying this distinction in the significational demands that produce the modernisms of the two national contexts is not a way to reify national cultural differences as such. Rather, it is a way to account for historically derived differences in the cultural production of national imaginaries, while the comparison addresses how these imaginaries necessarily operate in contexts that exceed that of an individual nation. In the pages that follow, juxtaposing Conrad's and Stein's texts will allow a delineation of the types of major and minor functions that are made possible from within the peculiar historicizing impulse of Stein's writing on sexuality, an impulse that is shaped out of a formation of empire that, emphatically unlike its British predecessor, does not announce itself as such.

## Lord Jim (and Mrs. Dalloway) on the Colonial Road

The image of a road, especially that of the sea voyage, in a modern British text can signify several important tropes of modernity (and nationhood within modernity) in the larger discursive "triumphalism" that Said theorizes in his "Note on Modernism" (discussed in chapter 1). These include economic development and expansion; the temporal progress of culture into a more and more civilized way of life; and, spatially, the heroic progress of culture in its civilizing progress across most of the non-Western world. However, at the same time, the road in its necessary relation to the colonies also makes visible or at least suggests the instability of the very national boundaries that it brings into narration. Along these lines, Fredric Jameson has argued in "Modernism and Imperialism" that the place to which such roads cannot lead (in English high modernism) is precisely the colonial site that nevertheless lies at the road's end and that this is what creates the formal structural occlusion of modernism, its lack of representational fullness and narrative development. However, I will argue that the analysis of a sea voyage modernist text like *Lord Jim* reveals that it is the English guilt and responsibility for the violence committed there, rather than the colonial scene itself, that is most difficult to bring into representation, precisely because the guilt contradicts the romantic heroics and triumphalism (Said) that characterize the representation of empire in its more realist renderings. In other words, I argue below that, in the British context, there is a realist, developmental representation of empire clearly presented as such and the failure of that heroic developmental narrative in more modernist texts registers the incipient breakup of empire (Sangari) rather than empire per se and that, in the U.S. context, juxtapositional, nondevelopmental writing as a problematic form of "completeness" is a particularly salient mode for the representation of the nation in an empire under erasure.

Both in "Modernism and Imperialism" and in his lengthy discussion of Conrad's *Lord Jim* in *The Political Unconscious*, Jameson draws a distinction between high modernism, which cannot bring colonialism into representation (*Howard's End* being an early, prototypical example), and the more popular adventure novel, which, Jameson asserts using the example of Conrad, "draws on more archaic storytelling forms" ("Modernism and Imperialism," 44) to represent the colonial site.[2] Indeed, there are important formal distinctions between high modernism and the adventure or sea voyage novel that should be recognized.[3] At the same time, however, it is equally important to account for the way in which Conrad's adventure novel can be considered as prototypically modernist as Forster's, even according to Jameson's description of that modernism, if it is not the more general colonial reality that we discover to be structurally occluded from modernist representation but, more specifically, the emerging issue of responsibility for colonial violence that, as Jenny Sharpe has argued, had to be renarrativized in the last part of the nineteenth century as nationalist movements gained strength and became militant in the colonies.[4] As we will see, it is the Englishman's guilt and responsibility for this violence that constitute the "truth" that is endlessly deferred in Conrad's novel, both in its content (we can never know for certain the truth of the past event through its recollection or representation) and in its form (the impossibility of closure even at the sentence level). The problematic of inscribing the nation according to a thematic and structural road (i.e., the novel) lies in the fact that this road constantly threatens to slip into the unrepresentable space of colonial violence, bringing with it the unwitting protagonist in his or her journey toward self-mastery and (national) identity. Once placed within the scene of colonial violence, as opposed to that of the colonial site per se, this self-mastery threatens to expose itself as attained only through the forced subjugation of people of other races. At the same time, national identity, a subjectivity of sameness that threatens to include the other in the terms of its own humanist definition, is only precariously stabilized as essentially different through precisely that same violence.

On the subject of British colonial discourse in the later nineteenth century, Sharpe has argued that "the civilizational mission cannot accommodate signs of violence except where they exhibit the native's barbaric practices" (*Allegories of Empire*, 6). According to this rationalizing logic, as colonial violence threatens to be represented in narrations of empire, it becomes the violence of the native. Sharpe historicizes this problematic by considering its significational value when deployed as a response to militant Indian nationalist resistance (beginning with the Indian Mutiny of 1857), after which the colonial violence exerted in the suppression of the revolts (Sharpe aptly terms this a *reign of terror*) was recoded into representations of native barbarism in order to rationalize the suppression of struggles for emancipation. During this period, violence begins to register the empire's vulnerability, as Sharpe demonstrates by framing the emerging racist colonial discourses of the late nineteenth century as "a defensive strategy that emerged in response to attacks on the moral and ethical grounds of colonialism" (6). Although it is not part of Sharpe's argument to emphasize this point, it follows that such violence also registers another, further vulnerability by operating as a harbinger of empire's possible fall. Sharpe's thesis appears to be contradicted by Conrad's ample representations of, for example, Jim's violence toward the natives (not to mention many other similar representations in Conrad's colonial fiction). However, a closer look reveals how Sharpe's argument sheds a helpful light on the discursive function of Conrad's narrative structure: because it is in contradiction to the "defensive strategy" of late-nineteenth-century colonial discourse, when colonial rather than native violence comes into representation, it brings temporal rupture into the narrative form and a cynical pessimism into the narrative voice.

In *Lord Jim*, when colonial violence is, in fact, represented, it comes into articulation in a way that constantly attempts to defer or deny the reality and responsibility of the disruption and exploitation of cultures and the bloodshed and deaths of the natives themselves; it is this deferral that produces a structural rupture in the temporality of the novel. Contentwise, the violence is deferred, after the incident on the *Patna*, into an ultimately futile attempt to salvage the heroics and romance of the imperial protagonist in his journeys and, by extension, the ever onward movement of colonial domination itself. This attempt is present, for example, when Marlow feels obliged to interrupt his story to say to his listeners: "Remember this is a love story I am telling you now" (*Lord Jim*, 221). The deferral of responsibility or guilt is most apparent, and most problematically carried out, in Marlow's narration of the trial scenes, where it takes the form of a complicated and multilayered critique of the possibility of uncovering the truth of the event. For example, the actual description of Jim's "leap"—perhaps better described as a "Fall" with a capital *F*—off the presumably doomed ship onto the lifeboat is understood as tragic not because of the incriminating truth of his abandonment of eight hundred Muslim pilgrims (whom the crew was not prepared to accommodate with lifeboats in the case of an emergency) but because Jim had abandoned his chance to be a hero. At the same time, however, the philosophical understanding of the truth or righteousness of heroism itself is constantly called into question in the trial scenes that cannot help incriminating "all of us."

The rest of the novel chronicles Jim's flight from this disgrace, following him across more and more remote colonial locations as he looks for a place where he can finally regain his status as a white master. And, once in Patusan, his legitimate lordship (which, paradoxically, he can achieve only in the extreme anonymity afforded by Patusan's particular geography) is secured through his killing a Malay native: "He [Jim] found himself calm, appeased, without rancor, without uneasiness, as if the death of that man had atoned for everything" (*Lord Jim*, 224). Here, Conrad has, in a series of complex logical maneuvers, managed to have this killing function according to a logic of atonement, even as the demand for atonement rather clearly attests to the criminality of the act. It is important to note that this logic, this endless displacement of the death of the native into the apparently politically neutral aesthetic structures of heroism and romance, never quite works; thus, we have Conrad's dense and convoluted style, which moves laboriously toward a truth that can never be found out in its entirety. In fact, instead of structuring the novel along a model of linear progression toward a goal, the search for truth seems to take on the form of this thematic leap that, in its long, repetitive narrations, takes Conrad further and further from the desired disclosures of any ideational "whys" (205) that could answer questions posed by the very form of the novel about the nature of identity and destiny.

These questions are also raised in the content of the novel through the trope of memory. In Marlow's self-conscious narration, memory is associated directly with the act of storytelling and the form that the latter takes on in his tale. The fallibility of Marlow's gaze in always seeing Jim only "through a mist" or "under a cloud" suggests a narrator ultimately incapable of fully knowing the subject of his story, thus shrouding storytelling, along with memory, in an essential mystery; Marlow often interrupts his story with comments such as: "I was confronted again with the unanswerable why of Jim's fate" (*Lord Jim*, 205). Most important, within the temporal structure of the text, memory as enigma is located as a specific moment within a larger conception of memory that includes it and one other prior temporality. The latter is a more distant, antiquated past still fully accessible to memory and characterized by "assurance," and the former is this more recent prior moment, perhaps the emerging modernist conception of the past, where that assurance has been called into question. In fact, in the narration's chronology as well as logically, the past characterized by assurance is placed *before* the *Patna*'s mysterious event occurs: "A marvelous stillness pervaded the world, and the stars, together with the serenity of their rays, seemed to shed upon the earth the assurance of everlasting security.... The propeller turned without a check, as though its beat had been part of the scheme of a safe universe. ... Jim on the bridge was penetrated by the great certitude of unbounded safety and peace that could only be read on the silent aspect of nature like the certitude of fostering love upon the placid tenderness of a mother's face" (19). This "marvelous stillness" and its corresponding psychic "assurance" (19) end abruptly with an unexplained bump, and, in marked contrast to the previous passages, the closing paragraph reads: "What had happened? ... Had the earth been checked in her course? They could not understand; and suddenly the calm sea, the sky without a cloud, appeared formidably insecure in their immobility, as if poised on the brow of yawning destruction" (26). In relation to the overall themes of the novel, the divide between the two temporalities marks the moment of a deferred recognition of not only the fundamental "untrustworthiness" of British leadership and heroism but also, and most sinisterly, the English subjects constitutive criminality, represented by Jim's fugitive-like flight into more and more remote areas. As Brierly exclaims to Marlow: "We are trusted. Do you understand? — Trusted! Frankly, I don't care a snap for all the pilgrims that ever came out of Asia, but a decent man would not have behaved like this. . . . We aren't an organized body of men, and the only thing that holds us together is just the name for that kind of decency. Such an affair destroys one's confidence" (56).

If what causes the emergence of a modernist critique within the temporalities of the English novel is, in fact, this deferred recognition, then the developmental narrative loses utterly the "assurance" of its goal. It is knocked off course by a sudden experience of "immobility," after which the causes of events and human actions are never illuminated and goals never reached. The goals are endlessly pursued, but this occurs through a narrative whose interminable twists and turns are structured around the *deferral* of uncovering the incriminating truth of its own subject matter. In this sense, the novel itself bumps into the same paralytic immobility that Conrad often describes, in this and other works, as a silent, almost transcendental pause before death, which, for example, the *Patna* inhabits while it appears to be about to sink.[5] This immobility is akin to Jameson's concept of *hesitation*, which he describes in "Modernism and Imperialism" as "modernism itself" (55). Although it is precisely this immobility, brought about by displaced terror and guilt, that precipitates the modernist sense of the present in this narration of British colonialism, I would like to argue that it does not, as Jameson suggests, also provide a general structural model for modernism itself in the British context; such a model would be more relevant to the writing produced by certain experimental U.S. nationals, such as Gertrude Stein. Rather, the "leap" that Jim makes in Conrad's novel provides a better model for the emergence of nondevelopmental writing that grapples with the increasingly threatened and uncertain future of the empire. Jameson's reading of hesitation as definitive of modernism in general and his neglect of what I'm calling the *spiraling fall* of narrative form in the British texts may be a projection of the U.S. structuration onto modernism in general.

In short, the power of the *Patna*'s immobility and the spiraling fall of the narrative that follows it seem to arise out of a terror and guilt that function at two levels of meaning: at the surface level, there is a thematic fear of discovering that "we" are not truly heroic and, therefore, not worthy of carrying out the burdens of progress, and, at a more cryptic level, there is a pervasive fear of discovering the actual violence that constitutes the truth of our laws. Because of this displaced guilt that structures this temporality of modernism, the British modernist can never "go home" (later we will see how the U.S. modernist can never leave home) because, as Marlow says, "going home must be like going to render an account": "To get its joy, to breathe its peace, to face its truth, one must return with a clear conscience" (166). Instead, he is to be found on the colonial road, traveling the gaping, obscure, and disorienting "Eastern roadstead" (that of British colonial expansion) that Conrad describes, in the preface, as the place where he first envisioned Jim, who is persistently claimed as "one of us," but who is forever exiled from the "commonplace" English countryside (vii). This more cynical stance on colonialism seems to provide a more critical representation, especially in its explicit critique of discourses of progress. I would like to submit, however, that this critique hides the more significant discursive function of the novel. That function lies in how its formulation of the narrative subject of empire dismisses other narrative possibilities: Jim's fall from grace on the eastern road stands in for *the* epistemological problematic of the novel, and, in his story, Jim, through Marlow's doubtful narration, gives us the voice of modernity (read modernist temporality). In occupying that position, the narrative voice serves a canonical function, marking off the possibilities for representing the heterogeneity of colonial histories for the colonial sites that operate simply as the setting and the impetus for the universalized end of time as developmental history.[6] This is felt as a loss; however, the resulting characteristically pessimistic and ironic narration actually functions as a *euphemism* for the violence and criminality of colonial histories because that pessimism attempts to present those histories as constituting the now sadly lost march of progress.

The discourse of the return and its impossibility, which marks the major function of Conrad's nondevelopmental temporality, suggests that the character of the Englishman or -woman abroad is part of the construction of national identity "at home." In this sense, the road or the sea voyage becomes an important vehicle through which not only the adventurer but also the domestic subject is figured. Just as the adventurer is figured in relation to home and the nation, so too is the domestic subject not only envisioned in relation to a wilderness that hovers nearby but also at times placed in a foreign setting that underscores its domesticity and femininity. In fact, in the latter case, the relation between domesticity and an imperialist subjecthood or national identity becomes apparent. An example of this is Virginia Woolf's character Mrs. Dalloway as she makes an early appearance in Woolf's first novel, *The Voyage Out*, in the cabin of a ship off the coast of England (later to sail to South America):

> "D'you know Dick, I can't help thinking of England," said his wife meditatively, leaning her head against his chest. "Being on this ship seems to make it so much more vivid—what it really means to be English. One thinks of all we've done, and our navies, and how we've gone on century after century, sending our boys out from little country villages—and of men like you, Dick, and it makes one feel as if one couldn't bear *not* to be English! Think of the light burning over the House, Dick! When I stood on deck just now I seemed to see it. It's what one means by London." (53)

In the word *House* in this passage, there is a telling slippage between concepts of home and the political center of the empire and, in the implicit reference to a lighthouse, another telling slippage between concepts of home and the nation's geographic boundaries. In all cases, the light of rationality shines as a beacon of domestic well-being and the fullness of national life in the metropolis. Like the quote from Stein that serves as the epigraph to this chapter, the further ironic effect of the obvious irony of this passage is that it renders effective the imperialist sentiment that it seems to disclaim through its critique of British patriarchal aggression. Both the irony and the slippage are further emphasized by the fact that these words are spoken by Mrs. Dalloway, who was to become one of the most famous domestic subjects of English literature (and of an internationally [read Western-] conceived canon of modernism). Taking into account Rosemary George's statement that the modern bourgeois individual is not only a woman—as Nancy Armstrong argues in her groundbreaking book on the unspoken class politics of domestic fiction—but also an imperialist, the rest of this chapter is concerned with the representational effects of the contradiction between domesticity and empire in the pre–World War II United States.[7] Although Jameson does not make this connection explicitly in "Modernism and Imperialism," the importance of the relation between the domestic sphere and the imperialist subject in

U.S. modernism is also suggested by the fact that, in his reading of *Howard's End*, he acknowledges almost parenthetically, in a long, final endnote, that the text that first prompted his thoughts on the relation between modernism and imperialism was *Lectures in America* by Gertrude Stein.

## Domesticity and the Empty Spaces of U.S. Modernity

Four years after *Lord Jim* was first published in 1899, Gertrude Stein was working on her first draft of *The Making of Americans*, from which the following is taken: "The home the rich and self-made merchant makes to hold his family and himself is always like the city in which his fortune has been made. In London, it is like that rich and endless, dark and gloomy place, in Paris it is filled with pleasant toys, cheery light and made of gilded decoration and white paint and in New York it is neither gloomy nor joyous but like a large and splendid canvas completely painted over but painted full of empty spaces" (*Fenhurst*, 160).[8] I would like to use this quote as a point of departure into a discussion of three of Stein's works, *Lectures in America* (1935), *Tender Buttons* (1914), and *The Geographical History of America* (1936), because it makes explicit the contrast between the different forms of historical erasure in the writing of the nation in English and U.S. modernisms. Just as Stein's description of the London home as "rich and endless, dark and gloomy" is evocative of the Conradian road, her description of the New York home as "a large and splendid canvas completely painted over but painted full of empty spaces" suggests a different figuration of nation and of literary form, one that is predicated on a self-contained, yet "empty," bounded space. This difference indicates possible cultural effects of the extent to which U.S. imperialistic histories are distinct from those of England and Europe. And, in precisely the spatialized contrast between the "endless" London cityscape and the self-contained nature of "a large and splendid canvas," it further indicates that these historical distinctions have been distorted into a premise for false understandings of the U.S. national formation as uniquely nonimperialistic.

By the time Stein was writing this draft of *The Making of Americans*, the United States had been developing a new foreign policy of "expansionism" that was deeply controversial because it directly contradicted the nation's originary anticolonial self-definition. Because until just before the turn of the twentieth century U.S. imperialism largely operated, in terms of the aims of its expansion, within the boundaries of a single continent, that expansion could appropriate discourses of progress from the European colonial context while paradoxically also misrepresenting U.S. expansion's geographic containment to claim that it is not an imperialistic one, not a process of wresting control from original inhabitants (which it also was), but one of claiming a right to and settling one's own territory. This kind of claim is not made in colonial discourses that proclaim the colony as a colony and that present the metropolis as clearly demarcated from the colony (although problematically so, as Conrad's endless roads eventually bring into articulation). When the United States began expanding overseas, it began to resemble an Anglo-European colonizer. Of course, this is not to say that the United States had become more imperialistic than it already was. But its imperialism, when it involved overseas expansion and formal colonies (Guam, Hawaii, the Philippines), came to resemble the form of imperialism—that of its own former colonial ruler—that it had defined itself against. It follows that this period's consequential crisis of national self-definition is overdetermined by the way in which it implicates the past and threatens to reveal the precariousness of the earlier anti-imperialist self-assertions (proclaimed politically in, e.g., the Monroe Doctrine of 1823). More precisely than the usual post–World War I periodization, the period of early expansion into the Pacific, beginning with the conquest of the Philippines in 1898, corresponds to the earliest group of writings by U.S. nationals that departed radically from dominant nineteenth-century aesthetic forms. These experimental writings, especially those that deal with national identity, as in Stein's case, participate in developing a discourse of the nation in response to this crisis of national self-definition that persisted into the 1930s.[9] Taking Stein's writings from this period as a case study, this chapter will argue that, in its canonical forms, while signaling the breakdown of nineteenth-century colonial narratives based on progress, U.S. modernism's fragmentation and juxtaposition at the same time become the vehicle for narrating twentieth-century forms of imperialism while attempting to keep them under erasure.

This narration is not seamless, however. The "splendid canvas completely painted over but painted full of empty spaces" is, as a modernist, palimpsested canvas, in part a surfacing of such contradictions because, among its layers, the foundational violence that has been largely "painted over" threatens to show through. This holds true as well for another example from Stein's work: the highly experimental *Tender Buttons*. Rather than being filled with images of the social and political realities that make the making of this bourgeois home possible, these modernist "empty spaces" are filled, instead, with the aestheticized modernist object. It is precisely this kind of painting over of empty spaces in the representation of national or domestic space—the latter already defined by Stein in her early draft of *The Making of Americans* as a microcosm of the national (*Fenhurst*, 160)—that functions in the U.S. modernist text as an attempt at erasing the imperialist formation of the domestic (in both senses)—and any sense of responsibility for that formation's violence and injustices—while at the same time addressing its contradictions. This fraught process of modernist erasure is accomplished not through rationalizing developmental narratives of progress that turn violence into heroics and civilizing improvement (although such narratives may be hovering in the background in contradictory, palimpsested fashion) but through the less rational logic of a "blank" ground or perceptual field that allows for the emergence of the importance of the modernist object, which must be presented as "the thing itself."[10]

Unlike those of many of her most influential contemporaries, however, Stein's texts contain yet another layer of complexity with regard to the presentation of objects and events in writing because her work also confronts the problem of how to represent experiences of nonnormative desire and sexual practices among women. As such, these experiences have no access to what Judith Butler has described as the (in this case, heterosexual) epistemological system legitimated as "reality" and, thus, cannot be incorporated into a structure of knowledge where a prior reality is expressed in textual representations.[11] Butler's argument might alert us to how Stein's insistence on what in "The Revolutionary Power of a Woman's Laughter" Jo-Anna Isaak has termed a *presentational* rather than a *representational strategy*—the former complicating the notion of a one-way relation between referent and representation and assigning the textual object as authentic an existence as the nontextual one—should be read as a strategy that challenges ontological normativity and, thereby, opens up the possibility for a performative relation to gender and sexuality.[12] In other words, this challenge to representation contests gender and sexuality norms without figuring the lesbian as an identity that can be represented.[13] Catherine Stimpson's discussion of how Stein "forgot" about the existence of her first novel can be read as an interesting example of the problematics of lesbian representation. In "The Mind, the Body, and Gertrude Stein," Stimpson describes how the story lines from *Q.E.D.*, an early text more explicitly about autobiographical erotic friendships between women, were later encoded into conventional heterosexual plots in "Melanctha" and *The Making of Americans*. She then goes on to describe how *Q.E.D.*'s own existence as a separate text was entirely forgotten until it was rediscovered and published, significantly enough, under the title *Things as They Are*.

However, I would not argue (as Stimpson seems to suggest) that the earlier novel is a more direct and authentic representation of "lesbian experience." On the contrary, Stein's "forgetting" of the earlier manuscript is an indication of the very complexity of the relation between nonnormative practices and those that are legitimated as the heterosexual real. Read in this light, her works that follow *Q.E.D.*—most notably *Tender Buttons*—can be read as a more thorough exploration of possible ways in which to write about such sexual experience because *Tender Buttons* takes as its subject both the sexual and social practices themselves *and* their complex, contradictory relation to the epistemological frameworks that legitimate certain practices as reality. In reading for the erotic in Stein's texts, then, the relation between sexuality and knowledge signals the importance of reading her characteristically modern preoccupation with the textual representation of the object as what now could be considered a postmodern critique of epistemology in the broadest sense. Her concern with the categorical (man/woman as well as many other binaries and lists), her critique of "fullness" in characters, and her lack of plot development, all of which seem to open up a kind of textual emptiness, must also be read in this light.

It is precisely these types of empty spaces, of course, that signify the beginnings in the Western canon of a modernist aesthetic that is founded on a radical instability of meaning. These empty spaces can be read as the absence of meaning or its indeterminacy, or, in Said's sense, they can be understood as the lack of a coherent metanarrative in the (Anglo-European) literary text that corresponds to the breakdown of the developmental, teleological narratives that support imperialist conquests and that, in the first decades of the twentieth century, are beginning to be threatened by early stirrings of nationalism in the colonies, as Sangari argues in her early article "The Politics of the Possible."[14] These writings, and Jameson's on modernism discussed in the previous section, demonstrate conclusively that, no matter how highly aestheticized, this textual emptiness does not serve a purely aesthetic function. Butler's formulation is also a helpful point of departure in considering the politics of modernist form because it illuminates how such empty spaces can register events that have no access to reality as such. However, I would like to emphasize that reality is legitimated by multiple, sometimes conflicting discursive frameworks and that these frameworks undergo historical shifts, resulting in overlaps that can produce contradiction and overdetermination. Modernist empty spaces can be read as produced through a historical overdetermination because they register events that are relegated to the unreal by both the dominant, developmental narratives of modernity and the emerging, modernist epistemologies that oppose developmentalism and, therefore, are doubly excluded from the representational framework.

The most relevant of these exclusions for our understanding of Stein's texts are nonnormative sexuality and the imperialism that consolidates "America" as a national entity. These two exclusions are far from parallel, however, and their absences exert very different influences on the significational functions of the formal structures of Stein's modernism. This distinction is most apparent in the fact that not just Stein but a notable number of modernist writers have attempted, however indirectly, to represent sexual relationships between women.[15] In contrast to such attempts in the realm of sexuality, the historical fact of imperialism, whether across the continent or into the Pacific, is under erasure, as discussed above, as the United States is presented as a self-contained, anticolonial national space as opposed to its colonial motherland. Both exclusions are structural, but differently structured, and they produce different types of textual emptiness. For example, when considered in relation to the historical erasure of U.S. imperialism, the importance of the unmediated presentation of the object for Ezra Pound (and the later modernists influenced by his theories on the relation between the subjectivity of the poet and the poetic object), and, in a more complicated way, the importance of the highly abstract object in Gertrude Stein's "portraits," suggests that these objects compensate for the historical emptiness of the modernist present by being framed against its multiple representational gaps. To take this a step further, these objects acquire their meaning as the thing itself precisely because they are set within a conceptual space/time that is radically empty. At the same time, these objects as fragments mask the relation of the history that they occlude to modernism's constitutive emptinesses. In this sense, the formal structure of modernism does not only articulate the breakdown of the developmental narratives that support imperialist expansion, as the readings that would posit modernism as politically subversive would have it. It also creates possibilities for replacing that metanarrative with new, more juxtapositional methods for representing U.S. national formation that keep its imperialism under erasure through the radically empty aesthetic of the fragment. Distinct from this exclusion of imperialist histories is the exclusion of same-sex relations between women in normative sexuality. When Stein's objects are considered in light of the problematics of the representation of nonnormative sexuality, the poetic object has a double function in relation to modernist emptiness because it articulates the representational crisis engendered by that sexuality as well as masking the absence of another representational possibility.

To account for the historical nature of this masking of representational exclusions, it is helpful now to return to Sangari's "The Politics of the Possible" (discussed in the introduction). Sangari points out an important difference between the postmodern (and modern) crisis of meaning in the West and "the inscription of the marvelous in the real" (217) in the novels of Gabriel García Márquez: the "cultural simultaneity" caused by foreign domination in areas that have experienced colonialism is significantly different from the "synchronic vision of culture" of the West, which is a result of the breakdown of a teleological model of time as a rational process of evolution and progress (219–20). An important aspect of this difference for Sangari lies in the fact that, whereas the First World version of the dissemination of teleologically based meaning into a chaotic synchronicity can easily propel writers into an apolitical posture, the Latin American "cultural simultaneity" in its articulation of a heterogeneity that includes effects of colonialism but is not contained by them does not produce the same preoccupation with a highly aestheticized and often self-consciously apolitical textuality. This, however, is not to say that one version of modernism is more political than the other. Rather, politics circulates differently in differently positioned modernisms. I would like to extend this argument by pointing out that the cultural politics of First World modernist texts also takes on different structural logics for different imperialist histories.

The difference that Sangari theorizes can, perhaps, account for the way in which the oppositional potential of modernism in the First World is to some extent swept back into an apparently neutral aesthetic that can be read as apolitical, internal, or radically subjective. As Sangari's argument suggests, however, such a reading overlooks how this modernist aesthetic serves an important ideological function within colonial discourses because its apparent neutrality is created through historical erasures. For this reason, it is important to read modernism's characteristic lack of narrative cohesiveness, linear story lines, and developed characters not only as the sites where developmental meaning breaks down, which is itself a valid reading, but also as the sites where national narratives subtly reassert themselves. In the British case, for example, the nondevelopmental inconclusiveness of Conrad's narrative form is presented as *the* crisis of the times, effacing how knowledge of colonialism is perceived by the colonized. And, in the U.S. case, we find a reaffirmation, even in Stein's radically nondevelopmental textual experiments, of the lifestyle of the bourgeois individual as a figure, at one level, of the problematics of national self-containment.[16] I noted in the introduction that, although this breakdown of developmental narratives and the reconfiguration of the certain aspects of those narratives can be explored in poetic texts, poetry is often overlooked in this connection precisely because of its lack of narrative form. I will turn to poetry later in this discussion of the representational problematic of Stein's work in order to account for how poetic brevity demands that individual words and phrases take on multiple, and at times contradictory, meanings, as is the case in *Tender Buttons*. Before turning to that series of prose poems, however, I will first consider how some of these hesitations make an earlier appearance in *The Making of Americans*, a novel that, in its last chapter, marks the relation between the breakdown of narrative form and the contradictions involved in the construction of U.S. national identity.

Although it may appear that modernist absences or empty spaces are not employed in the narration of *The Making of Americans*—since it is quite long and not at all empty in that it contains a large number of characters, events, etc. — the novel's narrative technique of repetition defies the fullness that is usually produced through narrative development. In this early novel, phrases and sentences are often repeated, sometimes in exactly the same words, and this repetition is further emphasized by introductory phrases such as "I have said that . . ." and "As I was saying. . . ." Here is an example from the first chapter of the novel:

> Yes, Julia looked much like her mother. That fair good-looking prosperous woman had stamped her image on each one of her children, and with her eldest, Julia, the stamp went deep, far deeper than just for the fair good-looking exterior. (14)

> I have said that a strong family likeness bound all three children firmly to their mother. That fair good-looking prosperous woman had stamped her image on each one of her children, but only with the eldest Julia was the stamp deep, deeper than for the fair good-looking exterior. (18)

Here, repetition not only hampers the narrative temporal flow but also reinforces a thematic repetition: Julia's resemblance to her mother. The concept of resemblance will, in Stein's later essays, be developed into a sophisticated critique of what she terms the *oneness* of the textual object or extratextual subject (which is also referred to as the *individuality* of the human subjects of her "portrait" poems), the beginnings of which are apparent in this novel in paradoxical statements such as: "Everyone then is an *individual being*. Everyone then is *like many others* always living, there are many ways of thinking of every one, this now is a description of all of them. There must then be a whole history of each one of them. There must now be a *description of all repeating*" (290; emphasis added). In such descriptions of individuality as a part of a process of resembling and repeating, Stein is writing against the fullness of protagonist characters (representations of "individual beings") that, in the Victorian or realist novel, develop over the course of the story line and are fundamentally distinct from other characters. Perhaps because of this lack of character development, the differences between characters in this novel have been read as differences among "types" rather than among "individuals."[17] Creating characters as types allows both the structural repetition and the theme of resemblance to heighten similarities among characters. This resemblance reaches its anticlimax in the closing chapter about the death of a character, which is discussed at length in terms of how "any one" will eventually become a "dead one" (907), thus homogenizing or equalizing all characters in death. It is this closing section on "dead ones" that definitively marks the death of the character in the repetition of its absence and that opens up another textual emptiness of the type discussed above.

If, as Jo-Anna Isaak has argued in "The Revolutionary Power of a Woman's Laughter," Stein's "entire work can be seen as an attempt to circumvent the end, the closure which is implied in the capitulation to the 'Law of the Father'" (46), then this final death of the character must be read not as an ultimate closure but as an absence that "completes" the text only by ending it with a pervasive sense of emptiness. Although this technique is a defiant and innovative departure from narrative structures based on character development and linear story lines, in this case by having a male character stand in for what Isaak refers to as the "Law of the Father," it also provides philosophical grounds for the exclusionary nature of Stein's portrait of Americans. By *exclusionary nature* I mean to refer to how Stein writes in this novel and in later expository prose that she was attempting in *The Making of Americans* to describe all the people that have ever lived in America while the novel centers on the story of two German immigrant families, the Dehnings and the Herslands.

This exclusion has been overlooked by critics who understand Stein's innovations as deriving from her less mainstream positioning (as lesbian, woman, German Jewish immigrant, etc.) relative to other early-twentieth-century canonical writers. Mary Dearborn provides a detailed analysis of the ways in which *The Making of Americans* is an immigrant ethnic novel (see *Pocahontas's Daughters*, 159–88). Dearborn's reading is illuminating in how it demonstrates the necessity of recognizing this text as a forerunner of a genre for which notions of Americanness, generation, and continuity and discontinuity are central themes. However, by considering the novel exclusively as an ethnic text, Dearborn loses sight of the ways in which the construction of whiteness is central to the writing of this German immigrant ethnicity and to the Americanness that it defines and is defined by. The final chapter's death of the character provides a good example of this as the exclusion of depictions of racialized labor (on which a significant extent of the progress of the generic "American family" rests) is justified in the logic controlling the sentence that opens the last chapter, generically entitled "A History of a Family's Progress." This sentence reads: "Any one has come to be a dead one" (907). The logic of representation here renders the purportedly inclusive heterogeneity (everyone) as "any one" in the form of a homogeneous, abstracted (and dead) white body. The opening paragraph of this chapter proceeds by extrapolating from the first sentence: "Any one has not come to be such a one to be a dead one. Many who are living have not yet come to be a dead one. Any one has come not to be a dead one. Any one has come to be a dead one" (907). The repetition of this generic *one* paints over textual space that would otherwise be inhabited with more traditional characters and their fates (the usual ending for a novel). At the same time, this aesthetic blankness functions as the kind of empty perceptual field within which the modernist object can be presented as the thing itself, or, according to Stein's terminology, an *autonomous entity*.[18] Dearborn does not explore how, as an unusual strategy of universalization, this dead white body stands in for the historical deaths that took place in order for the United States to eventually be established across an already-inhabited continent and for that land to become the setting on which the European immigrant family can make its progress.

The form and function of these empty spaces in the home become clearer in Stein's collection of expository prose *Lectures in America*, in which a similar concept is expressed through the implied metaphor of a movie screen. From the essay "Portraits and Repetition," this implied metaphor echoes the earlier image of a "splendid canvas." Stein's first step toward formulating this screen, however, is worked out in the opening essay of this collection, the argument of which consists of a detailed answer to the question that serves as its title: "What Is English Literature." In this essay, Stein argues that nineteenth-century literature is composed of phrases rather than sentences or paragraphs and that its primary function is to explain the relation between England's "inside" or its daily life on the island and its "outside," which she defines as everything England "owns." She sets up the relation between this national inside and outside thusly:

> As I say what happened was that the daily island life was more a daily island life than ever. If it had not been it would have been lost in their owning everything and if it had been lost in their owning everything they would have naturally

ceased to own everything. Anybody can understand that. They needed to be completely within their island life in order to own everything outside. (36)

And now how do phrases come to be phrases and not sentences, that is the thing to know. Because in the nineteenth century it does. . . . As they owned everything outside, outside and inside had to be told something about all this owning, otherwise they might not remember all this owning and so there was invented explaining and that made nineteenth-century English literature what it is. (40)

In the first of these quotes, Stein argues that "daily life" functions in English literature to enforce the notion of a national inside, thus preventing the existence of an outside subsumed within English ownership from challenging the stability of national geography and identity. The influence of Stein's essay on Jameson's is apparent in this thesis. In Stein's argument, however, the problematic is more contradictory: the English needed to be "completely within their island life in order to own everything outside," while at the same time "outside and inside had to be told something about all this owning" so that they would "remember" it. Stein does not speculate on exactly how the representation of internal affairs during a period of expansive imperialism might manage this inside/outside relation through the literary content; however, in accord with Matthew Arnold's famous thesis in *Culture and Anarchy*, it could do so by describing the daily life of the English as the most cultured and refined of all societies. Stein does, however, suggest that the paradox is resolved stylistically through the coming into primacy of the phrase (as opposed to the previous sentence and its completeness) in nineteenth-century English literature.

Below I outline how, in the distinction that she draws between nineteenth-century English phrases and twentieth-century American paragraphs, Stein theorizes a modernist completeness as a particularly American literary form. Her literary distinction attempts to illuminate purported differences between imperialistic and nonimperialistic national cultures. However, it would seem instead that it is precisely the attempt at drawing the latter distinction that results in a nondevelopmental literary form that is useful in narrating pre–World War II U.S. imperialism by putting it under erasure. My final analysis—of *The Geographical History of America*—explores how this erasure is problematized by the way in which Stein's modernist nondevelopmental temporality is "borrowed" from the failures of developmental history and, consequently, haunted by the histories of imperialist violence that the latter rationalizes and that both developmental and nondevelopmental forms fail to entirely suppress.

Stein describes nineteenth-century English literature as consisting of phrases, which, she says, are characterized by incompleteness. Earlier in "What Is English Literature," she describes a new sense of incompleteness caused by the insularity of English life, there being an entire outside that is also part of English experience but not "brought inside": "As they owned everything outside and brought none of this inside they naturally were no longer interested in choosing complete things" (34). Stein often writes that a paragraph (which contains a complete idea) is itself a complete thing and is useful in representing complete things, adding at one point in "What Is English Literature" that, if a thing is complete, "it doesn't need explanation" (43). The "incompleteness" of England itself is, according to Stein, what accounts for the way in which nineteenth-century literature utilizes an aesthetic of partial, explanatory phrases. As the respective parts constituting this incompleteness, "outside and inside had to be told something about all this owning . . . and so there was invented explaining and that made nineteenth-century English literature what it is." In other words, this incompleteness required a literature that could explain it, and a literature based on explanatory phrases emerged in order to take up that task. Stein has, thus, attributed to what she considers to be an incompleteness in nineteenth-century English literature the same reason that Jameson, following Stein, attributes to the radical incompleteness of English modernism. This reason is the distance between the colonies and the metropolis, the outside and the inside, causing what Jameson calls a *significational gap* in the high modernist text whose structure is formed by the impossibility of representing colonial reality. Stein apparently sees this incompleteness as already existing in the prose style (rather than the narrative structure) of earlier, Victorian novels. In this sense, both Stein's and Jameson's readings maintain that incompleteness is indicative of empire itself and not its vulnerability or its anticipated end: for Stein, such incompleteness is compensated for by a literature composed of explanatory phrases, while, for Jameson, modernist form itself is incomplete. Thus, when read alongside Jameson's, Stein's model allows us to see a degree of continuity between the two periods, rather than considering modernism, as it is usually described, as a radical break from past literatures. However, Jameson holds that the outside is unilaterally excluded from representation, whereas Stein acknowledges that this "owning" also had to be explained.

According to Stein's argument, the difference between nineteenth- and twentieth-century literature inheres not in a move from fullness to incompleteness, as contemporary modernist scholars usually have it. Almost directly to the contrary, Stein proposes that a literature of phrases was appropriate only while England was "certain" in owning everything in the nineteenth century, and she goes on to say that, in the twentieth century, literature began to be written in paragraphs: "The English have not gone on with this thing but we have in American literature" (49). In this way, Stein arrogantly locates all modernism written in English within an exclusively American context. Stein's observations on literary form in the two national contexts are, if not correct in an absolute sense, astute and provocative. However, the implications that are seemingly naturally drawn from these observations reveal a geographic brand of essentialism that makes American literature suited to the paragraph, an essentialism that allows America to be conceptualized as a "whole thing" and not dispersed, like the island nation England, across the globe in colonial conquests. In other words, according to Stein's logic, the literary self-containment of "complete things" is a marker of a nonimperialistic national culture contained in a single geographic space. This move assigns the nondevelopmental paragraph a new significational valence as a national literary form. Consequently, however, rather than operating seamlessly to obscure U.S. imperialism, the completeness of this cultural form both masks and signals the problematic of history in U.S. canonical modernism. Even as it buttresses exceptionalism, it also troubles the modernist text with the possible surfacing of precisely those histories of imperialist expansion — continental and intercontinental — that it painstakingly paints over in order to create the radical self-containment of the object as fragment.

I argue below that it is in precisely this troubled sense that the series of "paragraphs" that constitutes the entire text of *Tender Buttons* can be read. First, however, a passage from "The Gradual Making of the Making of Americans" brings us a step further toward understanding this formulation of "the American thing" by introducing a "space of time" that is characterized by "combination" and movement:

> It is singularly a sense for combination within a conception of the existence of a given space of time that makes the American thing the American thing, and the sense of this space of time must be within the whole thing as well as in the completed whole thing. . . . I am always trying to tell this thing that a space of time is a natural thing for an American to always have inside them as something in which they are continuously moving. Think of anything, of cowboys, of movies, of detective stories, of anybody who goes anywhere or stays at home and is an American and you will realize that it is something strictly American to conceive of a space of time that is filled with moving. (*Lectures in America*, 160–61)

Perhaps the most important metaphor for the "space of time" is that of "movies" since Stein also refers to the period in which she writes as "the period of the cinema and series production" (177). The two movements suggested here—the cowboy's movement within the boundaries of a continental frontier and the detective's movement across a space delineated by what can be discovered as the truth—can both be conceived within the larger temporal metaphor of the movie screen as "a space of time" within which one is "continuously moving." It is this movie screen that allows for such a contained movement (i.e., the movement of time contained within the film), and, in its essential blankness and strictly demarcated boundaries, it serves as the "space of time" within which the object (as a single isolated thing or a series of such things) can be foregrounded in a kind of cinematic movement that allows it to escape its frame (as in another essay in this collection, "Pictures," she suggests good paintings try to do [*Lectures in America*, 86]) while still being contained "within the whole thing."

This object is also the "whole thing" that is supposed to be capable of representing American experience, and *Tender Buttons* can be read as a series of such objects. This declaration of independence from (and even usurpation of) the cultural dominance of English literature is achieved, however, through its own strategy of literary colonization. In "Melanctha," for example, Stein appropriates Black English Vernacular as a "linguistic utopia that is a domain not colonized by England" (Bernstein, "Professing Stein/Stein Professing," 50) in a story that repeatedly affirms an absolute distinction between Negroes and whites and the "natural" superiority of the white race.[19] At the level of characterization, as A. L. Nielson points out, although

Stein's Negro characteristics in "Melanctha" are somewhat sympathetic in comparison with those of other white writers of the same period, "Stein's sympathy is the sympathy of romantic racism, and it is this that marks it as the signpost of modernism's discourse of the nonwhite" (*Reading Race*, 21).[20]

Although *Tender Buttons* contains no characters, not to mention dialogue, it is characterized by a less obvious but not less significant form of textual colonization in its radically experimental representation of the domestic sphere. To understand how this colonization works, therefore, it is necessary to understand the kind of experimentation that constitutes its form. Rather than utilizing a narrative form like that of "Melanctha," this text is made up of three sections, the first two (entitled "Objects" and "Food," respectively) consisting of a series of brief prose poems. Most of the prose poems are written in the form of a short paragraph. The paragraphs describe, in the first section, objects and, in the second, food items, although the extremely abstruse description that constitutes each poem renders the object or food item in question more or less unrecognizable. The final section, entitled "Rooms," is composed of one long and equally difficult prose poem. As critics such as Susan E. Hawkins have pointed out, the collection of prose poems in *Tender Buttons* collectively describes a home. Hawkins has emphasized Stein's contribution in rewriting the domestic sphere within the larger effort to create a women's literature. After a complicated analysis of Stein's syntactic experiments, she asks: "Is there anything else going on in *Tender Buttons* besides innovative technique and radical syntactic experimentation? And the answer is, yes; at a very comprehensible level Stein reveals to us, in an extraordinary way, the house we live in every day" ("Sneak Previews," 123). Stein's experimental refiguring of the home should certainly be acknowledged for its contributions to the larger feminist project of rewriting domesticity. Stein's most significant contribution to such a project is, however, the way in which the home in *Tender Buttons* is no longer the site of the daily experience of compulsory heterosexuality but, instead, transformed into the scene of what Elizabeth Freeman has termed an *erotic syntax* of lesbian desire. In "Queer Syntactic Strategy, Body Performance, and the Dialect of Lesbian Couplehood in Gertrude Stein," Freeman describes Stein's interest in the categorical and in lists as a way to examine "the structure of taxonomy itself" (2) and the relation of that taxonomy to the new sexual identities that served as objects of knowledge for scientific discourse in the late nineteenth century. In an argument that is too complex to summarize thoroughly, Freeman goes on to read the objects in *Tender Buttons* as, among other things, "nouns" that do not quite function as nouns and, therefore, signal the link for Stein between grammar, not lexicon, and sexuality: "By moving away from an erotic *lexicon* towards an erotic *syntax*, *Tender Buttons* abandons the static, the monumental, synecdochal quality of the noun which 'identifies' for the pulsions and rhythms of a syntax which 'performs'" (5). Freeman uses this syntactic analysis to show that Stein's objects, food items, and rooms reappropriate the setting for the heterosexual family for an erotics of lesbian couplehood that extends into the (Parisian Left Bank) lesbian community that is in the process of developing its own public sphere.

The problems with Stein's conception of the home are apparent not so much in the historical allusion to an emerging lesbian community as Freeman describes it as in the "we" that appears in Hawkins's analysis of this new "home." In a move typical of an identity-based feminism, Hawkins assumes that an unproblematic "we" can represent a women's literary movement. Unlike Hawkins, Stein does problematize the notion of women's identity and experience by thematizing the relation between nonnormative sexuality and the heterosexual real, which excludes nonheterosexual experience in order to function as the legitimated site of referentiality for knowledge of sexuality. However, by situating a critique of heterosexual norms within the domestic sphere without critiquing the other ideological functions of the home, there is a way this "we" subtly reconfigures itself in Stein's text.

Language play is an aspect of the construction of complete things in *Tender Buttons* that plays a significant role in its critique (and reaffirmation) of normative identity as a kind of self-containment. Formal self-containment in *Tender Buttons* is interestingly commented on in its content through the motifs of "spreading" and "widening," which first appear in the opening prose poem. Continuing throughout the three sections of the book, these motifs suggest the kind of movement in the textual presentation of objects that Stein would later—in *Lectures in America*—describe as the movement that allows an object (as the "American thing") to be simultaneously a self-contained thing and an aesthetic object that escapes a static and reductive framing. This movement is, however, intratextual, and its challenge to ideological and hierarchical classifications of objects (including human subjects) is highly linguistic. Even the rewriting of the home as a sphere of woman's power and pleasure and the nuanced critique of gender norms are presented quite explicitly as linguistic projects and as language games. The most obvious examples of this linguistic play are the lines "The sister was not a mister. Was this a surprise. It was" (65) and "Who is a man" (67). However, because Stein's concepts of identity and resemblance complicate the relation between the work of art and its referent, it is important to read the apparent aestheticization of this critique of gender norms mapped out by heterosexuality not as a failure of a potentially politically charged project but, rather, as the presentation of alternative gender formations. Rather than being read as representations of something real, prior, and extratextual, lines such as these should be read as entities in themselves with a significational force that is as real as anything outside the text.

Jo-Anna Isaak has, as we have seen, termed Stein's writing *presentational* as opposed to *representational*, and, although Stein does not use these particular terms, examples of a similar kind of distinction can be found in her own expository writings.[21] In the "Portraits and Repetition" chapter of *Lectures in America*, Stein explicitly complicates notions of referentiality in art by arguing that the value of a work of art lies not in its "resemblance" to a referent but in its own existence, which should be as independent from the referent as possible (188–89). And underlying her definition of in "Composition and Explanation" there is an implicit parallel between texts and things: both are examples of "composition." In other words, the textual object does not have a less authentic or immediate existence than the actual one; instead, both are mediated. The texts of her own compositions may be one location where it becomes possible for Stein to create a realm beyond that of proper names and norms, one where gender identity is freed up from biological determinism and where an improper gender identification does not entail a loss of "completeness."

Along with the emphatically textual meaning of the objects in *Tender Buttons*, the linguistic play that presents these objects also produces an aestheticized absence of meaning that, like their textual meaning, functions ideologically. To understand how this works what is necessary is not a lengthy close reading of the description of each object in its relation to the other objects but an analysis of Stein's textual frames, within which her objects repeatedly spread or widen. Stein begins the first series ("Objects") with a prose poem entitled "A CARAFE, THAT IS A BLIND GLASS." This is obviously an image of a container; however, the suggested containment is complicated by the last line of the poem, which reads: "The difference is spreading" (9). *Tender Buttons* thus begins with an example of how Stein's nonsensical style allows her objects to escape the boundaries of the proper (name, norm, etc.) while also accommodating the presentation of a complete thing. I would like to consider this first prose poem as a frame for what follows. In other words, this modernist carafe is a vessel that embodies Stein's new experimental language as itself a kind of frame—as a complicated strategy of containment within which objects continually move within their space of time. And the last section reveals how this language as a frame is also the home containing the "rooms" that constitute this text. In *Tender Buttons*, then, language itself is what the home or domesticity has been rewritten into: the poems written in this new, self-contained language are not representations of actual objects, food items, and rooms as much as they are themselves presentations of objects, food items, and rooms. If, in *Tender Buttons*, the bourgeois home is aestheticized, this aestheticization is not a simple retreat from everyday experience but a textual form of that experience. In other words, Stein's aestheticization is, ironically, a result of her refusal of representational meaning, a refusal that, in the case of *Tender Buttons*, results in a nonreferential presentation of everyday objects. Again, it is in this sense that her rewriting of the home and the gendered identities that inhabit it should not be considered a limited project that does not extend beyond the textual realm; rather, the textual should be considered as a real and compellingly articulate aspect of the social.

However, this shared ground between the work of art and the referent, according to which both have the status of "compositions," has other implications as well. The apparent absence of meaning serves an ideological purpose that is quite different from a critique of gender norms and that subtly restores its referentiality. As her language widens and spreads over any possible realities other than the textual ones that it creates, Stein successfully paints over any links between this home and the conditions of violence and exploitation that bring about the conditions of its existence, both textual and extratextual. Thus "the house we live in everyday" is "reveal[ed] to us" (Hawkins, "Sneak Previews," 123) as a nonreferential, completely aestheticized object that functions, paradoxically, to reassure "us" of its sanctity and exclusive claims to referentiality. In articulating this nonreferentiality that is necessarily fraught with the imperialist histories that are formative of the bourgeois home, *Tender Buttons* becomes the quintessential U.S. modernist text. This is not to say, however, that it is exemplary of a universally relevant modernism whose tenets are developed and defined in the West and then exported to the rest of the world as criteria for literary achievement. On the contrary, to see it as emblematic of the imperialistic historical configurations that structure modernist texts in the First World is to suggest that the notion of modernism itself, to the extent that it has been defined within Anglo-American and European epistemes, needs to be fundamentally rethought and, as Dipesh Chakrabarty has in "Postcoloniality and the Artifice of History," argued in the case of European historiography, provincialized. So far in this reading of Stein's texts from the first decade of the twentieth century through the 1930s, I have tried to provincialize her canon through a critique of how an underlying logic of American exceptionalism makes possible her theses on American cultural forms as well as her own representations of American modernity and domesticity.

That *Tender Buttons* becomes emblematic of the fraught relation between U.S. modernism and U.S. history happens not simply in spite of Stein's critique of hegemonic gender norms. Rather, because of its setting within what Rosemary George allows us to term a *recycled* home (see her "Recycling"), this critique itself ironically supports the twentieth-century imperialist discourses that continue to reproduce notions of the domestic sphere even as it suggests the breakdown of nineteenth-century colonial narratives of progress and development. Sexuality-based critiques and rewritings of domesticity such as Stein's are relevant to all areas of cultural criticism because the home is an important site of multiple deployments of patriarchal and heterosexual domination. However, because, in the U.S. context, the home is also a significant site of imperialistically derived forms of exploitation, a critical rewriting must also account for the ways in which in the domestic sphere a feminized whiteness is constructed and defined in opposition to the racialized domestic labor that also inhabits the home. Although Stein provides a salient critique of the domestic in these early writings, that critique does not consider the ways in which the subjugation of women in the domestic sphere not only occurs within heterosexist and patriarchal structures of power but is also significantly linked to the reproduction of labor relations formed through a colonial legacy of racialized exploitation. In other words, by critiquing conventional notions of domesticity through sexuality (by eroticizing the home as a setting for nonnormative sexual practices) and gender (by freeing up gender identity from biological determinism) but not through the axes of race and labor, Stein's new version of domesticity reinvests itself in the narratives of bourgeois individuality that inform the very notions of womanhood and identity that her texts consistently call into question. This is not to say that writing not set in the home avoids this problem; nor is it to argue that Stein is to blame for the discursive conditions of her time. Rather, it is to examine how these conditions operate as a structural element of canonical modernism, even in Stein's writing on nonnormative subjects. This is the case because it is precisely the failure of progress that is available for Stein to "borrow" in order to claim a kind of timeliness for her new formulation of the domestic by affirming nondevelopmental forms of self-containment as a kind of national or cultural characteristic emblematic of modernity. In doing so, she ironically reaffirms the exclusive concepts of identity that her texts attempt to deconstruct along with narratives of progress. How this borrowing is accomplished is the subject of the next section.

## The Allegorical Histories of America

Stein's choice of title for her 1936 text *The Geographical History of America* points immediately to the spatial and the temporal in its construction of America. The landscape of this text is pervasively flat, contains a repetition of figures in form as well as in content, and is inhabited more often by corpses than by characters. Such a landscape signals the temporal problematics of Stein's appropriation of the end of progress to construct a radical revision of sexuality in her oddly allegorical form of historiography. This appropriation is, I argue, most effective, but also most problematic, in the way in which, ultimately, her own allegorical histories of sexuality cannot be fully separated from allegorical histories of imperialism, which, as a result, inhabit the text as a kind of unacknowledged, ghostly temporality.

In the *Geographical History*, after a short paragraph about America, Stein writes: "Detective story number I. Will the world which is round be flat. Yes it is. When there was a sea the world was round but now that there is air the world is flat" (131–32). This short paragraph indicates how Stein's American landscape is characterized by a large, empty flatness, like a great expanse of plains seen from above: "In the United States there is more space where nobody is than where anybody is" (53). The connection between advanced technology (here suggested in the inference of an airplane as the site from which the world is seen) and America is a common one in Stein's writings, as is the connection between that technology and repetition (recall, e.g., her statement that the twentieth century is a period of "the cinema and series production"). The flatness and the repetition of U.S. modernity are, then, the products of rapidly advancing technologies, and they are crucial to Stein's formulation of both American space and modern space. The new technology of the movies in particular is associated not only with repetition but also with the American sense of space described above, which, we should recall, in *Lectures in America* she terms a "space of time that is filled with moving," using, as we have seen, movies, cowboys, and detective stories as examples of this American space. To theorize American space/time in this way is to associate it with forms of popular culture, such as movies, westerns, and detective stories. But it is also, as I will show below, to situate those forms in an epistemology of space that enables Stein to call into question the categorical frameworks that are the preconditions for the unfolding of meaning even in those popular forms. It is, thus, not exactly to represent the most ideological construction of America as an ontological entity, but to utilize a popular discourse about newness, discovery, and invention for purposes other than those of the nation even while relying on the givenness of America as constituted by such qualities in order to do so.

On the first page of the *Geographical History*, Stein begins her meditation on space by writing: "Let us not talk about disease but about death. If nobody had to die how would there be room enough for any of us who now live to have lived. We never could have been if all the others had not died. There would have been no room" (53). Space is described here as "room"—empty, expansive space available for occupation by the living as the setting for their life stories. However, if this space were filled with the stories of live characters, it would no longer be vast and empty—it would no longer be room. Instead of placing characters in her geographic landscapes, Stein again, as she did in *The Making of Americans*, replaces characters with corpses, whose appearances are first implied in this early passage and returned to repeatedly throughout. The corpse is an important figure in this geography because it marks the precondition of the room that characterizes American space. The fact that Stein opens this discussion of space with a reference to death demonstrates how, for her, the corpse or "dead one" is a particularly repeatable object. Its lack of the individuating stories that distinguish live characters from one another renders it generic, and, thus, the repetition of generic objects such as dead bodies replaces stories of individual lives. As repetition replaces narrative progression, this initial reference to death in Stein's American geography suggests temporal resonances different from those that correspond to landscapes characterized by life, variety, and fullness. To put it in Stein's own terms, in this landscape there is no beginning, middle, or ending: "Why is it always that there is a beginning and a middle and an ending: Because it is quite right that nobody can write" (120). In other words, the lack of character development signaled by the deaths in the opening pages corresponds to a general lack of narrative development and linear progression in the text as a whole. Instead, the history of the title, with its associations of progress, is embodied in the corpse, which, as in a detective story, begins the story rather than concluding or resolving it. The corpse begins the story, moreover, with a comment on the impossibility of beginning, beginnings being always indebted to endings: "We never could have been if all the others had not died." Thus, the usual temporal structure of narrative is flattened out into a logic of repetition—into the flat spatial dimension of the American landscape.

This repetition characterizes Stein's concept of the *continuous present*, the grammatically derived temporality on which Stein bases the narrative structure of her most experimental writings. According to this sense of time, the present does not develop out of a past and into a future but, rather, continues in a nondevelopmental movement. Stein maintains this temporality by employing the present continuous and present perfect continuous tenses, by repeating phrases and sentences in identical or slightly differing wording, and by focusing on the thematics of continuity and repetition. In the *Geographical History*, the difficulty of maintaining the present in narrative is suggested in such passages as: "So finally I became attached to one word at a time even if there were always one word after another" (195). Thus, repetition in a series provides an alternative to the temporal development of progress: "Progress is just that, it has come to go away and so here we are now . . ." (129).

This alternative temporality corresponds to what Priscilla Wald, in her chapter on Stein in *Constituting Americans*, has described as the importance of William James's notion of *hesitation* for Stein as she began her early writings. In an essay from *The Principles of Psychology* entitled "Habit," James defines *habit* as a mechanism that "diminishes the conscious attention with which our acts are performed" (*The Writings of William James*, 12). For James, this is a necessary factor of behavior, but, as Wald writes, summarizing James, "situations where habit proved insufficient, where there was 'hesitation,' awakened 'explicit thought'" (238). If habit involves diminished attention in the automatic flow of perceptions, a break in that flow of habitual behavior both enhances attention and enables the emergence of perceptions that are not already shaped by "preperceptions"—pregiven labels for different kinds of experiences. In other words, in the hesitation that arises from a pause in habit, new perceptions can be experienced and articulated. Wald goes on to speculate on the role that early Jamesian psychology played in Stein's language experimentation, writing: "James's interest in breaking habits of attention finds its fullest expression in the analysis and literary innovation of *The Making of Americans*" (268). If we take this connection more specifically into a consideration of Stein's use of the continuous present, we can see the ramifications of this alternative temporality for Stein's epistemological critique. Her use of the continuous present constitutes a type of hesitation that arrests the normative "beginning-middle-end" flow of narrative and prevents the occurrence of a linear development of plot, character, and meaning. This hesitation, moreover, in which the fullness of novelistic and realist meaning is arrested and flattened out, resonates much more fully with Jameson's statement from "Modernism and Imperialism" that a structural hesitation is indicative of "modernism itself" than does Forster's novelistic writing.

Stein's focus on the present as not structured through a linear relation to the past and future disrupts patterns of meaning expressed in the form of the novel in which characters develop over time into maturity—a developmental temporality that, as in *Are Girls Necessary?* Julie Abraham has argued, is dependent for its structure and meaning on the heterosexual plot. In other words, the meaningfulness of narrative is produced through the progression of the character through the sequential stages of gendered, heterosexual development. Nonnormative sexuality is excluded from these developmental processes and the meaningfulness that they produce. Stein's explicitly nondevelopmental temporality is, like the "complete" spatial form of her objects, a strategy for addressing experiences of what she refers to in *The Making of Americans* as "many ways of being and of loving" (505). However, the previous discussion of those objects has shown that developmental temporalities are necessary to meaning and representation because these processes posit reality as an ontologically prior field in relation to which representation itself is secondary. The representational process conceptualized in this way is, as Ferdinand de Saussure has argued, a linear one.[22] Perhaps for this reason Stein's epistemological project is aimed at articulating nonnormative forms of pleasure and the crisis of representation that they engender, rather than bringing the lesbian into unproblematic, realist representation. Stein's experimental prose never contains stories about lesbian characters structured according to a developmental logic; instead it articulates the problematics of nonnormative sexual practices to the heterosexual real and to representation through the use of a nondevelopmental temporality like the continuous present.

Stein's conceptions of space and time, and, consequently, her critique of identity, converge in the *Geographical History* in her claim that "there is no identity and no time and no interest in enough" (197). This claim appears in "chapter IV" of what is purportedly the story of her life. The chapters of this story are not organized chronologically, and this statement is from the *second* "chapter IV." The convergence of "no time" and "no interest in enough" suggests that Stein's nondevelopmental temporality is linked to a spatial logic of insatiability. This insatiability nuances her emphasis on self-containment and completeness in *Lectures*, *Tender Buttons*, and other texts: the idea of complete things corresponds to fulfillment not as satisfaction but as a kind of overflowing desire. In both cases, the promise of development that constitutes meaning, or, as Wald puts it, the "story" itself, is denied. This critique of spatial and temporal fullness presupposes, I would like to suggest, a crucial distinction between the allegorical histories that Stein writes and the historical meanings that she challenges.

Although Stein's landscapes are often the setting of something closer to absurdist comedy than tragedy, her "dead ones" signal the allegorical significance of her use of apparent nonsense at more than one level of signification. I would like to return for a moment to the spatial contours of Benjaminian allegory as discussed in the introduction and its landscapes of "overripeness and decay" (*The Origin of German Tragic Drama*, 179). Benjamin describes allegorical aesthetic form as nonprogressive and even as "self-indulgently hesitant" (183). This allegorical form is nondevelopmental, but not without history: history is embedded in its landscape as ruin or inhabits it as a corpse. It is only in this sense that it can be argued that Stein's geographic history is, indeed, historical: the vast and empty expanses of its geography are marked by the past only in the presence of death and corpses that function not so much as a reminder of what went before as an element of the continuous present. This is precisely the form of allegorical history: the past does not developmentally unfold into the full bloom of the present but exists in the present itself as ruin and decay. In this sense, allegory can be employed as an antihistorical history that challenges the fullness of historical meanings and contests the terms according to which representation is carried out. In other words, the *historical meanings* that Stein is challenging rely on processes of representation that are unacknowledged as such to allow those meanings to be seen as unmediated and factual. These representational processes are structured by a developmental movement toward the end and fulfillment. Stein's *allegorical histories*, on the other hand, acknowledge the signs of the past in the present while denying the story of progress and development that structures representational processes and knowledge formations.

It is in this ruinous landscape of the continuous present that Stein can formulate a conception of history in relation to nonnormative desires, identifications, and sexual and social practices in a nonrepresentational framework where "there is no identity." This conception of history is allegorical, first, because, on the one hand, it is denied development and, on the other, it self-indulgently denies fulfillment. Second, it instead inhabits an alternative temporality that challenges the developmental and an alternative spatiality that exploits the categorical: as such, it is an allegorical space/time of nonnormative sexuality. However, there are other allegorical histories, in addition to the allegorical time of sexuality and gender, that differently inform this geographic history. The dead bodies that occupy the wide-open spaces of this construction of American modernity can be read also as the allegorical presence of the histories of U.S. expansion across the frontier, which can be conceptualized as empty only through a discursive violence that supports that expansion.

Stein's modernist temporality is borrowed from the cultural processes of erasure that produce this American space/time as empty. The allegorical history of sexuality is most explicitly the subject of many of Stein's texts. However, the allegorical history of U.S. imperialism is a differently formed nondevelopmental temporality that Stein evokes as she borrows another nondevelopmental temporality—the new modernist temporality of the end of time—to make her own representational critique. Borrowing the end of time evokes the allegorical histories of U.S. imperialism because the former's radical temporal emptiness has emerged precisely in the attempt to erase the foundational imperialist histories of the United States as it began to embark on overseas conquests and expansion became a matter of controversy. What I would like to stress in conclusion is that the allegorical histories of imperialist expansion impinge themselves on Stein's acknowledged nondevelopmental time of gender and sexuality, a temporality that Stein achieves through her formulation of the continuous present and the empty space of her textual geographies. This pressure is exerted forcefully in the prevalence of the "dead ones" that mark Stein's empty landscapes with genocidal and catastrophic histories and, in Stein's terminology, in the indebtedness of the living to the dead.

# 3

## "Learning a Lesson in the Superficial Song Lyrics": Hsia Yü's "Underground" Poetry

>Suddenly it's quiet in all directions
>Only leaving one, easy-listening song:
>"Leaving on a Jet Plane"
>Humming along
>I want to let myself feel a little sorrow
>Learning a lesson
>In the superficial song lyrics
>
>     Hsia Yü, "Leaving on a Jet Plane"

WHEN ASKED IN AN INTERVIEW about the designation *underground poet*, Hsia Yü, arguably Taiwan's most innovative contemporary poet,[1] stated that she knew what the term meant when, after self-publishing her first collection and then immediately leaving the country, she later returned to find that her (not copyrighted) volume had become so well received that her poems appeared, uncredited, in stores on everything from magazine holders to cushions. Ironically, these poems had begun circulating as emblems of an emerging 1980s leisure culture that had little to do with the concerns that guided their composition. As Hsia Yü asserts in the interview, while she is not by any means anti–popular culture (she writes popular song lyrics for a living and has released her own alternative rock CD), it still should not be too much to ask that one's poems not appear on display as pretentious-looking commodities without one's knowledge (Hsia Yü, *Ventriloquy* 114). These remarks about the designation *underground* must be understood in light of the fact that Hsia Yü is one of the most well-known and critically acclaimed poets writing in Chinese today. In spite of her popularity and renown, however, in this chapter I take up the term *underground* as a point of departure for exploring how her poetics unsettles institutionalized knowledge formations, especially those produced through the apparatuses of education and marriage. Some previous discussions of her poetry have already shed helpful light on its critical edge with regard to its gender politics in particular (see Li, "'The Nation' in the Eyes of Taiwan's Women Poets"; and Yeh, "The Feminist Poetic of Hsia Yü"). However, the full significance of the way in which a critical poetics like Hsia Yü's makes interventions into modernist cultures is not easy to recognize within existing reading paradigms for poetry, even those offered by the theoretical discourses of postmodernism, feminism, etc., to the extent that these paradigms are unequipped to address the workings of neocolonial knowledge formations.

Like much of what I have been calling *modernist* writing, whether progressive or reactionary, Hsia Yü's poetry develops an embodiment of and a reflection on radical fragmentation. What I would like to demonstrate in the following pages, however, is that, through an interrogation of the quotidian, it implicates its fragments in a critique of neocolonial ideologies of identity (rather than reaffirming, like Stein's, a reformulated version of domesticity as a sublation of modernity's promise). Unlike Pound's, Stein's, and Cha's, Hsia Yü's experimental poetics does not develop an apparent or explicit focus on the experience of modernity. Because of this absence, her poetry illuminates, for the present study, the overly transparent nature of modernity as it is often conceptualized in canonical modernism, as if it ever could be already seamlessly in place, distinguishing the modern subject, or the West, as such. With this point of departure, I argue that Hsia Yü's attention to the "microstructures" of the everyday—the gendered, the sexualized, and the personal—itself provides a critique of the structures of knowledge and feeling that constitute the logic and affectivity of precisely those nationalist and other knowledge formations that constitute Taiwan's narratives of modernity.

I want to emphasize that making such an intervention without an explicit critique of the narratives of modernity and nation is not, as might be assumed, the mark of a more assimilative or less critical stance on modernity. On the contrary, it is the result of the discursive formation or conceptualization of modernity that is formed in Taiwan's postwar neocoloniality. Within this discursive formation, modernity cannot very readily be taken for granted as already in place, or as an established state of social, political, and economic existence and practice, or even as a transparently nameable object of a critical discourse, because modernity is already conceptualized as both the *sign* of a critical discourse aimed against historically instituted ("traditional") oppressions and the *goal* of progressive and democratic social change. Within this critical discourse that "modernity" names, modernity must function conceptually as a goal and not as an existing reality in order to support politically effective critiques of existing social conditions, which can then be seen as still "traditional," or as not yet modern enough. I'd like to suggest that it is partly by not naming modernity as its object that Hsia Yü's poetry finds a way to critique the lived conditions of modernity without rhetorically setting up the conceptual limitations of this modernity/tradition binary.

Additionally, although definitions of Chinese modernity and the question of Chinese and later Taiwanese identity have been two of the most central intellectual issues of Hsia Yü's time, her poetry, unlike, for example, Stein's, does not often take up the rhetoric of national identity, not even as appropriation. In the heatedly politicized intellectual circles of Taiwan, especially with regard to national identity and sovereignty issues, her poetry can be read as apolitical and ahistorical. Its cultural politics and historicity can be understood, however, even within the context of these complex discourses of national identity. With both the Chinese rule in Taiwan after Japanese colonialism and the ensuing development of the opposition promoting, respectively, *Chinese identity* and *Taiwanese identity*, these identifications both function as part of what is akin to a postcolonial political ideology (although not necessarily named as such), yet they name identities and alliances that are posited at times as mutually incorporative and at other times as mutually exclusive. The complicated postcolonial situation is exacerbated by the frequent denial of political representation for Taiwan by the international community. Further, with internal understandings of national identity split between Chinese and Taiwanese, a critique of one almost immediately rhetorically validates the other, even if there is no intended validation of either. What I would like to suggest is that, when discourses of national identity and modernity (the latter posited as in-progress modernization seemingly no matter how modern Taiwan becomes) are this thoroughly and deeply politicized in the interests of various state institutions and oppositional movements, the refusal to seriously take up that line of questioning is itself also a significant political act. In counterdistinction to a line of inquiry that appropriates discourses of nationality, Hsia Yü's poetry reveals how a sustained poetic engagement with quotidian detail, the personal, the popular, and even the apparently irrelevantly foreign is a particularly effective way in which a critical perspective on identity and modernity can emerge.

## "Leaving on a Jet Plane"

"Leaving on a Jet Plane" is one of Hsia Yü's earliest published works. (The title is a Chinese translation of the title of John Denver's hit song.)[2] A narrative and relatively less difficult poem, it was included in her first collection, which was circulated informally but widely in the 1980s by readers' recopying the original editions.[3] This poem, which appropriates and refigures the U.S. pop song for its own purposes, was itself later used as lyrics for a song by Sandee Chan, a well-known Taipei-based alternative rock musician and composer, in her 1995 CD release also entitled *Leaving on a Jet Plane*. (Despite her lasting critical acclaim, Chan remains on the margins of the mainstream, reputedly having refused to sell out to the mando-pop industry.)[4] In what follows, I read Hsia Yü's poem as both a reference to and an experimental refiguration of U.S. popular culture in Taiwan, a refiguration that spawns further experimental reincarnations like Chan's. I argue that the critical edge of the poem with regard to neocolonial knowledge formations does not disappear because of its lack of a macrostructural object of critique; rather, the poem takes up an "underground" sensibility in the representation of quotidian detail in love and school in order to offer a critical thinking through of the underlying logics of its context.

In Hsia Yü's early writings like "Leaving on a Jet Plane," this critical perspective is especially powerful when quotidian details form an alternative knowledge presented as at odds with both the content and the form of knowledge propagated by modern educational institutions. The intervention that the poetry makes in this regard must be understood in light of the importance of educational apparatuses to postwar nationalism in Taiwan. In "Making Time," the historian Marshall Johnson has persuasively demonstrated the vexed processes through which a Chinese national identity was constructed in Kuomintang (KMT) educational apparatuses. Although one might expect that literature and culture would be the primary academic venues through which such an interpellation process was carried out, Johnson, quoting Chiang Kai-shek, demonstrates how, in this case, it was the more scientific discourses of history and even geography that were most important.[5] Johnson suggests that the turn to geographic narrations of the nation in particular is a response to how apparent the contradictions of national space are in Taiwan's case (the KMT being removed from the site of the Chinese mainland where the Republic was established and had its history while Taiwan was under Japanese rule), asserting: "Nowhere else do fossils testify to the legitimacy of the state. In another Taiwan Miracle, nature is mobilized to enforce Taiwan's incorporation into the Chinese state, even before there were Chinese" (115).[6] Johnson draws on the work of Phillip Corrigan and Derek Sayer to argue that, in KMT nationalist geography and history, an underlying "doxa" was constructed that extended beyond KMT interests and purposes, shaping even the emergent oppositional identities:

> The crucial product of moral regulation was not opinion and explicit subscription to a credo, but *doxa*, an invisible dark-star knowledge, and to its gravity both heterodoxy and orthodoxy incline. The opposition of heterodox to orthodox (Taiwanese nationalism to Chinese nationalism) implies a true nationalism, . . . in short, the National structure of the prenotional world. Outside the field of opinion, doxic knowledge rests on historical relations deposited in bodies, and thereby embodied in the means of perceiving, cognizing, naming and operating on the world where "otherwise" is literally unthinkable . . . until objective crisis conjoins an effective heretical discourse. (111–12)

Throughout this chapter, I argue that such an "unthinkable" otherwise or "heretical discourse" is precisely the end to which is put the means of radical experiment in Hsia Yü's poetry. The formal difficulty and speculative nature of the poetry critiques the doxa of the nationalist interpellative knowledge structures that is hard to pinpoint behind its "factual" face. This is not accomplished, as might be expected, by addressing any issues of nationalism very explicitly. Rather, it is the less obvious and more underlying structures of knowledge, the doxa itself, that come under scrutiny and the values and structures of feeling that they support and help produce. "Leaving on a Jet Plane" provides a compelling illustration of this point because it uses the juxtaposition of textbook quotations (including a law of physics), a U.S. pop song, and its own subjunctive speculations to highlight the irony of this song's circulation in early 1980s Taiwan as an artifact of U.S. cultural imperialism while most people were still relatively confined by the travel restrictions instituted under martial law. In doing so, the poem also places value on what should be irrelevant and undesirable in terms of contemporary doxa by introducing a third term (a Romanian stranger) into the contradictory equation of national self versus foreign other/Western/"American," thereby upsetting this equation's fragile sublations.

The poem is composed of a juxtaposition, at the beginning, of the idea of leaving on a jet plane with mathematical/scientific principles and foreign allusions, followed by a humorous collage of homework topics and sentences. Together, the homework topics and references to travel and foreignness form a critique of institutional education and the objects of knowledge, identification, and desire that it promotes and excludes, while the representation of the everyday presents alternative knowledge formations and identifications/desires. Here are some passages from the first part of the poem:[7]

> On that day when I'm always going to run into such a person
> A neighboring table a dark little bar
> As an unfamiliar language is being spoken
> The perfectly straight diagonal lines split [the space] into
> Completely opposite quadrants there's such
> A person putting down a suitcase patiently
> Folding a cloth napkin into boats
> And women a very
> Exquisitely bored napkin
> Such a person
> And me
> Without any apparent reason
> Are in the same room
> Shadows slant, stretching into the distance

Waiting [until] amid random movements
[They] converge, and fall on a
Romanian's shoe
The Romanian's beard is like snow
The third snow after the revolution
To put it like this isn't enough, far away
The march's procession goes by
Seven drumstrokes inspire a passionate
Severance, where is the drum for stitching people up
Intensity like that of spring
Terrible chastity ah dragonflies the dragonflies
Have flown away the dancers enter
The people with nothing to say keep on drinking tea
In the dusk the sound of a sigh
Passed along by warm air
This shouldn't be too meaningful, yet there's no harm in
Some understanding some
Inextinguishability [conservation] of energy—to run into such a person
Yes
There could always be a day
It's possible
Very possible
In each other's weary eyes
Kindly glancing away there's no way
To do anything more
Suddenly it's quiet in all directions
Only leaving one, easy-listening song:
"Leaving on a Jet Plane"
Humming along
I want to let myself feel a little sorrow
Learning a lesson
In the superficial song lyrics

In these opening lines, there is a sense of possibility, figured as a chance meeting with a Romanian stranger, that is carried through the poem as a whole, while the idea of the chance meeting is juxtaposed—placed in the same line—with a law of physics, the conservation of energy. This law refers to how, in a given physical system, energy can change form but is always conserved, never increasing or decreasing in quantity. Although, in English, this law is referred to as the *conservation of energy*, I have translated it literally from the Chinese (*nengliang bumie*) as the *inextinguishability of energy* because, more than *conservation*, *inextinguishability* implies the sense of ongoing (even tiring) possibility important to these lines. In other words, the possibility of this meeting itself can be read through the juxtaposition as an illustration of the principle of the conservation/inextinguishability of energy. Descriptive phrases such as *diagonal lines* and *opposite quadrants* delineate the space of the bar, which contains, apparently, the neighboring table where the Romanian is sitting. This adds to the mathematical language of the opening lines and uses that language to emphasize a sense of difference. What I want to point out as an initial step in reading the poem is that these concepts from math and physics, which are familiar to any Taiwanese student, are applied here to an inappropriate subject (a chance meeting with a foreign stranger in a dark bar), upsetting conventional value systems and morality. Later, I discuss how other math problems and homework assignments are put to a similar use in the last half of the poem.

The literal act of leaving on a jet plane was not very common in postwar Taiwan while martial law was still in effect; international air travel would be more accessible to the general population in the late 1980s. Since direct travel to the mainland was forbidden, and since most of the island itself is easily traversed by ground transportation, air travel connoted leaving the country (it still does), and international travel was strictly controlled during martial law (Phillips, "Between Assimilation and Independence," 298).[8] This circumstance, in addition to the disorienting future subjunctive of the first line, creates the irony of the poem's title and thematics. It also creates a "what-if" mood for the whole poem that presents its content as a puzzle and at the same time a nonmainstream life philosophy that affirms adventure, chance, and risk. This is partly an effect of the language described above, which presents the poem in terms of a math problem or a scientific equation, while the mathematical language is also used, unexpectedly, to emphasize a sense of possibility and adventure in personal relationships. It is also worked out in other descriptions such as references to travel (the song, the stranger with a suitcase, the unfamiliar language), in the off-color setting (a small dark bar), in the preponderance of coincidence (without apparent reason, random movements), and, perhaps most strongly, in the fact that, rather than being one of the many U.S. soldiers for whom such places began to appear in the 1960s and who frequented them throughout the 1970s,[9] the stranger is from Romania, which, in the mid-1980s, signifies as a small, Communist, Eastern European country—in the context of this poem's production, Romania is emphatically not an important object of knowledge, identification, or desire.

The idea of leaving on a jet plane as a method of unfettering (with which it is associated later in the poem) evokes and even embodies a kind of sublation. In other words, the contradiction of lived and experiential space (i.e., that of national space discussed above) is not resolved but preserved by being displaced into a "higher" form of narrativized promise: the transcendent figure of the plane's takeoff.[10] In other words, on the one hand, the speculative nature of the poem and its title/refrain evokes, particularly for present-day readers, the neocolonial "hope" of emigration to the First World since such emigration was actually beginning to happen in the early 1980s, with a significant percentage of the elite student population remaining in the United States after receiving advanced degrees (Rubinstein, "Taiwan's Socioeconomic Modernization," 380). However, the poem's refiguration of the idea of leaving on a jet plane, especially as it is inflected by the would-be romance with an Eastern European stranger, runs counter to interpellative affirmations of both the national and the foreign (the latter because, when it is affirmed, it usually has to take the form of the dominant and the American). Further, the connotations of the takeoff are not material security, etc., but, rather, adventure, possibility, the unknown or the unfamiliar, and even revolution. The signification of *leaving on a jet plane* is glossed in the poem by the overall sense of energy and possibility, and this is contrasted to "the people with nothing to say" who "keep on drinking tea." While chance and adventure are affirmed, moreover, the attendant sublation of these themes is also complicated by the poem's unrelenting critique of the epistemological structures of the present in the form of institutionally produced knowledge formations and structures of identification. These are never presented as having been simply left behind; rather, they are continually challenged by the other aspects of adventure.

Adventure as alluded to by the references to a Romanian and a revolution may be typical as part of a leftist romantic imaginary;[11] however, such an imaginary is not typical of cultural production in 1980s Taiwan (oppositional, nativist literature tends to be focused on the local, and the opposition tends to be couched in ethnic terms rather than in classed or political terms like *Right* and *Left*). The romanticization of a small Communist country is not typical of what Kuan-hsing Chen has theorized using the term *little subjectivity complex*, referring to how the smaller or less powerful postcolonial or neocolonial sites (such as Taiwan) that have relatively strong economies but are cut off from the "big civilizations" (such as China) are left with a crisis of identification that creates a tendency toward identification with some former colonial or present neocolonial power (see Chen, "The Decolonization Question," 18). This helps explain the role of things American in Taiwan (even compared to other sites of U.S. neocolonialism in East Asia), a phenomenon that is often mentioned but rarely explained and that Chen has discussed, noting that, in postwar Taiwan, foreign equals Western equals American. Chen emphasizes how, beginning in this period, language learning had become part of both the educational and the administrative/political institutionalization of this equivalence: not only was there a strong emphasis on foreign-language acquisition, but American English had become by far the most important language to master and the United States the preferred site of advanced studies in any subject, with "unthinkable" "trickle-down effects" (see Chen, "Missile Internationalism," 179). Chen goes on to argue that this is not exactly a matter of colonial identification, even according to a critical colonial theorization such as Fanon's, but, rather, something even more complicated.

I would like to suggest that poetry offers a mode of critical reflection that can deal critically with the "unthinkable"—fragmented knowledge that would seem unmanageably complex in a strictly theoretical or sociological account. For example, Chen's "trickle-down effects" are illustrated in the poem's choice of an English-language song from the U.S. Top 40 charts as its title and theme and as the ironic source of an alternative knowledge. Ultimately, however, what the poem's use of the song illustrates is that it is impossible to anticipate how knowledge circulating in mainstream popular culture (English-language, U.S. or otherwise) is taken up and reshaped, as indicated in the reframing of the popular song with a chance nocturnal meeting with a Romanian stranger. This use of the song and its reframing affirm a hybridity of experience that contradicts, first, the homogeneity of nationalist doxa. Such homogeneity, moreover, supports neocolonial interests as well by shifting attention away from the interpellation processes of U.S. cultural imperialism in Taiwan that contribute to the little subjectivity complex. The poem focuses on the U.S. cultural text, ironizes its interpellative function ("Learning a lesson / In the superficial song lyrics"), and then appropriates a sense of energy and possibility from it, putting it to purposes that, in significant ways, run against the grain of both nationalist and neocolonial interests. This is because, if Cold War interpellation processes and the structure of value produced by them in Taiwan are hinged contradictorily between the national as local and the foreign as dominant, then Hsia Yü's poem has added another element (the Romanian) into the equation. The added significance might be hard to detect within U.S. Cold War paradigms of national versus foreign because, in the United States, the Cold War self/other interpellation operates along an ally versus enemy basis, according to which the Eastern European is constructed as one of the second terms. Romanticizing this Communist other is, thus, no surprise. However, unlike how it would signify in the U.S. context, the poem uses the figure of the Communist enemy both to romanticize it and to upset the exclusive attention to the dominant in postwar Taiwan interpellative constructions of Western modernity.

This kind of appropriation is carried further in the next section of the poem, where the idea of leaving on a jet plane is humorously, if subtly, framed within a Cold War popular spy narrative or detective story discourse:

> You know there's a stamp
> That once it left its stamp roll
> Then never again
> Returned, there's a lid
> That deserted its pot
> I want to write your address in the sand
> Keep you in my sleeping bag
> Before sleeping play a round of
> Crossword puzzles
> Harboring you in my book bag
> Along with a new volume of poetry
> Along with my hiking shoes

Binoculars and
Submarine
My earliest expectation
Toward the world
My secret love

"Fragments" of such a discourse (desertion, "harboring," "binoculars," "submarine," and "My secret love") help construct a poetic language (the poetry volume) that is compared to an intellectual exercise like a crossword puzzle, both of which become a source of alternative knowledge. The formative and interpellative power of such discourses for sexual identity is suggested in the lines: "My earliest expectation / Toward the world / My secret love."

A later section of the poem contains a pastiche of scenarios and sentences some of which read like direct citations from textbooks:

When all the flowers have forgotten your sleeping face
The constellations while I'm waiting to fly far away have almost all set
The last footprints have been erased by the confusion
The wind blows a book open
Page 8 line 9:
"In this way the affair was resolved."
Resolved.
Punctuate the following
Light watermelon stains. Watermelon is grown
In sandy ground, in the hottest season
When ripe it explodes, like you have
Toward me, like a teapot heating water whistles
When it boils. Yes such
A person one day suddenly
I completely understand, with him
We're each in our own
Different quadrants
Alone
Endlessly vast
Aging dying
Never never
Able to

> Interact—
> The crestfallen Chinese girl strolls back
> Sits in front of the window practicing
> French conversation: "Is this a horse
> Or is this a straw hat?"
> This is a bomb
> Bombs are falling in Lebanon
> The radical reformers obediently
> Go home for dinner
> When the equilateral triangle dissects
> The circle
> The chickens and rabbits don't understand
> Why they are in the same
> Cage;
> "Also, the post office is across from the bank
> To the right of the hospital
> The river under the bridge is flowing by
> The people on the bridge are walking"

The textbook statements above are unquestionable facts presented in short declarative sentences, and, as such, they constitute a marked contrast to the what-if or speculative mood of the rest of the poem. This allows a critical perspective to emerge on the factual presentation of information in educational institutions and pedagogies based on preparation for objective, standardized tests. This is especially true to the extent that, unlike the inappropriate use of the law of physics earlier in the poem, here the black-and-white nature of these sentences is shown to bring on the loss of a sense of possibility (especially the possibility for romance and even sociality): "We're each in our own / Different quadrants / Alone / Endlessly vast / Aging dying / Never never / Able to / Interact—" There is an oblique critique of this idea of absolute separateness and isolation in the suggestion, indicated by juxtaposition, that such "knowledge" produces the kind of domesticated, pragmatic compliance ("The radical reformers obediently / Go home for dinner") that will also come under critique in Hsia Yü's later poetry. The factual (as opposed to the speculative) nature of the doxa is presented in these lines as causing a sense of being caged in by a utilitarian pessimism; this, in turn, however, produces a need for the sense of possibility also affirmed throughout the poem—and even for liberation.

The following passage is from the closing section of the poem:

Is it possible for us to unfetter ourselves
In conversation
In front of the bank
Walking on the bridge
Or
Leaving
On a jet plane
Coming back to the beginning
A dark little bar
An unfamiliar language
A Romanian
Marching in formation
Yes
There could always be a day
It is completely possible
Someone will read to here
Someone will ask me
"Are you the drum
Or the drumstick?"
Now that is a stupid question
And it is not what I mean
I just want to say I could run into such a person
At the beginning it would be sincere and honest
And sorrowful too
But afterward things would change
Affairs always encounter
Some changes
It's possible
Very possible
Voilà

The juxtaposition of the earlier, educational doxa (which is nationalist in Johnson's sense) with the lines about unfettering ourselves suggests that one thing that the cynicism of the matter-of-fact nationalist doxa ironically produces, in addition to compliance, is a desire to leave the country or emigrate as a kind of unfettering. I would like to suggest in closing that one important contribution of the poem is that it does not deny but anticipates that desire and even shows how it is produced while at the same time offering an alternative sense of possibility in the Romanian revolutionary, the dark little bar, and the unfamiliar language (i.e., not Mandarin, but also not English). With these adventurous figures for possibility and the "earliest expectation" named as "secret love," the poem also suggests the importance of desire and sexuality to a critical engagement with the doxa of modernity; this relation is the subject of the rest of this chapter.

## Reticence and Dirty Words

Hsia Yü is, by all accounts, the most nonreticent of Taiwan's well-known female poets on the subject of sexuality. In addition to her persistent, ironic critique of institutionalized sexuality and romance narratives, some of her poems are written on topics such as short-term sexual relations, unfaithfulness, and female-to-male cross-dressing, while many have strong, strangely erotic overtones, the exact referentiality of which is impossible to determine. I would suggest that, in its entirety, her oeuvre makes an overall, and twice explicitly stated, call for "another kind of morality." In the following pages, I would like to show how this call is equally made through what I identify as a critical reticence in her poetics, which is, I will argue, at least as crucial as her more apparent nonreticence in challenging the tactics of what Jen-peng Liu and Naifei Ding, in "Reticent Poetics, Queer Politics," have theorized as a sexually normativizing reticence.[12]

Formally, Hsia Yü's poetics refuses closure and does not construct a recognizable subject for nonnormative acts. In other words, its grammar and structure could be more aptly termed *penumbrae-like* than *substantive* (Liu and Ding, "Reticent Poetics, Queer Politics"). "Leaving on a Jet Plane" is a narrative poem, and much of its content is recognizable. For this reason, it provides a good introduction to some of the issues and thematics that characterize Hsia Yü's oeuvre in that, in it, those concerns are more readily picked up by readers. However, her writing strategies for dealing with such themes are often quite different, and, before *Salsa*, it is her nonnarrative poetry for which Hsia Yü is most well-known. However, the most difficult of these poems have not been treated much by critics because they are so abstruse as to make interpretation almost impossible (they are even sometimes referred to in literary circles—rather negatively—as no longer being written in Chinese). In such poems, Hsia Yü makes use of the "looseness" of Chinese grammar (e.g., the option to omit the subject) to such an extent that even her content is elliptical, making it hard to pinpoint what exactly the referent might be. This silence or these gaps—with regard to conclusions, the construction of identifiable subjects, and even the contents of the poems—I consider as a kind of reticence that permeates the form as well as the content of her poetry. I submit that this formal experimentation (or "difficulty") is not evasive: it is not a symptomatic, unconscious manifestation of a suppressive reticence. Rather, perhaps most evocatively in its counterlinearity or lack of closure, it can facilitate the bringing into vivid legibility of nondevelopmental stories and their nonnormative and, sometimes, ghost-friendly or animal-like (Li, "'The Nation' in the Eyes of Taiwan's Women Poets") subjects in an apparently abstract (since not immediately recognizable) yet compellingly contemporary world. However, I will maintain, not that the poetry is exactly abstract in itself, but, rather, that this perception is a result of the way in which it "presents" (in the Steinian sense discussed in chapter 2) ideas, acts, and subjects that are not readily recognizable and, therefore, not seen as concrete. The reading offered below thus attempts to follow the reticent traces that are interwoven with the ironical and profane taxonomies of Hsia Yü's innovative poetics in order to understand how this poetics challenges sexuality-based meanings even as it addresses discourses of silence.

It is in large part this subversive reticence that allows Hsia Yü's poetry to be minor to several overlapping but formationally distinct paradigms of normative sexuality in Taiwan. An important one that has received much critical attention in recent queer theory produced in and about Chinese-speaking locations is that of familial and societal obligations—obligations that are met in ways that have changed in accordance with broader transformations in social conditions but that derive from the convention of arranged marriages. Although contemporary marriages are not often arranged, familial and social norms require all individuals to marry and place rather rigid restrictions on the choice of a spouse. These accounts therefore identify the family as a primary site for the suppression of homosexuality in culturally or nationally

"Chinese" locations at the same time as other social spheres are seen as relatively tolerant. An alternative to the positing of Chinese societies as tolerant with the exception of within the family, however, is Tao-ming Hans Huang's historiography, in his recent "State Power, Prostitution, and Sexual Order in Taiwan," of the legal regulation and management of sexuality in postwar Taiwan.

Through a detailed historical study of legal documents, legal commentaries, and media reaction to cases and events related to nonnormative sexual practices, Huang makes a convincing case for how the combination of Taiwan's geopolitical Cold War formation and a period of rapid industrialization brought about a contradictory need for the police to stringently persecute prostitution (a category through which the nonnormative came to be primarily conceptualized) and tacitly "administer" it for certain populations. Cold War militarization accounts for much of the latter need: the large population of low-ranking soldiers had no chance to bring their wives and families when they removed to Taiwan, so brothels were established for them (240), and the United States demanded legalized entertainment for the thousands of U.S. soldiers stationed or vacationing in Taiwan from the mid-1950s to the early 1970s. This period thus coincided with a dramatic increase in the number of bars (up by 93 percent from 1963 to 1966), which were strongly associated with sex work and stigmatized, and a general proliferation of different kinds of sex work establishments throughout society. At the same time, the martial law regime continued to have an official stance of aiming to eliminate all forms of nonmarital sexual practice (all of which could be suspected as prostitution) and, in order to do so, disregarded rights to private space and made illegal many establishments. As a result, Huang notes, many kinds of establishments were formed that did not appear to be sex work but might be—from barber shops to tourist agencies and from craft shops to catering agencies—to satisfy the great demand for it from both local and foreign/tourist/soldier populations (243–44). Huang also points out that the public outrage at the proliferation of sex work in an avowedly Confucian society was at two key points incited by U.S. media coverage of the Taiwan sex industry, which were taken as calling into question the legitimacy of Taiwan's Confucian moral society (244–45, 247). Although Huang does not go into this explicitly, perhaps also the legitimacy of Taiwan as a modern democratic society on the world stage was called into question by such exposés in the U.S. media. For the purposes of my study, I would like to draw out an implication of Huang's findings: the particular forms of sex work instituted during this period in Taiwan *and* the stringent policing of sex work are both partly determined through contradictory U.S. neocolonial demands. And I would like to suggest here that Liu and Ding's concept of *reticence* names a particularly useful discourse on the nonnormative when nonnormative sexual practices are both necessary to economic and geopolitical survival in neocolonial modernity and heavily stigmatized as throwbacks to feudalism at the same time (on this last point, see Ding's "Feminist Knots").

Another discursive formation on nonnormative sexuality is that of psychoanalytic and medical discourses, which operate according to normal and abnormal sexual and gendered identity categories that are developmental in structure and for which the developmental paradigm of modern romantic love and its subject of free will provide a cultural narrative (see Sommer, "Love and Country in Latin America"). Narratives of modern romantic love are evident in many arenas of cultural production (novels, films etc.), and I would like to suggest that, in this historically layered location, their affectivity is necessarily (although, apparently, contradictorily) deeply intertwined with familial and societal obligation. Psychoanalysis is the dominant academic discourse on topics pertaining to sexuality and gender, but, in the 1980s, the *practice* of psychotherapy had not permeated the society very deeply (and it still has not despite a recent growing awareness of high rates of depression and other forms of mental illness). Although I will not provide a comprehensive analysis of all these normative discourses, I would like to note how interwoven they are by calling attention to the way in which the normative demands of familial obligation, the categorizing strategies of psychoanalysis, and narratives of modern "free" love share a deeply developmental structure while the former and latter conflict markedly (they may all conflict somewhat) in their interpellations of sexual subjects. The former hails a socially obligated and positioned subject, and the latter complicates the subject's social construction and positioning with a value-laden, if less equally or deeply affective, individualism. This conflict can be somewhat resolved, and the paradigms can even become mutually supportive, if the newer "invisible" ideology of free love can be seen as a modern, liberating alternative to familial obligation, but, even when it does so, it is still apparent that the "free" choice will be most liberating if it meets up to familial standards.

In what follows, I focus primarily on the disciplinary tactics of reticence because it is such a useful mode of discourse for the contradictory demands placed on sexual norms and practices in Taiwan's neocoloniality and because it is the most often addressed, ironized, and countered in Hsia Yü's poetry. Liu and Ding's starting point is an essay by Ying-chun Tsai, "The Poetics of Reticence," on poetic discourse in the Chinese canon. Tsai, following Heidegger, defines *reticence* not as the lack of verbal statements but as a powerfully meaningful silence. His concept of reticence is similar to the Heideggerian one in that it "refers to a way of speaking that possesses a concentrated intensity and stands in contrast to the endlessly babbling chatter of the commonsense idle talk" ("The Poetics of Reticence," 1 n. 4). Tsai traces the rise of this poetics of reticence (i.e., "storing up" and "holding back" rather than directly stating an idea) as a convention in Chinese literature and literati culture—a convention that is, he suggests, particularly necessary in political situations within which direct critique is impossible. Significantly, his discussion of reticence closes by taking its readers into the twentieth century, "just four years before the establishment of republican China," and to the modernist writer Lu Xun's "now little heeded article on the demonic power in poetry," which, according to Tsai, Lu discovered "might be a weapon to resist conformist harmonies in an old empire." "This," Tsai concludes, "might be part of the politics of reticence that deserves our attention nowadays" (4–5).

In "Reticent Poetics, Queer Politics," Liu and Ding have brought Tsai's definition of *reticence* into a broader discussion (not limited to the world of poetry and literary conventions) of discourses on sexuality in contemporary Taiwan. Like Huang, Liu and Ding also question the idea that Chinese culture is relatively tolerant of sexual deviance. On the contrary, Liu and Ding speculatively inquire into the ways in which a suppressive reticence might be inadvertently maintained in theorizations or cultural representations that emphasize the important role of the family when the suggestion is also made that there is a relative tolerance in extrafamilial cultural institutions, in the political sphere, or in society at large, including the workplace. Liu and Ding theorize reticence primarily as a rhetorical strategy that is taken up effectively by subjects speaking in the interests of relative power or privilege. I would like to point out that, although they do not use this terminology, their focus, unlike Tsai's closing point about the critical reticent poetics of Lu

Xun, highlights the *disciplinary* functions of reticence, by identifying how it is deployed to suppress otherwise possibly legible signs of nonheterosexual, nonmonogamous, and short-term sexual relations. Because this reticence operates by ignoring and, thereby, disavowing the existence of nonnormative sexuality rather than naming it as abnormal, Liu and Ding demonstrate persuasively the remarkable extent to which reticence is hard to pinpoint as a suppressive force. Another reason for this elusiveness may be the intricate and sometimes contradictory way in which it interacts with other forms of normative sexuality in Taiwan: while reticence contradicts the naming strategies of medical discourses, it can still support the aims of those discourses as it exercises its disciplinary tactics within the deeply affective developmental paradigm of societal and familial obligation.[13]

Returning to Tsai's understanding of reticence as a poetic strategy for social critique in a contemporary context, I would like to suggest that, in its possibility for density and juxtaposition of images or concepts with little explanation, modernist poetry, and, perhaps, other forms of modernist writing, including Lu's fiction, contains great potential to operate as a form of *interventionary* reticence, challenging commonsense, taken-for-granted associations and linkages. It is these commonsense associations and linkages, moreover, that constitute the unspoken logic of the disciplinary reticence that Liu and Ding analyze. As a mode of reticent figuration, the form and content of Hsia Yü's poetry provide an acknowledgment of and a way to bring into legibility the existence of the nonnormative without forcing it into the more immediately recognizable discourses of sexuality, thereby reducing its complexity to either a familiar, substantive truth value or a reticently produced nonexistence, triviality, or trend (Liu and Ding).

Although this poetry is often reticent with regard to content and does not usually name its historical and social contexts, this chapter so far has been suggesting that it is precisely an articulate response to its context and should not be read as an unsituated example of a postmodern poetics. Hsia Yü's poetry has often been called *postmodern* because of its experimental nature, and, in this sense, it does correspond to certain definitions of postmodern aesthetics. Even though postmodernism tends to critique the idea of "newness," in Taiwan it is necessarily associated with Western influences that do connote innovation and change, and a discussion of her poetry that is guided by theorizations of the postmodern can, therefore, lose track of the ways in which it is not entirely "new" but carries on certain writing strategies developed in Chinese poetry conventions. Weng Wen Hsian has, in her "A Consideration of the Implications of *Xing* in the Creation of Modern Poetry," addressed precisely this problem by arguing that the main aesthetic device in Hsia Yü's poetry is not its innovation but its use of *xing* [興]. Xing is one of three writing conventions from the Chinese poetry canon, the other two being *fu* [賦, "narrative"] and *bi* [比, "metaphor"]. With regard to the xing, Weng argues that it has no clear Western equivalent, and she further explains that, while it is not metaphoric, neither is it literal or descriptive. It consists of an association or a juxtaposition of concepts or ideas usually implied in suggestive natural imagery: meaning or affect is produced in the relation of the images to one another and not by positing an identity between different classes. Because of Hsia Yü's innovative use of xing, her poetic form is, Weng argues, not a complete break from the conventions of canonical Chinese literature; instead, as Weng demonstrates, even some of the aspects of her poetry that have most often been labeled *postmodern* (e.g., the juxtaposition of images without explanation, followed by oblique commentary) also draw on those conventions. The reticent potential of xing should be apparent from this definition; in fact, Haun Saussy has described xing as "the figure that leaves the most unsaid" (*The Problem of a Chinese Aesthetic*, 129 [see generally 131–47]). I would like to suggest that Hsia Yü draws on xing (especially in Saussy's sense) and utilizes other strategies in order to construct a "minor" writing that is conceptual (not simply literal) and critical, that is, utilizing a conventional poetic reticence to challenge assumptions, including the assumption of the possibility of objective knowledge.[14]

In addition to this consideration of the formal elements of Hsia Yü's poetic project, and in order to begin to address the question of objective knowledge in that project, I want to point out the ways in which its stylistic craftsmanship is a response to and an engagement with the social conditions that partly determine configurations of gender and sexuality as well as their respective possibilities for transformation. A discussion of a postmodern poetics in Hsia Yü's work that does not historicize its understanding of aesthetics also risks overlooking how her poetry registers and challenges dominant assignations of value and meaning while producing new cultural narratives for "illegitimate" desires and "underground" sensibilities. For this reason, I would locate the importance of Michelle Yeh's article "The Feminist Poetic of Hsia Yü" in its demonstration of the way in which the practice of labeling Hsia Yü's poetry *postmodern* can, at times, cause critics to fail to recognize the political urgency of its questioning of gender norms. Yeh also contextualizes the poetry by documenting Taiwan's increasing feminist activism and scholarship throughout the 1970s and 1980s. However, the assumption that the poetry *reflects* this emerging feminist subject—an assumption based on the facts that the poetry is nontraditional in its gender politics and appeared during the same years that the movement began to develop—disallows the possibility of different types of progressive gender politics and, inadvertently, leads to reductive readings of the poetry's critical edge. I appreciate Yeh's helpful theorization of the "malleable" and generative qualities of Hsia Yü's poetry,[15] but I would like to point out that its questioning of gender norms does not necessarily posit an unproblematized category of *woman* as the agent of a feminist project. The latter, moreover, in Yeh's article remains taken for granted as a universally understood project and as an intentionality behind the writing.

Yeh suggests that modern gendered experience calls for a "malleable" language. One reason for this might be the immense and rapid changes that modernity brings for women in 1970s and 1980s Taiwan in forms of work, work relations, marriage and family conventions, and many other forms of gendered social organization.[16] For women of all economic classes, modernity promises a certain amount of liberation from traditional conventions and ethical codes. However, not only is this promise not delivered to all gendered subjects, but it is itself contradictory, that is, in the contradictory demands placed on women to function as agents in the reproduction of a national culture even as they are excluded from a national subjecthood that remains implicitly masculinist. For women of the expanding middle class, for example, some degree of a new form of autonomy may be gained through economic privilege, but the goal of liberation from patriarchy remains complicated by the oxymoronic constitution of a "female national subject." A further gendered contradiction is recognizable in the case of working-class women: because of the processes of rapid industrialization necessary to NIC (newly industrialized country) economic development, processes that rely on flexible and feminized labor forces, modernity's promise of liberation is out of reach for many female subjects.[17]

Women's writing of this period should certainly be considered a response to the changes and contradictions experienced by or familiar to female authors to the extent that it necessarily records and comments on them. However, using an expressive model to approach the question of women, modernization, and modern and postmodern writing has its limitations. First, it obscures the dynamic interrelation of culture and history, instead positing them as separate spheres, with cultural production as "fiction" (in this case, poetry) determined by what are considered to be the "facts" of historical conditions (in this case, an emerging feminist movement). Second, it does not account for the way in which the experimentation of the poetry itself challenges reflective definitions of *representation*. The central question of concern in my reading is, therefore, not the more realist one of how Hsia Yü's poetry might be expressive of the facts of women's experience during a period of rapid industrialization. Rather, it is how its stylistic experimentation puts particular strains on the limits of representation that determine what can be known as factual, as the opening reading of "Leaving on a Jet Plane" illustrates.

Below, drawing on a distinction made by Gayatri Chakravorty Spivak, I would like to elaborate on how, if further inquiry into the historical determination of Hsia Yü's innovative technique avoids an expressive model of analysis, it might lead us to a different question: In what ways might the poetry's experimentation actively engage the contradictions that inhere in the "microstructures" of gender and sexuality while also speaking to the nonidentical forms of contradiction and disjunction in the developmental narratives that underlie the "macro" politics of modern national identity?

Only if we do not use an expressive model of analysis can we approach the question of how the reticent, "demonic power" of Hsia Yü's poetry is in alignment with its more explicit aspects without reading the poetry reductively—as reflecting reality rather than engaging it. This combination (reticence and explicitness) can be read in more complexity when taken as a form of what Gayatri Spivak has termed *taxonomic practice*. Engaging in taxonomic practice means "striv[ing] moment by moment to practice a taxonomy of different forms of understanding, different forms of change, dependent perhaps on resemblance and substitutability—figuration—rather than the self-identical category of truth" ("Three Feminist Readings," 28).[18] The significance of this practice is made clear, for example, in Hsia Yü's famously nonreticent statement: "Women have no dirty words of their own" (*Ventrilo-

*quy*, 116). This statement thus illustrates a particularly explicit, even obscene, way in which a practice of taxonomy can be carried out in order to begin to "redefine microstructural exchange" (Spivak, "Three Feminist Readings," 31). Another, more difficult aspect of this taxonomic intervention is suggested by the distance between the spoken word and the subject of speech implied in the title *Ventriloquy*: this formulation of the author's relationship to language, poetry, and the dirty words coined in that poetry paradoxically refuses the construction of a female subject. I would like to suggest that this refusal may stem from the way in which Hsia Yü's writing derives from a sexuality-based critique even when that critique is somewhat in antagonism with a feminist project, in that the latter often requires a female subject to function as the object of patriarchal domination and the projected subject of feminist liberation. This refusal to construct a female subject, moreover, may be one reason why Hsia Yü has been described by many critics, including Chung Ling (*Modern Chinese Muses*), Liao Hsien-hao ("Materialism's Mutiny"), and Michelle Yeh ("The Feminist Poetic of Hsia Yü"), as the first of Taiwan's female poets to write about love and romance while radically breaking away from the conventions of a "woman's poetry."[19] Her poetry, for example, often utilizes linguistic characteristics of Chinese in the construction of sentences that do not have a grammatical subject but that nevertheless "voice" what could be considered a strong feminist critique of the demands that normative sexuality places on women in particular.[20] In other words, her writing investigates conditions of gendered oppression without being based on a normative category of *woman* as the subject of feminist practice, perhaps in part because the production of that category serves the interests of normative sexuality, and, instead, critiques the production of the sexually normative as an ideological project (as we will witness in the reading of "Making Sentences") at the level of microstructural relations. Hsia Yü's poetry can, thus, elucidate how gender and sexuality should not be theorized as interchangeable categories. Further, the inevitable tension dramatized in this poetry (between an emphasis on creating a language "malleable" enough to compensate for women's lack of expletives, on the one hand, and the critique of the tenability of the category of *woman*, on the other) demonstrates to contemporary feminists the difficulty and, equally, the necessity of attending to both agendas, even as they conflict with one another.

In addition to being a crucial part of a nonreticent "practice of taxonomy," this absence of a female subject is also a powerful use of reticence as a vehicle through which formations that complicate identity can become legible on their own terms. In its depiction of a distance between the speaker of the words *I do* and the words themselves, for example, the poem "Ventriloquy" addresses how the processes of subject formation in institutionalized sexuality can produce alternative forms of identity, or perhaps a nonidentity, for some subjects:

> I walk into the wrong room
> And miss my own wedding.
> Through the only hole in the wall I see
> All proceeding perfectly: The groom in white
> She with flowers in her hand, the ceremony
> The vows, the kiss
> Turning my back on it: fate, the ventriloquy
>     I worked so long and hard at
>     (tongue, that warm-blooded water creature
>     squirms domestic in its [small] tank)
> And the creature says: [Yes,] I do
> (Bradbury, *Fusion Kitsch*, 85)[21]

The meaning of this poem turns, in part, on the multiple meanings of *bei zhe* [背著] and the ambiguous referent of its object, *ta* [它]: Bradbury translates this clause as "turning my back on it" (with connotations of casting away or rebelling against), which is the main meaning of the line, but *bei zhe* also means to carry on one's back. According to the structure of the sentence it appears in, the pronoun *ta* [it] most obviously refers to "fate," but, within the poem as a whole, it can also refer to the ceremony being described. This layered ambiguity suggests that what reads as a literal (because the bride is in another room) turning against fate (that of marriage and the skill of ventriloquy that allows the bride to say the vows during ceremony) can also be read as meaning that the burden of that fate is still being carried precisely because the ventriloquy is so well learned that the vows can be spoken when the subject has turned her back on it or is even absent. Alternately, what looks like compliance (the domesticated tongue) is also a kind of opposition in that it allows this distance to be maintained even as the vows are spoken; however, this opposition is a reticent one that, in the context of the ceremony, has no visible or audible traces except in the eyes of the bride herself, who, hidden behind a wall and unobserved, observes her own obstructed distance from the ceremony and hears her ventriloquized words, which are spoken with such skill that the ceremony proceeds "perfectly." In this sense, the invisibility and inaudibility of the poem's rebellion against marital fate vividly illustrate Liu and Ding's theorization of the ways in which moral values such as virtue and harmony are the affective and domesticating tools with which reticence deploys its suppressive force: nothing in the ceremony itself is upset or incomplete, and it harmoniously concludes its performative function for the (virtuous) couple and the witnesses.

Precisely because the poem is such a striking illustration of the effects of this suppressive reticence, however, it also supports Hsia Yü's call for "another kind of morality," a phrase that appears in a particularly sexually explicit poem from *Ventriloquy*, "Me and My Unicorn," in a passage that ruminates on how "self-understanding" of one's "fate" only "makes one's back ache," while "poetry is better than self-understanding" because it is "more steadfast," "what it creates" having "another kind of morality" (72; my translation). This phrase ("another kind of morality") appears again in Hsia Yü's next collection as the title of a poem composed of six made-up (and, therefore, illegible) characters (*Friction Ineffable*, n.p.). Not only does this irony parody contemporary morality, but it also critically links morality with language and discourse, illuminating the ethical stakes of the poetry's taxonomic practice; and, in "Me and My Unicorn," the transformative possibilities of such a taxonomic practice are compared favorably with simply understanding one's fate. The critical treatment of fate in "Ventriloquy" is a part of this practice: in the context of the ceremony represented in the poem, the rebellion unfolds in a reticent form that illustrates the failure of the affective apparatuses of institutionalized sexuality but also allows fate to proceed uninterrupted to its performative conclusion in the vows; however, the poem itself carries out the difficult task of tracing the reticent workings of institutionalized sexuality as they are instanced, somewhat ironically, in the affective force of the ceremony's performative utterances. The willing choice of a free subject (我願意, "I do"; lit., "I am willing") that underlies romance narratives is, thus, complicated in its performative utterance in this marriage ceremony by the ventriloquy that first places the speaker at a distance from her own words and then presents the tongue's movement as tamed or domesticated. This distance and uncomfortable (squirming) domestication do not resonate with the developmental closure that, in conjugal union, produces a gendered subject; more than that, in speaking precisely the narrative that, again ironically, it should, it places in strained juxtaposition the developmental paradigms of, on the one hand, individualizing romance ("I do") and, on the other, familial obligation (the tamed or domesticated tongue that says what it is supposed to) and, thereby, aggravates the conflictual processes of subject formation that might otherwise be alleviated in a compensatory logic in which the romance and free choice of modern paradigms become seen as a nonideological alternative that is replacing conventional familial and social positionings and demands. The layered meanings of *bei zhe* do not replace some suppressed desires (e.g., not to marry) with a representation per se but, instead, vividly narrate the complex mechanism of reticence within the most paradigmatic instance of institutionalized sexuality, including how the maintenance of that institution relies on a compensatory logic among competing discursive systems.

As I mentioned at the beginning of this chapter, Hsia Yü's use of formal experimentation and fragmentation does not emphasize any explicit link to the developmental discourses of modernity and progress. In my readings of "Leaving on a Jet Plane" and "Ventriloquy," I have not addressed temporality directly. However, I have emphasized these poems' refusal of both normative identity/desire categories and the corresponding developmental resolution, or, alternatively, sublation, produced by closed forms. In this refusal, the poems dramatize, without resolving, specific cases of microstructural temporal contradiction. Below, I close this discussion by reading her 1983 poem "Making Sentences" to show how it presents discontinuity in the microstructures of sexuality as what, in "History, Allegory, Sexuality," Chandan Reddy has termed an allegorical *repository* of macrostructural contradictions in colonial modernities.[22]

Also from *Memoranda*, the series "Making Sentences" (all translations by Natalia Chan and Amie Parry) uses the name of a common homework assignment as its title. This homework assignment instructs children on how to use particular words with the correct grammatical patterns. All the poems in this series are written as sentences for this kind of assignment: the titles are single words or phrases that the short poems, which all consist of a single sentence, are built around. For example, the first poem in this series,

"不得不" [Cannot but], takes as its subject the ramifications of this pedagogy in terms of its effects on the subject formation of the children:

> Cannot but
> leave footprints
> humbly and kindly
> on their not yet dry cement
> hearts

This opening poem suggests that both the words chosen and the linguistic structures used in the sentences composed with them are supposed to be capable of shaping the minds of the young students in important ways. Here, education is understood as precisely an ideological apparatus, and, as a state apparatus, it is one that plays a central role in the formation of national subjects. The poems in "Making Sentences" also reveal the ways in which interpellation processes rely on a temporality that is based on continuity. Structurally, this temporality takes the form of grammatical and linguistic patterns (e.g., the sentence) that emphasize causality and linear development. At the level of content, all the titles except the last one explicitly address the theme of continuity: "就" [Then]; "然後" [Afterward]; "每當" [Every time]; "繼續" [Continue]; "以後 . . . 之前" [After . . . before]; and "其他" [The rest]. After the initial implicit reference to education in the content of the first poem, however, the subject matter becomes that of romance and sexuality, suggesting, at first glance, that these poems are about the successful interpellation of normative sexual subjects: further, framing the "continuity" of sexual development with a reference to a state apparatus suggests that sexual identity formation is an important aspect of the interpellation of national subjects. I will return to this connection later; for now, it is important to note that, although, at first glance, the unifying theme of the poems seems to be continuity, a closer reading reveals (1) a thematic of discontinuity that suggests that notions of continuity are inappropriate to certain experiences of romance and sexuality (as in the poem "Then," in which the speaker of the words "I love you all" has apparently been unfaithful—as evidenced in the plural "you"—and is in the process of leaving) and (2) descriptions of the restrictions caused by the enforcement of continuity in institutionalized monogamy (as in the lines from "After . . . Before" that read: "forever / of all the words I've heard / causes people the most sorrow"). This thematic of discontinuity dramatizes the breakdowns in normative sexuality's logic of development, and this creates, I would like to suggest, the possibility for readers to reinterpret microstructural relations in a manner that does not attempt to alleviate their inner contradictions.

This critique of continuity is perhaps best illustrated in the poem entitled "Continue," which reads:

> Let the music continue to play
> affecting three silent sunflowers
> below the dash
> between the esophagus and the intestine
>
> The road from tragedy to forgetting
> is the starting point of all failure

In this poem, it is music that "continue[s]," but music has already been described in the previous poem ("Every Time") as "circuitous," as something that "dissolves metaphor" and that is opposed to its linear logic: as music continues, it is also disrupting the continuity of language (metaphor). In this sense, music is referred to as an alternative arena of cultural production not entirely contained by the linear structure and meaningfulness of language. It also has a bodily effect that facilitates the "forgetting" of the closing lines: "The road from tragedy to forgetting / is the starting point of all failure." If the tragedy caused by "forever" (described in the next poem) is forgotten, then these romantic narratives can go on uninterrupted, meaning that forgetting is a failure in that it entails a capitulation to the regulatory narratives of sexuality. At the same time, however, this "failure" also refers to the failure of continuity itself to the extent that "the road from tragedy to forgetting" does not arrive at total forgetfulness. Rather, the tragedy, not wholly forgotten, is marked on the body (in "the dash / between the esophagus and the intestine"), and, instead of arriving at forgetfulness, the road is always in a constant movement toward it. Continuity in this poem takes the form of both the cause of tragedy (i.e., the "forever" of the following poem) and "the road from tragedy to forgetting," or the process of forgetting the tragedy, which is itself brought about by romantic continuities. In both cases, continuity is undercut by the way in which, by definition, it must maintain itself precisely by remaining perpetually in process and never arriving at its promised goal of fulfillment and completion. In this way—in the conclusion that it reticently does not reach—Hsia Yü's poem dramatizes the inner contradictions of a logic of continuity at the microstructural level of narrative sexual development.

On the one hand, by illustrating how these romantic narratives ultimately do not and cannot produce the normative version of fulfillment that they offer, the poems reveal the impossibility of reaching these conclusions through their developmental logic. On the other hand, their framing of these narratives with reference to an ideological state apparatus also indicates, I would like to suggest, that the vexed continuity of sexual development and its promise of fulfillment function as an attempted sublation of the irresolvable macrostructural contradictions of national identity and its interpellative apparatuses. When these apparatuses utilize the logic of sublation (as opposed to resolution), the contradiction of national identity is not addressed directly or on its own terms; rather, it is masked by being "preserved in a higher form," in this case, in the exalted (microstructural) ideology of romance in normative sexuality.[23] Sublation, then, is a particularly powerful form of reticence because it alleviates the immediacy of modernity's temporal discontinuities and sense of belatedness by "naming" another type of development and its promises of fulfillment. The distinct discontinuities and contradictions that in these poems complicate nonnormative sexual development, however, make that sublation, at best, difficult to effect. Further, if the gendered contradictions described earlier are not sublated into phantasmatic identification, they could, under the right conditions, make apparent the temporal contradictions of sexual development even for normative sexual subjects. Thus, the discontinuities of the "stories" told in these fragments perhaps join the call for "another kind of morality" as the recourse to sublation in the ideology of romance becomes especially fraught in the subject matter that they address. These thematic and formal discontinuities thus indicate the contradictions of normative demands within microstructural relations while simultaneously marking the failure of the sublation of macrostructural temporal contradiction into the narrative development of normative sexuality.

In this sense, these poems illustrate the temporal contradictions of sexual fulfillment and of national progress, producing a variety of discontinuous and disidentified experiences that cannot be incorporated into their own developmental temporalities and assigned the meaning that they would assume if they were incorporable. Simultaneously, not only does the reticence deployed through developmental normativity not succeed in relegating all nonnormative sexuality to nonexistence, but it might also have unanticipated effects to the contrary, effects that are not easily managed. Both in its content and in its structural nonlinearity, "Making Sentences" figures the almost incoherent relations among experiences of the fragmentary and of the meaninglessness of certain everyday objects and events for the sexual subject for whom sexuality to some extent escapes the meaningfulness of institutionalized sexual practices. Some of these experiences are the subject of the last poem in the series, entitled "The Rest":

> The rest are all fragmentary things
> tape, a pen cap
> cut paper
> crookedly drawn lines
> fingernail clippers
> toilet tissue
> ceaselessly dripping
> water from on top of an umbrella
> dust
> sounds
> love

In these closing lines, "love" has become a fragmentary thing, part of a list of miscellaneous items, rather than constituting the scene of narrative development. The placement of these objects in an arbitrary list, without comment or explanation, creates a form that enables them to defy the meaningfulness that they might take on in a narrative logic. For example, rather than having a meaning determined by the development of a sentence, the word *sounds* refers back to the music in "Every Time" and "Continue" as a mode of articulation not entirely structured by causality and linearity, in contrast to the kinds of "sentences" that are the subject of the poem's critique. The logic of "sounds," as opposed to that of sentences, also indicates how the poem challenges the totality of meaning in sexually normative fulfillment and replaces that fullness with a fragmentary, reticently disconnected series of objects and events. This dramatizes the ways in which microstructural relations are as determined by breakdowns and disjunctures in developmental narratives as they are by the developmental logic itself. This list thus frames the nondevelopmental experiences of sexuality in the preceding poems as "memoranda" (the title of the collection) or as ordinary, everyday experiences like the items on this list—experiences that are, however, disavowed by institutionalized sexuality. The exertion of this disavowal, like the tragedy of the "dash" described above, is marked on the body, leaving traces of a discontinuous materiality that, like this list itself, cannot be incorporated into the logic of normative developmentalism. Both in content and in form, "Making Sentences" demonstrates, in Lisa Lowe's words, how "a surplus of materiality" can be utilized as "what will not be ordered, what will not coagulate and cohere" (*Immigrant Acts*, 111). As well as dramatizing the contradictions of developmental temporality, then, in all that is not concluded, resolved, or sublated in its strategic use of the fragmentary to critique discourses of continuity utilized by cultural and educational apparatuses to determine microstructural relations, "Making Sentences" also brings a nondevelopmental, allegorical temporality into articulation. Because this allegorical temporality does not replace a dominant reticence with an immediately available but reductive naming strategy, it can help us reimagine new terms for microstructural relations.

The list of objects that constitutes the formal structure of "Making Sentences," like the form of many poems in *Memoranda*, allows memories of ordinary, everyday events to be set down in a form that is explicitly nondevelopmental. The objects presented in this form necessarily become fragments (not framed and made meaningful by narrative) that, rather than attempting to figure a new kind of universalism or self-containment, instead present the failure of sublation in the stories of nonnormative sexual subjects such as those presented in these poems. Reading thus becomes a process of recognizing the fiction of normative sexuality's promise of fulfillment, which is an important aspect of microstructural narrativity in the broadest sense. The reticent suppression of nonnormative sexuality in this sense takes the form of a disavowal of the internal failures of microstructural narrativity and its consequential inability to sublate macrostructural contradiction. These poems, then, open up the possibility for a reading of the microstructural that also engages its allegorical relation to macrostructural contradiction as the latter's site of failed sublation. This allegorical discontinuity in the poetic task of making sentences is emblematized in this alternative homework assignment, which itself is a figuration of how Hsia Yü's experimental poetics gives fragmented form to knowledges that otherwise might not come into representation at all. Knowledges such as these are underground in relation to readily recognizable representations of sexuality, modern interpellation apparatuses, and common sense. Hsia Yü poetry makes these microstructural knowledges legible without compromising their critical edge by refusing to perform a canonically modernist erasure of the failed sublation of macrostructural contradiction. Such an erasure would, despite its own flaws, render its own functions and their breakdowns invisible. Instead, Hsia Yü's poetry ventures beyond the perimeters of a canonical emptiness by making legible the failures of the sublation function of normative identities while presenting alternative identifications, desires, values, and knowledges.

# 4

## "For the Other Overlapping Time": Pound's Ideogramic Universalism and Cha's Countermodernist Translation

Our [U.S. writers'] best asset is a thing of the spirit. I have the ring of it in a letter, now on my desk, from a good but little known poet, complaining of desperate loneliness, envying Synge his material, to-wit, the Arran Islands and people, wishing me well with my exotics, and ending with a sort of defiance: "For me nothing exists, *really exists*, outside America."

Ezra Pound, "The Renaissance"

Words cast each by each to weather
avowed indisputably to time
If it should impress, make fossil trace of word,
residue of word, stand as a ruin stands,
simply, as mark
having relinquished itself to time to distance

Theresa Hak Kyung Cha, *Dictee*

EZRA POUND'S ASSERTION that the best asset of American writers is a spiritual conviction that nothing really exists outside America is, perhaps, not so contradictory to his own "exotics" and Orientalism as it might at first appear, once we take into consideration the universalism that directs the historiographic project underlying his poetic experimentation. I would like to read Pound's assertion here in light of Bruce Cumings observation about U.S. culture: "A deep, abiding and often unexamined 'consensus' is so rooted in the United States that it is not a matter for conscious reflection (i.e., it is a species of Gramscian hegemony), and therefore Americans conceive of themselves as people without ideology. A people that thinks its goals are self-evident and universal also has trouble grasping that it is bound by its own history and particularity. Benedict Anderson wrote that 'no nation imagines itself coterminous with mankind,' which suggests that the imagined community of the nation is finite in this sense. But the minute he says it, it occurs that the United States might be an exception to that rule" (*Parallax Visions*, 4). Pound's universalism, by definition and by its very determination within the U.S. national imaginary that Bruce Cumings has brought to light, cannot recognize the historical particularity that brought it into being as such. This chapter attempts to "provincialize" Pound's internationalism (Chakrabarty), by juxtaposing the canonical erasure of Pound's modernist translations with the translation thematized in Theresa Hak Kyung Cha's 1982 historiographic novel *Dictee*. I read Cha's novel and its experimental form as taking up and making legible elusive but persistent knowledges in a practice of writing that is interventionary in relation to the erasures of modernist culture.

## Beyond the Empty Theater of the Present

*Dictee* includes scenes depicting a movie theater and the experience of cinematic viewership, scenes that are dispersed throughout the nondevelopmental, fragmented, multigenre, and multilingual narrative. On a first reading, some of these depictions might appear to take place in a single setting and to be monolingual. However, in an early instance, the theater's film has subtitles (translations of an original script), and, in the section entitled "Memory," the spatial and temporal singleness of the modernist, cinematic setting itself becomes a vehicle through which the erasure of other settings and other times is, paradoxically, illustrated. Not only does the novel locate erasure in cultural narrative such as film, but another type of narrative is also critiqued: that found in English-language macrostructural U.S., Korean, and Japanese History (with the capital *H*) and even in documents written in

English to challenge that History, but written in its own language and discursive terms.

This empty theater in *Dictee*, and its screen that blocks out other times and settings, evokes Stein's modernist canvases painted over with empty spaces to describe, through the metonym of the New York home, the American setting. It also, and more closely, resembles Stein's descriptions of American space as empty spaces filled with movement, spaces that are implicitly metaphorized as a movie screen (with cinema as one of Stein's markers for twentieth-century modernity in the United States).[1] In the final section of chapter 2, I argue that, in constructing her contained yet moving empty spaces, Stein borrows a historically produced internalized emptiness, and its disavowing deployment into discourses of American exceptionalism, to make another kind of epistemological intervention into the use of categorical knowledge in normative sexuality. I also argue that the allegorical histories of U.S. imperialism from which this space is borrowed are not entirely left behind and outside the continuous present tense of Stein's writings. In other words, those allegorical histories remain as a phantasmagoric presence that cannot be seamlessly dissevered, for example, from the corpses that populate her *Geographical History of America*, even though the more explicit function of the corpses is to flatten out the novelistic character, its internalized gender identity, and the accompanying logic of narrative development.

Like Hsia Yü's critical poetics, Cha's epistemological interventions into quotidian knowledges offer a more critical alternative to Stein's project of borrowing from allegorical histories in order to bring their phantasmagoric presences into another kind of epistemological intervention. Cha's text, like Hsia Yü's, provides a way of writing about gendered experience without reaffirming a conventional woman's voice, and her writing is equally difficult and experimental. Unlike Hsia Yü's, however, Cha's writing takes the form of a more explicit political critique and historiographic intervention. I argue below that Cha's novel traces the complex, almost incoherent web of relations among sexual universalist narratives and postcolonial, nationalist, and neocolonial historical narratives. *Dictee* is an Asian American, Korean immigrant text explicitly concerned with providing a "counterscript" to History and its imprecise language: "Not physical enough. Not to the very flesh and bone, to the core, to the mark . . ." (32). In its rendering of events, History distorts "to the point where it is necessary to intervene, even if to invent anew, expressions, for *this* experience, for this *outcome*, that does not cease to continue" (32). Cha's novel intervenes historiographically in the challenge that it poses to the tenets of American exceptionalism by showing the imperialistic role that the United States has played in Korean history since the turn of the last century. It also indicates how epistemological violence is deployed to blank out the memory of material and physical violences, including those enacted on colonial, postcolonial, and/or gendered subjects, making Cha's historiography an epistemological project from the outset. Unlike Stein's, however, Cha's addresses and directly critiques some links among gendered identity, imperialist histories, and nationalist discourses, instead of borrowing from one to intervene into another.

Cha's novel incorporates and describes a modernist historical emptiness that has its roots in the one that provides Stein with material for her experimental formal strategies. This modernist emptiness continues to haunt new nationalist narratives in the second half of the twentieth century as the contours and discourses of U.S. imperialism undergo significant shifts after World War II and with the Cold War. The explicit acknowledgment of the U.S. presence on the world stage especially in East Asia necessitated some developmental narratives (especially, perhaps, temporal ones of postwar progress in industrializing regions). However, it is important to recognize that the discursive erasure of U.S. imperialism and neocolonialism in Asia continued in the sense that U.S. military presence and maneuvers were couched as containment strategies and sharply distinguished from the concept of imperialism, still understood according to the earlier model of formal colonialism. In the literary sphere after World War II, modernist narratives, like Pound's in that period, continue to perform historical erasures in an increasingly radically nondevelopmental format. Cha's text delineates the epistemological limits of these political, historical, and cultural erasures, partly by metaphorizing them as an empty theater, and partly by referring to what lies beyond the window and on the other side of the blank screen that is created by these erasures in the cultural sphere. The movement from one setting, apparently absolutely singular, to the dimensions beyond and, invisibly, within it is, I argue, an epistemic translation at the material, even physical "flesh-and-bone" level of the historiographic project.

The section entitled "Memory" brings us to the brink of this translation.

It begins with an enigmatic definition of (apparently) memory: "It is an empty theater" (149). The definition is followed by a description of the sensations of the protagonist, who is seated in a theater just as its movie begins; this description culminates with the lines: "She follows no progression in particular of the narrative but submits only to the timelessness created in her body. . . . She remains for the effect induced in her. Fulfilled in the losing of herself repeatedly to memory and simultaneously its opposition, the arrestation of memory in oblivion." With these lines, Cha describes an interpellation process that produces unanticipated effects in the contradiction that inheres in the simultaneous experience of opposing "oblivion[s]." To begin with the second example, the arrestation of memory in oblivion is one effect of the narrative structure of film. This effect is unanticipated because the interpellation should produce the narrative effect of past, present, and future that would contain memory in its past, yet structural because the film's narrative is built precisely on the erasure of memories such as the ones this novel presents as its past. This past is not a narrative past in the sense that it does not progress into the present in a developmental movement; rather, it, or the memory of it, has been arrested. Memory of the past informs the present as a static image that disrupts the narrative flow and its demand for identification and plunges the subject into a temporal oblivion.

The "opposition" of this form of oblivion is the experience of "the losing of herself repeatedly to memory." Here, Cha describes another unanticipated effect: instead of producing a self in the present, this interpellation process produces a loss of self in the repeated emergence of memory. This loss of self is not a simple procedure because the memories to which the self is lost are a part of its formative elements and provide a paradoxical fulfillment. The distinction between self and memory is crucial, however, because it makes explicit how, even when submitting to the interpellative demands of film narrative, this viewing subject experiences repeating memories that, in their repetition, disrupt the developmental flow. If the former interruption of narrative is constituted by stasis, this one, as a series of repeated memories, does entail movement, yet it is a movement not structured by a narrative development. Like the motif of the theater that appears intermittently throughout this novel to describe the experience of these memories, the memories themselves are structured according to a logic of repetition rather than development. Thus, the opposition or contradiction lies in the two forms of oblivion: one is the erasure of histories such as the ones that constitute this subject's memories; the other is the content of those memories that persist in the present, a content that is partially constituted by erasure and loss and to the memory of which the present self is lost. The latter oblivion (the incomplete content of the memories) is structurally recalled, moreover, precisely by the fact that the apparatus must repeatedly perform the former (historical) erasure in order to take on its developmental form and produce a meaningful narrative.

Although this passage from "Memory" does not explicitly thematize translation, as many other parts of the novel do, I would like to suggest that it is one of the clearest depictions of the interpellation processes that can produce what Tejaswini Niranjana might call a *subject in translation* when translation is interventionary.[2] Niranjana defines *interventionary translation* as textual practice that challenges and disrupts the representational logic of translation as a humanist enterprise that, in the colonial context, can ground universal history. Cha's novel, as itself an interventionary translation, narrativizes contradictory effects of interpellation processes as temporal disjunction, overlapping times, temporarily "lost" subjects, and arrested, yet repeating, memories. Niranjana's notion of interventionary translation clarifies how Cha's novel does so, rather than attempting to mask, through the construction of a unified subject that develops over time in a linear narrative temporality, the nonequivalence of languages and national subjects that are positioned as such by imperialistically formed geopolitical relations. Niranjana's critique is aimed at developmental narratives; however, Cha's novel responds to the role of translation in grounding universal history by providing a counterscript that not only resists developmental narratives but also exceeds a nondevelopmental, modernist empty present. In doing so, it suggests that, whether deployed in creating colonial or imperialist meaning or, alternatively, in bringing decolonizing (in Niranjana's sense) meaning into neocolonial modernity, the act of translation is a task that a modernist poetics can carry out as well. Before discussing Cha's intervention, I first return again to the work of Ezra Pound, this time to understand the degree of difficulty involved when universalism is to be grounded by translation across the great East/West divide in another kind of nondevelopmental historiographic project.[3] To put the question more specifically (and somewhat against the grain of Pound's internationalism), what allegorical shadows might seep into the modernist text when the as-yet-unformed spirit of American literature is pedagogically summoned forth in the ideogramic writing of history?

## A Shadow of Perfection

We last left Pound's most famous personae faced with two possible outcomes for the would-be modern poet trained in Victorian verse: either floating in a decadent, phantasmatic South Pacific ocean, completely adrift from modern society and culture, or attempting, as well as possible in the dim electric light of mundane drawing rooms, to produce the virtu. Neither is a satisfactory outcome, and, as Hugh Kenner has noted in *The Pound Era*, "Hugh Selwyn Mauberley" retrospectively as a "eulogy" marks an end to one Vorticist era of experimentation (71) and prepares the way for a more truncated and abstruse ideogramic method. This method Pound defines in *Guide to Kulchur* as one that can "reveal the subject to the reader" by "presenting one facet and then another until at some point one gets off the dead and desensitized surface of the reader's mind, onto a part that will register" (51). This juxtaposition is an expansion of Imagist and Vorticist principles, taken to a more densely concise form based on what Pound, following Fenollosa, understood to be the composition of Chinese characters as visual, as active, and as embodying immediately understandable meaning.[4] Ideogramic method has been linked to Pound's historiographic concerns by Akiko Miyake, who writes in the preface to her *Ezra Pound and the Mysteries of Love*: "Seeing the whole *Cantos* as one enormous ideogram can help us recognize it as a critical study of history pervaded by Eleusinian values" (xi). Chou Zhao-ming offers an interesting angle on this aspect of Pound's poetics by demonstrating persuasively that the ideogramic method of his historical poem (the *Cantos*) is always intertwined with an "enigmatic method" (or riddle method), resulting in his translations having "the function of riddles" ("The Other Solution," 232). In addition to the inclusion of passages translated from classical Chinese, part of what makes the whole *Cantos* an ideogramic exercise is the insertion of Chinese characters and Japanese kanji into the text, at times with and at times without accompanying translations in English. Even when accompanied by a translation, the ideogram appears in its original form because it signifies something that cannot be translated precisely enough by using the usual methods. I refer to this direct and, as Chou argues, enigmatic use of characters as itself a kind of modernist, experimental translation, and I consider the underlying, ideogramic structure of the poems to be based on this experiment, forming a kind of translative writing.

It may be that this method joins, and transforms into strengths, the two unsatisfactory predicaments mentioned above. Rather than drifting into nonexistence, the poet is supplied with premodern myth, significance, and meaning (in the form of characters from non-Western languages), while he also maintains some facility with the less than adequate resources and conditions for craftsmanship in the twentieth century. Although this method may be Pound's answer to the predicament of the modern poet, the concerns of my study lie elsewhere because this answer itself marks a problematic in the great divide that it must cross. My reading of "Mauberley" in chapter 1 stresses the standstill of the dilemma produced by allegories that cannot, yet must, be overcome and the consequential "exit" from culture. The present brief discussion of Pound's later method shifts our focus from that standstill and exit to the threat, lurking just beyond, of shuttling movements not only out of culture but also into the presumed singularity of the truth of the present, through the act of innovative translation used as a method for writing historical poetry. Again reading Pound against the grain of his professed critical stance toward the United States, I consider the increasing difficulty and fragmentation of his poetry as reflecting increasing modes of erasure in U.S. nationalist narratives as the United States dropped its isolationist self-definition in the 1940s but continued not to name its imperialistic relations with much of the world. My task here is, thus, to unravel how, as a translation across the East/West divide, ideogramic historiography produces gaps that can be entrances for the impure shadows of history or links to other, nonsingular dimensions beyond the modernist temporality of the universalized fragment. As such, these unexpected effects should be read alongside the incompleteness that Gertrude Stein identifies as part of American geographic history and the allegories residing in it, which she evokes but does not name.

To understand the significance of universalism in Pound's modernist translation (or ideogramic method), we must revisit Niranjana's study of translation in colonial discourse. In *Siting Translation*, Niranjana illuminates how colonial translation suppresses colonial histories by establishing and maintaining an ontological relation between representation and reality as well as a corresponding developmental temporality as the preconditions for universal history. In an in-depth study of the politics of translation in British colonization of India that reconsiders Paul de Man's and Jacques Derrida's poststructuralist theorizations of translation (largely by reading their readings of Walter Benjamin's essay "The Task of the Translator"), Niranjana has outlined how the familiar, centuries-old debates centering on fidelity versus freedom reveal that, in the traditional sense, the act of translation assumes that meaning can be transferred from one language into another. In this sense, translation is premised on the notion of a universal signifier that can be represented in different languages by different signifieds. Niranjana notes that this has prompted Derrida to suggest that translation is the most basic task of philosophy as a humanist enterprise, thus exposing the intimate relation between translation and Western metaphysics. Niranjana extends Derrida's theorization by examining how, in the colonial context, the translation of Hindu texts produces "strategies of containment" by "creating coherent and transparent texts and subjects, . . . making them seem static and unchanging rather than historically constructed" (3). Further, Niranjana investigates the ways in which metaphysical representation is caught up in a mutually constructive relation with the teleological model of history within which colonial sites are "fixed" in the past and that erases and suppresses the heterogeneity of colonial histories. Niranjana not only describes how traditional understandings and practices of translation are complicit with colonial discourses but also posits further that "Western metaphysics itself (and the 'historicism' that is emblematic of it) seems to emerge in a certain age *from* colonial translation. The concept of representation put into circulation by eighteenth- and nineteenth-century translators of non-Western texts grounds, for example, the Hegelian theory of world history" (25). This is not to claim that all facets of colonial discourse originate in translation; rather, it might be to consider translation as a technology (in the Foucauldian sense) that not only regulates but also actively generates epistemes within particular historical conditions. Niranjana's nuanced discussion of the politics of translation in the Britain/India colonial context thus alerts us to the generative capacities of colonial translation's strategies of containment. It also reveals the ways in which the same logic of equivalence that underlies translation also masks the asymmetrical political relations between the various Indian languages and English in that colonial context.

Niranjana's discussion of translation and colonial history demonstrates how translation is always a political act. Pound's modernist translations, however, are carried out in circumstances that must be distinguished from those of the translations in Niranjana's discussion. In the case of the United States in the first decades of the twentieth century, when Pound began his study of the Chinese language and Chinese literature, nationalist ideologies presenting the U.S. relation to China as one of diplomacy rather than militant expansionism and economic opportunism positioned translators of Chinese texts differently in relation to their objects of study. As noted in the introduction, in the wake of the impending fall of the British Empire, the United States had little to gain by naming its new form of imperialist strategies as imperialist.[5] At the same time, as Zhaoming Qian has thoroughly documented (see *Orientalism and Modernism*), English-language resources were scarce for would-be Anglo-American Sinologists of Pound's generation, whereas centuries of formal colonialism in India necessitated more thorough study of its languages. These conditions present the translation of unfamiliar Chinese texts as a project whose nationalist investments and ideological ramifications are strongly distorted by denials of any kind of conquest, even though Pound's study of Chinese was an ongoing exploration of a largely unknown language of great importance to national interests. My point of departure on the subject of Pound's expatriate and often explicitly critical stance toward the United States is that his translation project, which critiques Anglo-American modernity partly through "translating" Chinese history as a political model, is for that very reason informed by a specifically nationalist discourse.[6] However, the denial of empire in that discourse makes it possible for Pound to refrain from acknowledging the importance of those expansionist interests to his poetics (e.g., even as he incorporates Chinese figures into an internationalist canon). This is the case even in his allusions to the dilemma of American letters, which is presented as an internal, domestic dilemma, from which one can turn to foreign traditions for solutions, and within which he positions himself as aesthetically representative. Added to the disavowal of imperialist expansion in the U.S. setting are the broader pressure and strain placed on culture at the beginning of the fall of the British Empire that I discussed in chapter 1. Perhaps this combination of circumstances contributes to the *loss*, in Pound's modernism, of the developmental structure of nationalism derived from a colonial discourse partly generated through translation as historiography (the process that Niranjana deconstructs), even as his translative task remains universalist.

Pound's famous imprisonment for treason at Pisa after World War II, the subject of the *Pisan Cantos*, frames the postwar scrutiny of fascist convictions such as Pound's in a particularly powerful way.[7] It is, therefore, not surprising that Pound's ideogramic poetry increasingly bears out the contradictory nature of his modernist translations as historiographic task. Let us look briefly at a passage from the first of the *Pisan Cantos*, into which Pound inserts the character *xian* [顯]. Because this character contains the sun radical, and because it means "to display, to manifest," it is representative of the function of Chinese characters in Pound's later poetry to provide luminous details that manifest or display the mystery of unchanging truth in history:

> The great scarab is bowed at the altar
> the green light gleams in his shell
> plowed in the sacred field and unwound the silkworms early
>    in tensile 顯
> the light of light is the virtu
>    "sunt lumina" said Erigena Scotus
>    as of Shun on Mt Taishan
> and in the hall of the forebears
>    as from the beginning of wonders
> the paraclete that was present in Yao, the precision
> in Shun the compassionate
> in Yu the guider of waters
>
>                       (*The Cantos of Ezra Pound*, canto 74, pp. 428–29)

In *The Spirit of Romance*, Pound defines *the virtu* as "a glow arising from the exact nature of the perception" that has "an effect upon the air, upon the soul, etc." (90–91). "The light of light" is that which reflects light itself, the latter being the light of exact perception, of reason or truth, which can bring fullness of meaning into modern writing. The green gleam of the scarab resonates with other uses throughout the *Cantos* of luminous color, especially the green, blue, and gold attributed to the glow of mythological significance or spiritual meaning, to evoke the vision of the virtu, as can be discerned clearly in these lines from the earlier canto 5:

> "Et omniformus": Air, fire, the pale soft light
> Topaz I manage, and three sorts of blue;
>    but on the barb of time
> The fire? Always, and the vision always . . . (*The Cantos of Ezra Pound*, 17)

It is this kind of color that Pound found lacking in American literature and that he attempts to incorporate as "pure color" through translation: "No American poetry is of any use for the palette. . . . Undoubtedly pure color is to be found in Chinese poetry, when we begin to know enough about it; indeed a shadow of perfection is already at hand in translations" (*Literary Essays*, 218). On the basis of Pound's use of color in these and other cantos, we can speculate that "pure color" is what can present the virtu in poetry but that it is difficult to craft out of the materials available to the twentieth-century poet of a "botched civilization" (*Personae*, 191). For example, such pure color is taken from another non-Western tradition in the passage from canto 74 as the green glow of the scarab in its shell (the shell suggesting the hard and precise contours of the image). In that canto, just as the scarab, the sacred field, and the silkworms are luminous ("'sunt lumina'"), so the names Yao, Shun, and Yu (known to Pound as the legendary Chinese emperors from the second millennium BC) are associated with the "precision" and divine spirit ("paraclete") of the virtu, and, as great leaders, they represent the legitimate authority of the bearer of truth and reason.[8] All references in this passage are made contemporaneous as what is represented by different historical or legendary figures does not change over time, has not changed since "the beginning of wonders." If access to this unchanging dimension of light and truth is more difficult in modernity, it is the poet's task to rediscover or rekindle it, and one way to do so is through what I have termed the *modernist translation* of Pound's ideogramic method. Such translated references, like Yao, Yu, and Shun, are, thus, always associated with the virtu's luminous pure colors, if not by juxtaposition, as in this passage, then through a logic formed through repetition. Repeated throughout the *Cantos* we find (alongside the ideograms of the later *Cantos*) pines and sequoias, crystals and balls of light, as well as images of prayer and contemplation in ancient or Oriental forest and temple settings where the mysteries are still given a definite setting. These images repeat as fragments; their task is to embody universal truth that repeats itself through time as the mystery of "the light of light." This is implied often by their juxtaposition with references to particular historical circumstances. The latter, however, are also presented as fragments—taken out of any narrative historiography and placed next to apparently unrelated references and even languages. The fragmentation of Pound's epic historical poetry has a double source: it is a consequence of both his use of nonnarrative images of the truth that illuminates history and the incorporation of historical fragments that purportedly contain some glimmer of transhistorical truth within them. It is this paradox of a twice-fragmented historiographic universalism, which becomes most apparent in Pound's modernist translations of non-Western texts, to which I now turn.

The mystery of truth presented as the virtu and repeated as fragment is precisely what Pound, through his own process of insertion, must use, as Maud Ellman has convincingly argued, to "blank the blank" ("Ezra Pound," 248) that usury has inserted into history through its own process of erasure. Ellman demonstrates how, for Pound, usury's task is to perform two erasures: it tries to erase the real value of the original mysteries through "interest," understood aesthetically as the production of false value, and it also erases its own history (that of the production of false value). According to Ellman, the difficulty is that the mysteries themselves are a kind of blank because they cannot be known; thus, for the poet writing a historical epic, the blank of usury must be canceled (or blanked) by the other blank of unknowable truth, resulting in a poetry of densely layered emptinesses difficult to unravel. Ellman concludes by remarking that, as far as Pound was concerned, usury, or darkness, does not have a dialectical relation to truth and that, "rather than a dialectic, history consists of a single principle of light" (259). She thus demonstrates that, for Pound, the singularity of truth cannot be opposed by a true antithesis, while at the same time this nondialectical concept of history remains a teleological one. Ellman does not continue this thread of her argument, but her insights indicate that Pound's teleology is one based on the direct manifestation of truth, suggesting that any moment, even the immediate one, can bring the anticipated ending or closure. It is an epiphanal and universal (but nondevelopmental) teleology. In Pound's modernist translation, the goal of presenting history as the manifestation of truth within an epiphanal and nondialectical telos results in truth presented as universalized fragments framed by a nondevelopmental history.

Although the *Cantos* include references to and excerpts from texts of many languages, to a certain extent the problematic of this universalism is most evident in Pound's modernist translation of non-Western texts in particular, often Chinese, since this is the non-Western language that Pound studied for many decades.[9] This tendency is borne out most clearly in canto 8, when it is Kung (Pound's name for Confucius, following the romanization) who "remembers": "A day when historians left blanks in their writings, / I mean for the things they didn't know" (*The Cantos of Ezra Pound*, 60). Kung represents the ultimate bearer of truth, yet the translation of these lines, like the knowledge described in them, brings Kung himself into Pound's poem as an unknown blank, unexplained and unannotated, like the ideograms that dot the later *Cantos*.

It is worth noting, finally, that Pound's practice of translation had unanticipated but, perhaps, inevitable ramifications. Let us consider for a moment Bruno Latour's theorization of translation as a practice of mediation and as resulting in the proliferation of hybrids and their networks, a practice that, nevertheless, for moderns and modernists, is caught up with the act of purification (*We Have Never Been Modern*, 11). Pound's experimental translation of ideograms is supposed to produce difference that reveals universal truths found (via Fenollosa) in nature (the East) before the alienating effects of money economies in the modernization process. However, in carrying out its mediating task, translated difference (e.g., as ideogram) appears as a manifestation of the truth that is, at the same time, a fragmented noncoherence and whose illegibility creates an epistemological blank.[10] Especially given the historical conditions of this entry into the East/West divide, this difference cannot but be antagonistic to a singular principle because its very presence evokes the absence of the contexts and histories out of which it has been excerpted. Not only is incoherence at the margins of this poetic text that so values reason; it runs throughout its translative structure, beginning with canto 1's invocation of the Homeric sea voyage. In the first lines, "And then went down to the ship / Set keel to breakers, forth on the godly sea," the "And then" opens the *Cantos* with a grammatical fragment that leaves open the question of what came before the represented action. I return to the opening lines of the *Cantos* to close this discussion by suggesting that this task of modernist translation produces meaning as shipwrecked fragments. The fragments are shored against the ruin of time, yet their lack of context leaves blanks open for the entrance of other times and settings, as the unreadable (for most of Pound's readers) ideograms allegorically invoke the unspoken histories of conquest that are the impetus for the voyage.[11] The shadows of these other, also nondevelopmental histories enter as unspoken allegories through the blanks left open in the attempted universalism of the translated fragment.

## Counterscript

In 1994, Norma Alarcón and Elaine H. Kim edited an anthology of four critical essays and one photo-essay on *Dictee* entitled *Writing Self, Writing Nation*. Their preface outlines a double goal for the collection: first, to offer a corrective to critical work on *Dictee* that minimizes the Korean and Korean American historical contents and contexts of the novel; second, to create a forum through which the novel would receive more attention from Asian American scholars (the papers were first written for the 1991 Asian American Studies Association meeting). Kim's essay in the collection, "Poised on the In-Between," begins by suggesting that *Dictee* is difficult to categorize as Asian American because much of it is set in Korea and because it resists constructing an immediately recognizable Asian American or Korean American subjectivity. Unlike earlier readings of and reactions to *Dictee*, those in this volume present the novel as an important artifact in Asian American cultural production precisely because it provides its readers with a way to connect Asian American and Korean nationalist struggles while maintaining a strong sense of their different histories.[12]

In her contribution to *Writing Self, Writing Nation*, an article entitled "Unfaithful to the Original," Lisa Lowe argues that Cha's theme of dictation illustrates the layered contradictions that inhere in the national, colonial, and religious demands for homogeneous subjects that are "faithful" to an original, absolute subject. Most important, Lowe demonstrates how the process of dictation—of molding subjectivities–often produces subjectivities that are not entirely "faithful" to this original. Moreover, since these national and colonial regimes and religious doctrines require a masculine subject, the failure of dictation is especially apparent in the contradictions that arise when the subject undergoing interpellation is gendered female. Most significant for my study, Lowe also describes the ways in which translation in *Dictee* exposes "the nonequivalence of the French and English text, . . . thematiz[ing] the failure of translation as a *topos* of faithful reproduction" (41). She also demonstrates how this failure of translation in the reproduction of equivalent, faithful colonial and national subjects is analogous to the implicit failure of developmental teleology in colonial and nationalist discourses. In my reading of *Dictee*, I draw on Lowe's analysis of gendered contradiction in nationalist interpellation processes because it opens up possibilities for a reading of sexuality in the text's treatment of translation positioned across a complex micro/macrostructural matrix. On the one hand, I account for the ways in which the novel traces intricate relations between developmental time and identity (as interiorized truth) in sexual and nationalist narratives in its depiction of heterosexual gendered interpellation. This is not to assign to particular forms of institutionalized sexuality a primary, universalized value. Rather, it is to address how the novel suggests that sexuality can *perform a universalizing function* within neocolonialist and nationalist discourses by defining their modernist and developmental structures as the perimeters within which representation can occur.[13] At the same time, I argue that Cha's nondevelopmental aesthetic is not reducible to the universalist project that is attempted in canonical modernism's nondevelopmental teleology.

*Dictee*'s critique of normative sexuality and gender identity is carried out in the translation that occurs among colonially sedimented layers of languages (English, French, Korean, and Japanese kanji) and between discontinuous geographic sites. I first discuss the intervention that this translation makes at the macrostructural level of its historiography and then turn to how the novel traces the complex ways in which historiography is carried out to a significant extent, albeit almost imperceptibly, at the microstructural level. First, the historical formation of *Dictee*'s subject in translation is traced partially through a feminist genealogy of Korean women living under and in nationalist struggle against Japanese occupation. In the chapter "Clio History," this genealogy begins with an account of the "short and intensely lived" (30) life of Yu Guan Soon, an early nationalist revolutionary. The account of her life is interrupted by a 1905 appeal to President Roosevelt from Korean Hawaiians to intervene against Japan in support of Korea; this petition exposes the extent to which the United States was responsible for Japanese military presence in Korea by reminding the president that a treaty between Japan and the United States during the Russo-Japanese War (1904–5) is what initially opened Korea to the Japanese militia. Between the biography and the petition is another appeal, this one to English-language readers of these histories, that contains a short meditation on the effectivity of the words (and, later, the images) that make up these historical texts:

> To the other nations who are not witnesses, who are not subject to the same oppressions, they cannot know. Unfathomable the words, the terminology: enemy, atrocities, conquest, betrayal, invasion, destruction. They exist only in the larger perception of History's recording, that affirmed, admittedly and unmistakably, one enemy nation has disregarded the humanity of another. Not physical enough. Not to the very flesh and bone, to the core, to the mark, to the point where it is necessary to intervene, even if to invent anew, expressions, for *this* experience, for this *outcome*, that does not cease to continue. (32)

The ironic address, written in English, "to the other nations who are not witnesses," presents a narrative subject already in translation, one who throughout the novel addresses not only the moment of this appeal but also the legacies of French imperialist expansion in Korea, of Japanese colonialism, and of increased U.S. military presence in East Asia after postcolonial "liberation." As a passage from an early 1980s text, this appeal is made after increased Asian immigration to the United States was brought about by the 1965 U.S. immigration legislation that changed restrictive quotas. This legislation converges with displacements that occurred in the wake of the Korean civil war and North/South division, which, in turn, were partially facilitated by the U.S. military presence. This address thus registers the irony of "recording" a history that itself determines that its audience will be the subjects of "other nations" who "cannot know" its content. The "History" referred to here is described as inadequate to meet the task of *interventionary translation*; instead, it is shown to function in ways that serve dominant interests. The use of a capitalized *History* refers to the developmental macronarrative that erases those events that would call into question the ongoing march of progress and to which *Dictee* offers a "counterscript" (18). In this passage, History is clearly presented as a humanist rhetoric that erases the materiality of the events by framing Japanese colonialism in Korea as one "enemy nation" pitted against another. The phrase *enemy nation* employs and critiques the rhetoric of the Cold War, and its new tactics of historical erasure, that was to be deployed by the U.S. government against East Asian nations later in the century (a fact at the time of the writing of *Dictee*). Further, in its logic of national equivalence (like that of Cold War rhetoric itself), this statement evens out asymmetries at the national level within East Asia, asymmetries that partially derive from the ongoing effects of Western imperialisms, which were carried out to differing extents and with different effects in different sites. Cha not only depicts the ways in which teleological History excludes the vast heterogeneity and catastrophe of colonial histories (as has also been theorized by postcolonial theorists) but also posits that the "words" of this History are not sufficiently physical, no longer material. *Dictee*'s historiographic project becomes the difficult one of ensuring that the force of the physicality of the stories to be told will not be lost "in translation" even as the humanistic task of philosophy as translation (the neat correspondence between a universal signifier and particular signifieds) is critiqued. Thus, it is at the most material and physical level that *Dictee*'s epistemological project comes into play: in order to produce a translation that can tell these stories under such circumstances, new "expressions" must be invented. The novel's experimental form, including the difficult "words" and images that Cha uses to tell its stories, is an attempt to invent expressions for the "outcome" that continues as colonial legacies continue to determine the conditions of neocolonialism.

In its form and its difficulty, Cha's novel critiques the notion of writing as representation that Niranjana discusses as partially deriving from and, in the colonial context, grounded in colonial translation. This process of representation assumes that cultural texts are a reflection of a unified reality that exists prior to and is unaffected by its representations; it also assumes a reality that is constituted by entities of symbolically equivalent value in the sense that all are signifieds. These entities' status as signifieds also universalizes them as their equivalent value is derived from an ontological realm separable from and prior to both language and reality (otherwise, the value of these entities would be affected by historical contexts and, thus, differentiated and made nonequivalent). Since language simply reflects reality rather than affecting it or mediating subjects' relation to it, each language is understood as reflecting the same universal or ontological truths that are manifested in particular realities, making possible and grounding the concept of world history. Niranjana's argument demonstrates how this logic of representation can be challenged by interventionary translation, or writing as translation, in which history is composed of heterogeneous, nonequivalent sites. Far from being separable from reality, writing as translation becomes an active engagement with it and functions to mediate subjects' relations to other subjects and to history. This notion of translation, then, suggests not that there is no reality or history but, rather, that language or representation is an active element in reality and history, with the result that the signifier cannot be entirely separated from the signified. What writing as translation reveals is not a unified reality but, rather, how, in positing a unified reality, representation masks the heterogeneity and hybridity of different historical sites after colonialism. As *Dictee*'s experimental form exemplifies (as do its other forms of experimental representation), "writing" becomes an epistemological, anti-universalist project as well as a historical act. In Cha's words, what I am calling *writing as translation* (following Niranjana) is a process in which the writer's task is "to extract each fragment from each fragment from the word from the image another word another image the reply that will not repeat history in oblivion" (Cha, *Dictee*, 33).

This image that Cha describes as extracted from another image in the process of constructing a language that can make legible a counterhegemonic historiographic project has strong resonances with Walter Benjamin's concept of the allegorical image and its role in the writing of a nondevelopmental history (discussed in the preceding chapters). In "Allegory and Trauerspiel" (in *The Origin of German Tragic Drama*), Benjamin theorizes the allegorical image as an image that contains in its present form the violent marks of the past and, thus, breaks the continuity of history. Niranjana reads this early essay of Benjamin's on translation in light of his later, Marxist-influenced historiographic project through his formulation of the allegorical image and suggests that there is a conceptual symmetry between the task of the translator and that of the historian. That is, the translator must grasp the fragment that "claims" the translator through its translatability, which brings it nearer to the redemption of pure language, a task that Benjamin clearly distinguishes from the translation of meaning. The historian must grasp the nonreferential, allegorical image that claims the historian by containing the constellation of the past in the present before the past is forgotten, a claim that is taken up with the endlessly deferred goal of redeeming the past. According to Niranjana, both tasks imply a critique of representation, and the translator's task is, thus, rewritten into the later critique of developmental history partially through the centrality of the allegorical image to the writing of a new historiography: "My argument is that although Benjamin used the fiction of a pure language toward which all translations are aimed, the amphora or vessel of the original work is either shattered continually or was never 'whole' to start with. Thus, the task of the translator is to reveal the original's instability. The critique of re-presentation implied here is echoed in Benjamin's theory of historicity, which depends on the critique of *adequatio*, on the shattering of the continuum" (*Siting Translation*, 156). Niranjana synthesizes the tasks of the translator and the materialist historian in her theorization of interventionary translation as decolonizing historiography, and the temporality of the allegorical image, or the image containing "now-time," is the vehicle of this synthesis: Niranjana speculates that "translatability"—the "claim" of particular texts on the translator—is "perhaps a figure for the past charged with 'Messianic time' that recurs in [Benjamin's] later writings. Only if a text is translatable can it demand that its *claim* be fulfilled. Only if a past image possesses 'now-time' (*Jeztzeit*) is it redeemed. The notion of 'now-time,' the constellation of past and present, shatters the continuity of teleological history" (119).

Niranjana's discussion of the importance of translation for Benjamin's allegorical image might lead us to consider for a moment how two statements, one from Pound and one from Cha, draw attention to a similar concern with images, with the fragmented and nondevelopmental. Pound's statement runs: "The hurried reader may say I write in cypher and that my statement merely skips from one point to another without connection or sequence. The statement nevertheless is complete. . . . Having said this, perhaps the reader will believe me when I say one must begin study by method . . . A narrative is all right as long as one sticks to words as simple as dog, horse and sunset" (*Guide to Kulchur*, 48). Some forty years later, Cha writes: "Time fixes for some. Their image, the memory of them is not given to deterioration, unlike the captured image that extracts from the soul precisely by reproducing, multiplying itself. . . . The present form face to face reveals the missing, the absent. Would-be-said remnant, memory. But the remnant is the whole" (*Dictee*, 37–38). Cha's later statement can be considered in relation to the politicized aesthetic of her fragmented, multilingual text. In this sense, her use of fragments, her passages in French and Korean, and her use of kanji respond to an earlier modernist writing strategy emblematized by Pound's image as poetic ideogram. I have discussed how, poised on a great cartographic divide, Pound's translated image as ideogram, with the loss of its linguistic and historical contexts, ironically furthers the singularity of the modernist present even as it attempts to represent all historical truth. Cha's use of apparently similar aesthetic forms and images (including kanji) differently takes up the canonical modernist critique of developmental narrative for a distinct political goal: to take issue with the facts and certainties of History that have abstracted, erased, or obstructed knowledge of the materiality and physicality of histories deemed illegitimate. Although this goal is historiographic, accomplishing it means presenting readers with the fictionality of facts. For this reason, unlike Pound's historiography (which is simultaneously scientific and spiritual/mythological), Cha's must resist reconstituting a new, nondevelopmental universalism even in its depiction of the materiality of the remnant.

Niranjana has theorized Benjamin's allegorical image as a mode of translation: "Benjamin claims that while historicism 'presents an eternal image of the past,' historical materialism shows 'a specific and unique engagement with it,' since 'it has recourse to a consciousness of the present that shatters the continuum of history.' For Benjamin, this destruction of continuity is characterized by the allegorical image, in which 'the past and the now flash into a constellation,' making possible, perhaps, what Spivak would call 'transactive reading' and what I have called 'translation'" (*Siting Translation*, 111). Beyond evoking the aesthetic similarity, Niranjana's reconsideration of Benjamin's allegorical image allows us to account for the importance of translation for Cha's remnant, which is also the whole, in counterdistinction to Pound's image as ideogram. Cha's "would-be-said" remnant is the memory that constitutes, I would like to suggest, a kind of moving center to this nonlinear narrative.[14] The memory as remnant claims redemption and translation; its many translations radiate outward from this moving, elusive center like the peals of sound in the novel's closing lines—". . . to break the stillness as the bells fall peal follow the sound of ropes holding weight scraping on wood to break stillness bells fall a peal to sky" (179)—apparently echoing, at one level, Pound's eddying ripples.[15] However, if we take Cha's peals of sound as emblematic of the thematic structure and formal qualities of *Dictee*, they redeploy and differently politicize the modernist fragments that would otherwise, precisely because of their decontextualization from historical narrative, assert a self-contained universalism. Rather, Cha's translations of remnant and memory "into Their tongue, the counterscript," reveal the "screen" that structures the divide and the singularity of a modernist present on one side of it. The translation radiates outward and beyond the window and the blank screen; however, it does not simply bring us, in multicultural fashion, from one already-existent system of knowledge into another. Rather, it moves not from one knowledge formation to another adjacent to it but from a singular and one-dimensional modernity to the settings and histories covered over and denied, ironically, by the one-dimensionality of the former's appropriations. At the historiographic level, at the time of the writing of *Dictee*, historical denial was no longer taking place in a larger denial of expansion; rather, it was to be found in the neocolonial humanistic rhetoric of the Cold War, which, in its vigorous global mapping, might not appear to possess any blanks. Thus the importance of Cha's epistemological critique as an interventionary translation. Cha's counterscript—to both the new History, with its hidden erasures, and modernist historiography like Pound's—as it intervenes epistemologically in order to go to the very flesh and bone, must also relinquish words to time and distance. How it does so is the subject of the following sections.

## Expulsion, Eclipse, and the Invisible Present

I turn now from the discussion of Cha's intervention into the macrostructures of History to a consideration of how, in doing so, *Dictee*'s experimental form mobilizes the microstructures of sexual contradiction. In "Unfaithful to the Original" (discussed earlier in this chapter), Lisa Lowe has demonstrated how *Dictee* further specifies Stuart Hall's theorization of overdetermination by taking as its subject the overdetermined contradictions produced by the competing hailings that interpellate gendered subjects in postcolonial Korea and Asian America. Her reading opens up the possibility for understanding how sexuality in *Dictee* is presented according to its specific overdeterminations. Reading Lowe in conjunction with Spivak (on macro- and microstructures) allows us to address how Cha's allegorical form exposes the ways in which gendered interpellation is deployed in the construction of national identity to naturalize the temporal and spatial logic of nationalism at the microstructural, and, apparently, "apolitical," level.[16] What I would like to explore in this regard is how Cha's allegorical depiction of this universalizing function of the interpellative processes of institutionalized heterosexuality also reveals the conflicts and contradictions of those processes in both their developmental and their modernist modes. *Dictee*'s focus on translation traces the interpellation of gendered subjects within contradictions of developmental temporality (or "History") and its opposite, a modernist emptiness and discontinuity, in the historical overlap that forms the temporal structure of this immigrant text: "Forward. Ahead. And somehow bypassing the present. The present redeeming itself through the grace of oblivion. How could she justify it. Without the visibility of the present" (140). If sexuality functions as, for example, a vehicle through which modern temporalities are naturalized, then, in its depiction and critique of these processes, *Dictee* takes on a countermodernist stance distinct from a modernist or modern stance. In other words, it does entail a critique of modernity as a modernist text would, rather than being premised—in a modern spirit—on the logic of assimilation to modernity that erases the nondevelopmental or embedded and nonexcerptable contents of histories that cannot be accommodated in the assimilation process. However, *Dictee* also counters the erasures performed by the nondevelopmental aesthetic of emptiness deployed in the modernist critique.

This countermodernist stance is facilitated through two overlapping scenarios: first, as its subject "records" the contradiction of the production *and* expulsion of female subjects from the nation and, second, in the cinematic viewing of the "eclipse" of the universalized gendered subject. The emptiness of Cha's narrative both references these erasures and suggests possibilities for new forms that can bring into articulation the stories that can be told not through a realist logic or a strictly modernist one but only through a particular combination of these genres. By considering *Dictee*'s form and images as allegorical, then, I am referring to its use of nondevelopmental formal structures that derive partly from canonical Western modernism but that it differently develops and mobilizes into a multilayered critique of colonial and postcolonial forms of domination, including the cultural apparatuses that interpellate modern gendered, racial, and national subjects.

In order to attend to the layered yet specific historical determinations of Cha's novel as well as to its epistemological critique, I would like to address once more Spivak's argument from "The Politics of Translation" (already discussed in chapter 3). In this article, Spivak stresses the "rhetoricity" of non-European women's writing and its potential for carrying out its critique at the level of ontology, which can undercut the "logic" (of colonial discourses) within which certain experiences can come to be known as factual and others cannot. To consider *Dictee* as a *non-European* (in the context of Spivak's article this designates "non–First World") woman's text in this analysis is not to ignore locational concerns but to follow the locational trajectory of a writing whose content and context spans Korean and U.S. locations. It is important to do so in order to appreciate the variety of positions that, potentially, can garner their distinct critiques. In "The Politics of Translation," Spivak draws on Benjamin's essay on translation, the influence of which on poststructuralism is, as we have seen, the impetus also of Niranjana's theorization of interventionary translation. Using Spivak's term to reframe my argument in the preceding sections of this chapter, we can see how the experiment of Cha's *anti-ontological* writing is a contribution to the type of epistemological, historiographic intervention that Walter Benjamin has labeled *allegorical*. *Anti-ontological* indicates another level of analysis, moreover, because Cha extends the historiographic functions of the allegorical, as does the "writing in translation" that Spivak theorizes, by bringing it into what Spivak calls the differently, more incoherently formed *microstructures* of sexuality. Below, I argue that, as *Dictee* depicts the microstructural contradictions of heterosexual narratives, it figures the contradictory demands on heterosexual female subjects revealingly as the layered "eclipse" (118) of that normative subject as "non-body" and "non-entity" (112) even within its own universalizing narrative and, simultaneously, points toward a similarly eclipsed yet (paradoxically) necessary alterity (Lowe).[17]

The nonrealist narration of the realist narrative of the film in the chapter "Erato Love Poetry" exposes the "eclipse" of the main character, the wife, within the very narratives that universalize and interpellate this normative female subject. Cha's narration continually emphasizes the affective processes of watching the film on a generalized female viewing subject: "Upon seeing her you know how it was for her. You know how it might have been. You recline, you lapse, you fall, you see before you what you have seen before.

Repeated, without your ever knowing it. It is you standing there" (106). In this passage, we can see how the wife's role as normative female sexual subject is precisely what makes her subject universal, but at the same time it is also what negates her access to the status of subject: "He touches her with his rank. By his knowledge of his own rank. By the claim of his rank. Gratuity is her body her spirit. Her non-body her non-entity" (112). The "non-entity" of these lines is brought to its final form in the wife's suicide at the lake, implied by her disappearance and in the "rising mist" of the final scene, which begins to blot out the image of the white-suited waiter as he begins looking for her. Cha's emphasis on these layered blanks (the suicide, the white mist and lack of visual images) and the emphasis on repetition of and within the apparently linear story line illustrate how the representational paradigm of heterosexual normativity (which, apparently, grants fullness of meaning, narrative development, and the emergence of a full subject) as it is deployed on female subjects depends on an aesthetic of "emptiness" within which repetition complicates development and the subject herself paradoxically emerges at the end of the film as doubly invisible (by the suicide and by the mist) and silenced (106).

This nonrealist repetition has another function as well. Repetition is also fundamental to the interpellation processes that are depicted as the protagonist is described, at the beginning of the chapter and periodically throughout, as though a camera were filming her as she enters the theater and begins watching the film and as her affect mirrors that of the wife in the film. Thus, the readers of *Dictee* witness, and, perhaps, participate in, the processes by which that female subject is endlessly reproduced. This reproduction is facilitated in part by the translation of the subtitles, which make sense of (*translate* in the broadest sense) film images produced in a particular cultural and national context for subjects of other localities. The importance of these translations is further emphasized by the visual impact of the sparse text on the largely blank pages in this chapter, which makes the text of the novel itself resemble subtitles on an otherwise blank movie screen. Perhaps this process of perfectly equivalent reproduction is what Cha refers to as "successive refraction of *her*" (89): the reproduction of multiple identical female subjects. However, as *Dictee* illustrates by the material conditions and history of its protagonist, this process is not seamless. If *Dictee* is a text that, like the subtitles of a film, makes sense of foreign and possibly incomprehensible images, then its "translation" is an interventionary one that refuses the equivalence and fullness that would be produced in a realist rendering of the film narrative. Instead of narrating correspondence between its protagonist and the universalized female subject of the film, Cha's "translation" of knowledge of "the other overlapping time" from a "different place" (99) reveals a fundamental nonequivalence, and, at the same time, that universal subject itself is, even within the bounds of its own narrative, exposed as a nonentity. This kind of critique of the fullness of gendered identity and the development of sexual narratives is reminiscent of Stein's in its use of emptiness and in its focus on the repetition of gendered types. However, because of its more comprehensive approach to the ontological, universal categories of gender or sexuality are, in *Dictee*, not subtly reconstituted in nondevelopmental form along racial or class lines, as I argued is the case in some of Stein's texts. Instead, the specific microstructural knowledges of imperialistically derived histories, otherwise suppressed by both developmental and modernist representation, are brought into legibility, such as that of the nonequivalence of the viewing subject to the subject reproduced in the film's interpellative apparatus. This nonequivalence is evoked most powerfully in the memories of "irreplaceable" events and locations on the other side of the screen.

The eclipse of the normative female subject in the film, moreover, is layered with another, perhaps unanticipated effect of this process of mirroring in the brief possibility of a "gaze" between the two women in the audience: "Medium Close Up, directly from behind her head. She turns her head to the left, on her profile. Camera pans left, and remains still at the profile of another woman seated. Camera pans back to the right, she turns her head to the front. The screen fades to white" (96). The layered mirrorings in this passage make a simple reflection untenable: the script language of the narrative allows the text to trace the movements of the protagonist of the novel as if she were the protagonist of the film and as she mirrors that protagonist. This mirroring is, in turn, mirrored by the two profiles of the women in the audience as their gaze is momentarily transferred from the screen to each other. This suggests that the very process of the reproduction of the normative subject also produces the possibility for a nonnormative "gaze" or desire that would be alterior to that normativity. This gaze is, however, quickly eclipsed as "the screen fades to white." In Cha's narration, the negation of the possibility of the gaze between the two women mirrors the negation of the female subject of the film in language as well as in content (both are replaced by a white blankness). This negated possibility of nonnormative desire might be read as an effect of a contradiction that further suppresses its subjects into heterosexual norms rather than coming into crisis under the strain of transgression.

As well as tracing some strands of the distinct formation of microstructural contradictions in heterosexual interpellation processes, *Dictee* also illustrates points of overlap and interconnection between these contradictions and the breakdown of the developmental macrostructural narratives of development and progress. This scene in the theater described in detail in "Erato Love Poetry" first appears at the beginning of the previous chapter, "Melpomene Tragedy," thereby placing the scene of gender and sexual interpellation in direct relation to (in front of) the suppressed history of the student demonstration in which the protagonist's brother is killed. In the opening lines to the tragedy, which foreshadow the following chapter's use of film script language to describe the actions of the protagonist, Cha suggests that the time and space of the film "replaces" memory: "She could be seen sitting in the first few rows.... Closer the better. The more. Better to eliminate the presences of others surrounding better view away from that which is left behind far away back behind more for closer view more and more face to face until nothing else sees only this view singular" (79). However, traces of "that which is left behind" remain in the theater as the film's own processes of erasure recall memory's position "beyond" the emptiness: "Beyond the empty the correct setting, immobile" (79). As discussed in the first section of this chapter, the "emptiness" of this theater articulates the erasures of the violence of Japanese colonial and U.S. neocolonial histories as well as Korean nationalist violence against "its own" people (women and student demonstrators). This emptiness and its erasures are, as we have just witnessed, deployed through a repetitive modernist aesthetic that permeates the developmental temporality in the film's narrative. The juxtaposition of the theater scene with that of the demonstration suggests that the interpellation of female subjects through heterosexual narratives that bring about the eclipse of that subject also, in the noncorrespondence of *Dictee*'s gendered subject with that of the film, produces the possibility of another female subject who simultaneously inhabits the microstructural contradictions of heterosexuality and the breakdowns in the macrostructural narratives of progress. This subject would be the "diseuse" who can tell layered stories: that of the expulsion of woman from the nation, that of noncorrespondence with universalized femininity and the eclipse of woman within the microstructural narratives that produce the universalized female subject, and that of the suppressed histories of colonial, neocolonial, and national violence carried out in the name of progress. By telling these stories, this diseuse would "restore memory" (133).

Describing, perhaps, the recalcitrance of memory at the beginning of "Melpomene Tragedy," Cha writes: "Nothing equivalent. Irreplaceable. Not before. Not after" (79). Now we can begin to discern one of the intricate interrelations between the macrostructures and microstructures of interpellation processes as they come into play in hailing the subject of *Dictee*. That is, the distinct and differently formed inner contradictions of the film open a space in its narrative where the "correct time" and "correct setting" can bring their own "incision." Cha's placement of the letter after the theater scene (the "rhetoric" of juxtaposition) without a smooth transition suggests that there is no simple severance of memory by the singular developmental trajectory of the film. Rather, the nonequivalence of the suppressed history (memory) to the film's temporality might make its own incision into the process of erasure at the point where the film's development itself is complicated by repetition and emptiness of another kind (gendered and universalist). Thus, the letter to the mother, to be read as a history and a document of the feminist genealogy traced by these chapters, interrupts the narration of the process of erasure, and the scene of the theater unfolds onto the suppressed memories that persist beyond it.

Cha's feminist genealogy, carried out most explicitly in this letter, begins earlier in the novel with the account of the life of the female revolutionary Yu Guan Soon. It is taken up again in the chapter that follows "Clio History," entitled "Calliope Epic Poetry," with a realist depiction of the exilic condition that the protagonist's mother was born into, after her parents' flight to Manchuria during the Japanese colonization of Korea. The narration stresses the linguistic dimensions of a life in exile and the persistence of the use of the mother tongue within a temporality of waiting for postcolonial liberation and the recovery of nation and national language. However, this recovery is also described as the recovery of a "land that is not your own" (45), a statement that might be referring to the fact that the mother was born after the advent of Japanese colonialism and her parents' subsequent exile. Read in light of the novel's feminist critique of nationalism, it could also be an indication of the distinct ways in which women involved in the struggle for national independence were once and are to be "expelled" from their "own" nation.

Perhaps this deferred feminist critique of the persistence of patriarchal domination in postcolonial nationalism, which, on the one hand, may have to be deferred, at least within the realist developmental narration of this chapter, because it cannot be carried out until after the fact of liberation, is, on the other hand, taken up in the surreal imagery of the mother's dream. This surreal imagery contrasts with the "realist" language of the mother's life story and takes on allegorical meanings within the interpretive possibilities of the moment of its occurrence. Like the temporality of nationalist anticolonial struggle, this dream presents a vision of an alternative, perhaps future, society; however, in the dream, we find a vision of an alternative that is not contained by the colonial/liberation reversal. The dream takes place as the mother, as a young woman, is seriously ill and possibly dying. In the dream, the mother is transported to another place that is "still" and where there is no struggle, and the people in this other place are wearing clothing that is not recognizably Korean or foreign. She is approached by three women who offer her food; the food, like the clothing, is described as neither domestic nor foreign. At this point, the narration of the dream begins to be interrupted at key points by the biblical parable of Christ's temptation by Satan in the desert. Because their clothing and food are not Korean or foreign, these women's national identity is not recognizable; this suggests that the community depicted in the dream is not the postcolonial future of the recovered nation. To accept the offer of food would be to join that unknown community, an act that, within the available logics of a preliberation moment, is equivalent to the death of the (nationalist, anticolonial) subject: the mother refuses the offer and comes back to life and to her parents. Another available interpretive logic is a religious one (the dream is presented through a religious lens in Cha's narration) that, ironically, derives from previous imperialistic histories. According to the religious parable, the strange women's offer of food is a sacrilegious temptation, and the women are analogous to Satan, while the mother becomes a Christ figure. Perhaps her refusal to take the food and her identification with Christ are analogous to the other acts of (often-gendered) self-sacrifice, particularly those committed in the name of the nation, that permeate the novel. Another overlapping interpellative logic is the microstructural one of heterosexual generation and filiality. This one is (ironically, considering the nationalist struggle described in this chapter) "imaged" in the two Japanese kanji (for "father and mother"), each of which takes up an entire page following the narration of the dream. The dream itself ends with the words: "You come back [from the other space of the dream and from the imminent threat of death] to your one mother to your one father" (53). By isolating these actually interrelated interpellative apparatuses, we can understand how the dream seems to have an important double function in the novel. First, it prefigures a feminist critique of nationalism. Second, in an exilic context during Japanese colonization of Korea, it traces some of the distinct but complexly interrelated macro- and microstructural interpellative logics (here, religious as well as nationalist, heterosexual, and filial) that produce female subjects as also, and contradictorily, nationalist preliberation subjects.

It is significant that the non-sensible language of the dream interrupts the realist narration of the mother's life. As a layered allegory (e.g., biblical, filial, and historical), this experimental structure can narrate the dream in a nondevelopmental form in which the story is repeatedly interrupted, as its progression follows not a logical sequence of cause and effect but, rather, one of association and unaccountability. The allegorical narration of the dream thus enables Cha to translate its images into narrative without producing the developmental story within which heterosexuality is universalized in the emergence of a unified subject of interiorized depth demanded by a realist form. Instead, the interpellation apparatuses (e.g., religious with nationalist) can be depicted as in conflict with one another in relation to Korea's colonial histories: as the nationalist demands for self-sacrifice, for example, overlap with and paradoxically reinforce imperialistically derived religious narratives of self-sacrifice. Narrating this conflicted epistemological framework in the nonrealist narrative of the dream also foreshadows the interruption of the theater scene with the narrator's letter to her mother, which is written in a straightforward prose until it begins to tell about the demonstration, when it takes on a nonrealist form. In the surreal language of the mother's dream, as in the many other nonrealist passages in the novel, interventionary translation of gendered and heterosexual interpellation processes is carried out through an allegorical temporality.

In this section, I have attempted to show how, by giving narrative form to the contradictions that exist for subjects at least doubly removed from the original national or colonial subject, this microstructural allegory counters the representational paradigms of developmental history. At the same time, its counter-Historical nondevelopmentalism makes a historical intervention as the narrative remarks on or incorporates the formation of competing discursive systems and the nonequivalence of material conditions with interpellative demands.[18] Rather than asserting a truth beyond the materiality of what remains, as does Pound's poetry, the fragmented images in Cha's allegorical writing give a countermodernist form to embedded historical memory. The nonrealist passages of the dream and the demonstration, for example, both interrupt a chronological narrative temporality, but their constitutive fragments, which are importantly "to the very flesh and bone" (32), are also remnants, and as such they are "relinquished" to the time and distance of their circumstance and mode of remembrance. They are not universalized, like Pound's ideogram, as important because purportedly containing a humanist, transhistorical truth (transcending circumstance and conditions of formation). This does not mean that the specificity of Cha's intervention makes it also one-dimensional; rather, even as "remnants" (there are many) are brought into discourse in Cha's novel, their respective distance and time constitute a multivalent temporality that is not overcome in a modernist recourse to a singular dimension of truth. The multiple levels of allegory in the dream (e.g., nationalist and religious) speak to and evoke the interpretive possibilities available in the moment of its formation, and the allegorical meanings are, thus, embedded in these possibilities. The sudden use of modernist form in the scene of the demo is addressed to the suppression of that history and renders a new knowledge of that event.

A related consequence of this redeployment of modernist technique is that the erasures performed by the modernist aesthetic discussed earlier are not reproduced in the same way in Cha's nonrealism. Instead, modernist form is used to address the discursive processes, modernist and developmental, that create the invisibility of the present. A more modernist writing in *Dictee* contrasts with other writing modes (the modernist and developmental aspects of the film's story, official versions of history, etc.) incorporated into the novel and then narrates the gendered erasure carried out in their formal structures. Further, these countermodernist passages illustrate how the process of gendered and historical erasure can itself be "erased" in the modernist aspects of their representation. This process is elusive and hard to narrate because its result is precisely to make invisible its own apparatuses. I would like to suggest that this difficulty is a factor in the aesthetic complexity of *Dictee*: we find a layered whiteness and emptiness in Cha's writing that are formally similar to what Ellman calls Pound's *layered blanks* but that address the "erasure of history" to the different end of developing a language for the words of the diseuse of microstructural historical memory. In the passages discussed above, the eclipse and expulsion are narrated with both developmental and modernist techniques and with the interruption of the former by the latter. The layered whiteness that ends the description of the film addresses not only the gendered eclipse but also the film's aesthetic and affective erasure of the eclipse, an aesthetic erasure that sublates the gendered eclipse into the film's development and the logic of tragic conclusion. It is this logic that allows the film's interpellation to be carried out nonetheless (as "successive refraction of *her*"). Instead of presenting a canonical and transhistorical image of the feminine to offset the modernist breakdown of character development when it is detected in developmental narratives, this formal interruption of the process of sublation is a way to initiate the writing of nonequivalence to the "multiple refraction" in what I've been calling the *nondevelopment* of allegorical form. The allegory of the self-negation of universal gender in the film, and the layered form and specificities of the mother's allegorical dream, both resist the one-dimensional universalism inherent to modernist critique.

## Mercurial Light: The Claim of the Image

In addition to the incorporation and critique of realist narratives such as developmental history, *Dictee* also contains a different kind of realism in its last chapter. In this section, I discuss the last complete chapter, "Polymnia Sacred Poetry," arguing that it reimages the previous chapter's "mercurial light" and countermodernist repetition as the counterrealist narration of the appearance and disappearance of the woman at the well. By *counterrealism*, I am indicating that, on the one hand, the subject matter is already positioned as counter to realism in the sense that it is excluded from what has been established as real yet, on the other hand, the narration uses a modified realist representational strategy, perhaps to counter the erasures discussed above. However, this realism is of a different type than the realism against which the novel makes one of its interventions. This is so because, if, in its developmental and modernist forms, the present contains as "invisibility" what it has expelled and eclipsed, then, when the representationally excluded becomes to some extent represented in the realist sense, its image forms a kind of interventionary epiphany that changes the contours of realism.

"Polymnia Sacred Poetry" opens with the appearance of a woman drawing water from a well, toward which a girl is walking. The girl has been walking since daybreak, across a hot, dry landscape; this scene foregrounds the way in which the woman's movements recall the more abstract ritual from "Terpsichore Choral Dance" of drawing water from stone and earth. After a brief conversation, the woman hands the girl several bundles of medicine and gives her instructions on how, on her return to the village, to administer the medicine to her mother, who is sick. The content of this chapter, then, is the passing on of medicine among gendered subjects whose relations include a familial one and a very brief acquaintance. In the knowledge from which it is derived, in the power that it represents, and in its marginalized mode of transmission, this medicine figures one genealogy of suppressed knowledge. It, and the knowledge that produces it, is neither the primitivized premodern nor an antimodern romanticized reversal of Western knowledges. Instead, it is a figure for the words of the diseuse, which can bring into discourse the knowledge, derived from sources not without relation to the imposition of a historical modernity but also not completely reducible to it, that can, nevertheless, go "to the core" in a "counterscript" to it. This connection between the unknown woman's medicinal knowledge and the words of the diseuse is suggested in the way in which the images of a paradoxically dark illumination, or fulmination, in "Terpsichore Choral Dance" are to some extent reimaged in "Polymnia Sacred Poetry" in a kind of elusive concreteness. In other words, the line "Her eyes were dark and they seemed to glow from inside the darkness" (169) may be a realist echo of a more abstruse passage from the previous chapter: "Shone internally. As the light of the eclipse, both disparition. Both radiance. Mercurial light, nacrous. . . . Luminous all the same." This passage is followed shortly by one that repeats the lines: "To core. In another tongue" (157). The mercurial light indicates the content of the translated words (in another tongue) of the diseuse: layered stories difficult to represent, as is the paradox of a dark illumination, because they bring us beyond the bright haze of the "opaque screen" that determines what can be recognized as real.

The appearance/disappearance of the woman at the well happens only at "a good distance" (167) from the village, which, as a village, may itself be only at the margins of the encroachment of modernity. Not "outside" it, she indicates another relation to modernity. Her appearance/disappearance recalls and, perhaps, is a response to the gendered exclusions of previous chapters because her appearance has a healing power (brings and passes on medicine) and indicates another genealogy of knowledge. According to the version of official knowledge instituted in U.S. neocolonialism, for example, she is not supposed to exist (to be real), nor is her medicine supposed to work. If the attempt at her exclusion is a part of the imposition of neocolonial modernity, *Dictee*'s final scenes suggest that its establishment is not complete or seamless. This is suggested both in the passing on of the medicine and in the description of the road and the screen: "The heat rises from the earth, diminishing the clear delineations of the road. The dust haze lingers between earth and sky and forms an opaque screen. On the other side of it and beyond" (167). That the "clear delineations of the road" have been "diminish[ed]" indicates that the chronotopal or spatial-temporal contours of narrative have been blurred, and the setting of realism thus seeps out of its developmental demarcations. The "opaque screen" formed by a "dust haze" also complicates the setting, and the scene is designated as being "on the other side of it [the screen] and beyond." This setting, whose narration is one of the most "realist" in the novel, seems to respond to that of the movie theater and the sense of losing and remembering what is on the other side and beyond its blank, white screen. In it, a certain kind of knowledge is passed on and the perimeters of reality challenged.

This challenge constitutes an important example of how *Dictee*'s difficult historical intervention still manages to relinquish words to time and distance rather than reasserting a canonical universalism. The discussion in the preceding sections demonstrates how Cha's historiographic intervention is accomplished by tracing connections among macro- and microstructures; yet none of the various female characters becomes a representative female subject. Instead, emphasis is placed on processes such as expulsion and eclipse, and the woman at the well's appearance is followed by her inexplicable disappearance. In the mother's life story and Yu Guan Soon's, a narrative development is utilized, but, even in these cases, there is no transparent characterization whose gender can be universalized and, therefore, made representative. In fact, that very effect is critiqued in the ironic reference to History's records of Yu's revolutionary life: "The identity of such a path is exchangeable with any other heroine in history" (30). This statement, followed by the other historical narratives in this chapter, is then interrupted by the evocation of the memory of those "who will not know age," a memory that cannot be adequately addressed by History since it "maintains the missing. Fixed between the wax and wane indefinite not a sign of progress" (38). Also, the juxtaposition of so many different women's stories helps prevent the homogenizing effect of a representative gendered subject, especially as the first one is that of a female member of the opposition who lived in defiance of gender norms in order to carry out her revolutionary tasks. Ultimately, one effect of these juxtapositions and the emphasis on various kinds of disappearance is that another emphasis is placed on the transmission of knowledges that are not only suppressed but also elusive in their content, knowledges that cannot register as fact or be clearly "represented" by what can be readily recognized as a Historical agency. Instead, another kind of historiographic agency is presented in the difficult words and finally unrepresented form of the diseuse, whose critique of sexual narratives calls into question the establishment of the factual in the broadest sense, the very basis of the macrostructure of History. At the same time, these words carefully carry out the difficult translation of the materiality of suppressed histories, the events taking place on the other side of the screen that otherwise demarcates the dimensions of the known and the knowable.

# Conclusion

## The Cultural Uses of an Interventionary Poetics

AS A LAST NOTE on the preceding chapters, I would like to call attention to both the means and the desired ends of this study in order to clarify the ways in which I have conceived of it as a step toward a more critically formulated exercise in comparative poetics. First, the distinct types of cultural politics that I have identified modernist form as taking up are not limited to poetics, but I have focused on poetics in this project in order to attend to an area of cultural production neglected by the field of postcolonial studies and because more poetic texts have significant potential for narrating disjuncture and contradiction, as I stated in the introduction, and as each chapter bears out. In addition, I have intended to take an important point in modernist literary criticism into a discussion of the possible range of cultural politics that modernist form encompasses. It has often been suggested that, in its use of nonlinear structures and in its subjective fragmentation, modernism constitutes an assault on common sense—on assumed, taken-for-granted knowledge formations, on the naturalness of what is taken as fact, and so on. This important insight into modernist form's interventionary possibilities understands modernist culture as a kind of "nonsense" that offers an antagonistic challenge to regimes of sense, rationality, and fact and their seemingly objective discursive authority. This authority is quite difficult to challenge, moreover, precisely because it positions itself, however untenably, as objective while placing anything outside its perimeters as nonsense, rendering it apparently ineffective. Thus, the importance of the modernist achievement is emphasized and applauded. My intention has been not so much to challenge this reading as it applies to canonical modernist texts as to complicate it by showing how another form of authority arises as modernism takes on a canonical function. This is the authority of the modernist fragment that exerts a new and exclusionary universalism in its reaffirmation of its own status as an end, which I hope to have demonstrated must be distinguished from "nonsense" in its minor forms. At the time of this writing, in Taiwan, where I live and work, among many other more interesting forms of cultural production, so-called postmodern narratives of psychic fragmentation like the confusedly neo-fascistic *Fight Club* are attracting alternative audiences by appealing to their need for the cultural expression of a critique of bourgeois values. At such a moment, it seems especially important to be able to make this distinction as clearly as possible, even when the two functions might be competing with one another within a given cultural text. My study of poetics has been intended not to carry out this task in its entirety but to outline the ways in which such a distinction in cultural politics can be made in the more poetic fields of literary fragmentation and to locate the canonical in moments when more reactionary or fascistic tendencies are not disguised by pluralist ideologies and are more readily recognizable than they are now, although they persist in new and sometimes very appealing forms.

Secondly, while heeding the imperative to "always historicize," I have not considered any of the texts analyzed in the previous chapters as reflecting their contexts in a simple sense; rather, whether I read them as performing a more canonical or more minor cultural politics, each text was chosen because it can be read as in some way reacting critically toward its own time and as engaging with its time in a dynamic way. It seems to me that this is the necessary second step (after historicization) in a politically responsible reading practice for any kind of cultural work—and a most essential one for a comparative project. If such a step were not taken, the heterogeneity of each social and historical context would be homogenized into the representative logic that allocates difference to a comparison *between* sites, thereby tending to erase differences within each site. Instead, I have tried to account for differences between and within different sites by choosing texts that read "against the grain" (Spivak, *In Other Worlds*, 189) within their respective contexts in socially and politically significant ways and by not taking as assumed their actual contexts of production and circulation. I developed my method in this study partly as an alternative to the common way of reading a canonical modernist text as representative of the voice of Western modernity, a reading that consolidates the canonical cultural politics of the privileged reading of the text and forecloses other readings that might highlight the contradictions of the construction of such a voice. However, my primary consideration in this regard has been to respond to the need for scholarship on modernism and postcoloniality to address the wider range of cultural politics that modernist form can accommodate. My desired outcome in doing so is to account for the more astutely critical and decolonizing uses of fragmentation as an effective and powerful mode of representing neocolonial knowledge formations.

In carrying out this project, I have designed the chapters of this book to be read in a nonmodernist manner, from beginning to end. They do not necessarily have to be read in this way. However, although something of what is designated by the term *minor modernism*, and its cultural significance with regard to previous theorizations of modernism, can be inferred from the term itself, it would not be as clear for a reader of one of the later chapters who had skipped the introduction. And, for a reader of the second, third, or fourth chapter who had not read the first chapter, which historicizes literary forms of modernism written by writers from the United States and Taiwan, some of the literary historicization important to the development of the arguments in these chapters would be missing. Most important, however, is the overall development of the argument about minor modernism as a critical mode of representation in neocoloniality, which is developed from chapter to chapter and through critical juxtapositions that are designed to illuminate the varying and, at times, starkly contrasting cultural politics of texts that share a similar form and, often, even seem to share an object of critique (i.e., *modernity*).

The layout of these chapters does follow an overall movement from a more reactionary critique to one that engages institutionalized social injustice and attempts to imagine more equitable alternatives rather than desiring the reinstitution of hierarchical social orders. However, this is not at all to say that the first text is most reactionary or that the last is most progressive. Yü Kwang-chung, for example, is certainly not more reactionary than Pound.

On the contrary, his poem is placed first because his ambivalent rendering of the imposition of modernity on a Pacific island as a mysterious and seemingly endless suspension bridge, which is virtually unknown to English-language readers, frames in a much more critical way Pound's "loss" of the virtu in modernity (and simultaneous loss of modernity), which is quite famously and intertextually figured as a shipwreck on a South Pacific island in "Hugh Selwyn Mauberley." Similarly, although other readers familiar with both might make this argument, I do not think that Cha's text is more critical or even more politically engaged than Hsia Yü's (although that is certainly the case if a more narrow definition of *politics* is used). Rather, Hsia Yü's complex take on the microstructural quotidian and the sexual helps us read that aspect of Cha's text even where it is less meticulously explored. And, most important, Hsia Yü's refusal to appropriate political and nationalistic discourses of her time even for the purposes of critique helps us not take the terms of modernity for granted in reading Cha's more explicitly political themes. Cha's, then, is not the last word of this project in terms of the type of critique that it affirms most strongly; rather, when framed by Hsia Yü's lack of nationalistic language and implicit questioning of nationalistically determined critiques, Cha's text can be read less as an "American" text (although it is also that) and more like another kind of critically positioned text (vis-à-vis U.S. hegemony) that challenges neocolonial structures of knowledge derived partly from U.S. Cold War investments in the East Asia region. It is the latter positioning and contextualization of texts that this study can, I hope, foreground: beginning with a study of modernist poetics in two national sites whose shared histories are obscured by the knowledge structures of U.S. neocolonialism in postwar East Asia, what is gradually revealed is the unevenness of the neocolonial relations of power between the two sites and, at the same time, the limits of nationalist structures of knowledge in dealing with modernist cultural production. In doing so, what I ultimately hope to have uncovered is, first, the implicit ideological *uses* of those limits in canonical modernism's attempt to use fragmentation and disjuncture as a new, nondevelopmental way to reconstruct and reaffirm its own cultural self-containment and exclusivity and the inherent contradictions of this task. Finally, I have intended to show how nationalist structures of knowledge come under critique (Cha) or prove to be inadequate (Hsia Yü) in a critical poetics that takes up the task of questioning structures of knowledge and identity in Cold War neocolonial modernities at both micro- and macro-structural levels. Although beyond the scope of this study, such a task could certainly be taken up in other fields of decolonizing cultural production as they intervene into or reveal other generic exclusions of modernist cultures.

# Notes

### Introduction

1. The studies linking modernity to modernism that have been particularly influential for my project include Matei Calinescu's *Five Faces of Modernity*, Raymond Williams's *The Politics of Modernism*, Ricardo J. Quinones's *Mapping Literary Modernism*, and Michael Davidson's *Ghostlier Demarcations*. David Harvey's *The Condition of Postmodernity* begins with a discussion of modernism that has influenced my understanding of modernist space and time (however, I find the clear distinction between modernist and postmodernist poetics problematic). Although this is not a study of modernism per se, I also draw on Fredric Jameson's *The Political Unconscious*, which contains a substantial chapter on Joseph Conrad. However, in chapter 2, I show that Jameson too schematically distinguishes Conrad's oeuvre from "high modernism."
2. As Michelle Yeh does in her important article "The Feminist Poetic of Hsia Yü." Ironically, in her readings of Hsia Yü's work Yeh utilizes a feminist paradigm of interpretation that has undergone little transformation in its relocation even as she argues that Hsia Yü's poetry is representative of a local and specifically Taiwanese feminist discourse. I will discuss the merits of Yeh's article in chapter 3, but here I would like to point out that the use of this paradigm also leads to reductive readings with regard to the poetry's aesthetic and conceptual complexity.
3. For a discussion of U.S. "imperial anticolonialism," see Williams, "Imperial Anticolonialism." For a helpful overview (and critique) of the internal colonialism model, see Omi and Winant, *Racial Formation in the United States*, 44–47.
4. In *We Have Never Been Modern*, Bruno Latour has helpfully pointed out that *modernist* has meant *antimodern* and that both are opposed to the modern yet firmly within its "constitution." As an alternative to these terms, he offers the "hybrids"—what the modern constitution both proliferates and denies in its work of translation, which purifies the poles of subject and object (10–12). The argument (not Latour's) for modernism's "antimodern" inherent subversive potential can be taken too far. For example, in a book that is illuminating in many ways, Ricardo J. Quinones makes the insupportable claim that modernism and fascism are "polar opposites" (*Mapping Literary Modernism*, 119). It is this kind of indiscriminately exonerating reading of modernist cultural politics that I am responding to in attempting to discern its canonical and minor functions.
5. Calinescu defines the *foundation* of modernist culture as "the identity of *time* and *self*," which is in "irreconcilable opposition" to modernity's "objectified, socially measurable time of capitalist civilization" (*Five Faces of Modernism*, 3).

6   This concern with both kinds of modernism as a response to modernity is part of my reason for not using the term *postmodern*, along with its periodizing function, which is less appropriate for a study of non-European or Anglo-American sites of literary production since, in these other sites, such aesthetic forms all tend to happen at once. However, my argument concerning noncanonical modernism may be somewhat in agreement with politicized theorizations of the postmodern that see it as a differently positioned critique of modernity, including those that also designate it as *posthuman*. See the introduction to Halberstam and Livingston's *Posthuman Bodies*.

7   Anne McClintock's relatively early "The Angel of Progress" anticipates this kind of problem in its discussion of the homogenizing tendency of the term.

8   The by now familiar impasse characteristic of this binary is that each side is often seen as possessing answers to the problems that have arisen in the "other" sphere. For example, in mainland China in the 1920s and later, many May Fourth intellectuals had faith in the ability of "Mr. Democracy and Mr. Science" to solve China's modernization problems. Meanwhile, U.S. modernists (writing at the same time as the May Fourth intellectuals, but continuing into the "postmodern," post–World War II era) believed that the adoption of Chinese and other literary techniques considered primitive would help restore to Western literature the mythic or spiritual dimensions believed to have been lost in what has been termed the *alienation* of modern Western society. By using examples of this binary logic from the early decades of the twentieth century, I do not mean to imply that it is no longer a prevalent conceptualization; on the contrary, contemporary examples abound. This kind of reciprocity functions according to a logic of sameness that, in spite of the apparent paradox, structures any argument based on absolute difference and binary relations. Within this binary, *difference* is an opposition, a formulation that can allow for difference only as the site of the "primitive/native/barbarian" or the "savior." In either case, it attempts to produce cultural homogeneity at the moment it is reduced to a mirror for "our" problems.

9   Chen points out that "behind the West lies a racist concept, white; the West contains no unity except color" ("The Decolonization Question," 19). Although the East/West epistemological structures underlie modernist writings, it is beyond the scope of the present study to account for and analyze their complex formation. Naoki Sakai has provided an in-depth analysis of the construct *the West*, arguing that it is neither "a geographic territory with an affiliated population" nor "a unified cultural and social formation." Rather, Sakai argues that "it is only our essentialist insistence upon its geographical and cultural uniformity that evokes the putative unity of the West" ("The Dislocation of the West," 72).

10  In "Through the Open Door," his exceptionally well-researched account of U.S. modernists' preoccupation with China, Steve Bradbury has shown how this phenomena extended beyond visiting museum exhibits, or even attempts at studying the language, and included actual tours of China for certain poets and

11  As has been suggested in Liao, "Borrowed Modernity."
12  My understanding of the problematic of postcoloniality in East Asia has been influenced by my participation in the University of California humanities in-residence research group "Nationalism, Colonialism, and Modernity: The Cases of Korea, Japan, and China," which took place in spring 1995 and was organized by Theodore Huters.
13  V. G. Keirnan notes Taiwan as an exceptionally successful example of the implementation of U.S. neocolonialism (see *The New Imperialism*, 224).
14  For my understanding of sexual alterity, I am indebted to Reddy's "Homes, Houses, Non-Identity" and "The Migrating Present."
15  Gayatri Chakravorty Spivak has written that what makes a postcolonial writer interesting, and her work of political significance, is not her representativeness but the extent to which she is "unlike her time" (*In Other Worlds*, 189). Spivak further explains this choice with a statement that differentiates such writers from those who more smoothly perform what we might call a *major function*: "I remain interested in writers who are against the current, against the mainstream. I remain convinced that the interesting literary text might be precisely the text where you do not learn what the majority view of majority cultural representation or self-representation might be." Likewise, the literary subjects of the minor texts discussed in these chapters might be considered allegorical rather than representative in that they are not always able to claim any recognizable subject position because they, and the knowledges they impart, are recalcitrant with regard to available epistemological paradigms of subjectivity. Throughout the following chapters I attempt to demonstrate that, in part, it is this recalcitrance that enables these texts to provide interventions into existing knowledge structures.
16  In my understanding of the workings of overdetermined contradiction and its articulation in antagonistic cultural objects, I am drawing on Lisa Lowe's introduction to *Immigrant Acts* and on her discussion of Theresa Hak Kyung Cha's *Dictee* in chap. 6.

The concerns of minority discourse have been brought into dialogue with Marxist formulations of contradiction in Lowe's work. In *Immigrant Acts*, Lowe demonstrates how the same conditions that produce gendered subjects in oppositional Korean nationalism (as reproductive units for the nation) also produce the demand for absolute equivalence among national subjects and how women are, thus, simultaneously interpellated into and distanced from national identity, producing a contradiction that could come into crisis. In the U.S. context, Lowe demonstrates how political, legal, and economic conditions can place racialized women in a position of nonidentity or alterity in relation to national equivalence—a position from which collective movements might emerge if this contradiction is not sublated through the pleasure of phantasmatic identification and, instead, comes into "rupture." She argues further that, when political conditions do not permit overdetermined contradictions to come into rupture in the political arena, overdetermined political contradictions can "erupt" in cultural texts. In a modification of Louis Althusser's theorization of ideology in the well-known article "Ideology and Ideological State Apparatuses," she emphasizes how, "as an Asian immigrant cultural text, many of *Dictee*'s formal features imply links and questions that are excluded and undeveloped in Althusser's strictly theoretical formulation of interpellation." She further demonstrates how formal features such as a "non-linear and non-developmental" (145) narrative can mobilize in a more precise manner these gendered contradictions in a critique of the layered structures of dominance that constitute U.S. patriarchy and the U.S. racial state. In this and other articles on Asian American cultural production, Lowe focuses primarily on novelistic narratives. (*Dictee* is considered to be a novel, albeit an extremely experimental one whose experimental structure is precisely what allows it to represent contradiction; more conventional novels are read for how they articulate the demand for reconciliation to narratives of the national subject while, at the same time, the material contradictions that they necessarily register to that subject's trajectory also call it into question.)

## 1 The Historicity of the Fragment

1 For Bakhtin, who invented the term *chronotope*, one quintessential literary chronotope is the road (see *The Dialogic Imagination*, 98). Also related to our concerns regarding the significations of roads in modernity is Marshall Berman's discussion of the new boulevards in the modern city, i.e., Paris (see *All That Is Solid Melts into Air*). Reading Baudelaire, Berman argues that the modern boulevard is "a perfect symbol of capitalism's inner contradictions: rationality in each individual capitalist unit, leading to anarchic irrationality in the social system that brings all these units together" (159). In *Changing Song*, Miriam Silverberg builds on this passage from Berman in her analysis of Nakano Shigeharu's "In Front of the Policebox." Silverberg provides a historical reading that addresses the context of rapid industrialization and its relation to the development of modern states in Asia: roads are built by the state to help build the nation, suddenly making accessible remote, local settlements and integrating them into the nation. The road can, therefore, serve as a tool of state surveillance of the public and a means of situating individuals in an alienated relation to one another. Silverberg makes the latter point in her summation of the ending of this story: "The people [in the street] break the shared circle they have formed in order to disperse. Passive before the power of the state, they return to their disconnected yet fully controlled positions within the urban crowd" (183). However, her reading also demonstrates how the street becomes a potential site

for emerging public spheres, where "a portion of the crowd transforms itself into a grouping when an increasing number of people break out of their routine to become witness to 'the incident'" (182).
2  I would argue that the binary of Westernization (as modernization)/tradition is both evoked and called into question by these poems.
3  The Chinese who removed to Taiwan after the KMT (the Kuomintang, or Nationalist party) lost to the Communists in 1949 are referred to as *mainlanders*, a term that distinguishes them from local Taiwanese, Hakka, and indigenous peoples. This history is outlined below.
4  Shang Ching's "Uncovered Footfalls" uses footsteps to illustrate a unilateral forward temporal movement and an arrested temporal movement. This poem (in the original Chinese and with an English translation) is collected in Shang, *The Frozen Torch*.
5  Originally from mainland China, and now residing in the United States, Wai-lim Yip is one of the most prominent of Chinese modernist poets. He lived in Taiwan during the height of the modernist movement in the 1960s and has remained one of its active participants.
6  In the important article "1960s Modernist Literature?" Ko Chingming points out that the only aesthetic form from Western literatures that was significantly new for Chinese writers was realism (not modernist or postmodern experimentation). Similarly, Weng Wen Hsian's "A Consideration of the Implications of *Xing* in the Creation of Modern Poetry" (discussed in chapter 2) stresses that what are labeled *postmodern* aesthetic forms in contemporary texts may actually be carryovers from the classical canon.
7  Homi Bhabha (*The Location of Culture*, 238) on the time lag from which Fanon writes.
8  For the UN recognition of the People's Republic of China rather than the Republic of China in 1971 and the withdrawal of U.S. recognition of Taiwan's statehood in late 1978, see Wang, "A Bastion Created, a Regime Reformed, an Economy Reengineered," 438–41. For a brilliant analysis of the vexed issue of sovereignty in Taiwan, see Solomon, "Taiwan Incorporated."
9  For a helpful outline of Taiwan's modern history, see Spence, *The Search for Modern China*, 53–58.
10  For an illuminating analysis of the political stakes involved in the use of the ideological concept *We are all Chinese*, see the anonymous article entitled "Fake Taiwanese People."
11  The Fukinese are the original Chinese emigrants to Taiwan. Their descendants are now referred to as *native* Taiwanese.
12  In "Rewriting Taiwanese National History," Ping-hui Liao includes an account of the demographics of military, government, and higher-education positions, demonstrating that "cultural and symbolic capital is still very much in the hands of the mainlanders" (284). For an analysis of the formation of the industrial working class in Taiwan, see Hill Gates's *Chinese Working-Class Lives*. Gates's analysis is particularly thorough on the histories of ethnicities in Taiwan (26–

49), the role that ethnicity plays in popular understandings of class difference (54–62), and the utilization of traditional and changing family structures in the formation of an industrial working class and the effects of this development on women's lives in particular (103–44). In *Parallax Visions*, his recent book on U.S.–East Asian relations, Bruce Cumings provides a brief but helpful survey of studies documenting the demographics of class and politics in post-1949 Taiwan (82).

13 The development of nativism in Taiwan's literature is complicated since it originated as a call for a return from the changing society and culture of rapid modernization to a native Chinese culture, a return that was later challenged by a movement that centered Taiwanese culture as "native" for Taiwanese people. The latter school often pits prose and socialist realism against modernism's poetry and abstraction (although some of its writers have used modernist techniques, most notably the poet Pai Ch'iu). When scholars use the term *nativist resistance*, they are referring to this later debate. See Yvonne Chang's *Modernism and the Nativist Resistance*. Sebastian Hsien-hao Liao has charted the earlier developments in "Nationalism at the Crossroads."

14 The idea of two Wests was first brought to my attention by Ko Ching-ming in an independent seminar.

15 For a theorization of Taiwanese identity under Japanese colonialism, see Leo Ching's important *Becoming "Japanese."*

16 The first principle in "A Retrospect," basically Pound's Imagist manifesto (first published in full in 1918), is "direct treatment of the thing whether subjective or objective" (Pound, *Literary Essays*, 3). In this essay, Pound further states that "the natural object is always the adequate symbol" (5). It is also here that Pound comments that the Imagist principles were arrived at by H.D., Richard Aldington, and himself in 1912. The naïveté of this attempt seems to be parodied by Virginia Woolf in the opening paragraphs of *Orlando* (first published in 1928): "He was describing, as all young poets are for ever describing, nature, and in order to match the shade of green precisely he looked (and here he showed more audacity than most) at the thing itself, which happened to be a laurel bush growing beneath the window. After that, of course, he could write no more. Green in nature is one thing, green in literature another. Nature and letters seem to have a natural antipathy; bring them together and they tear each other to pieces" (16–17).

17 In the introduction to his *Ghostlier Demarcations*, Michael Davidson outlines the frequency of the appearance of phantasmagoric images, and even the term *phantasmagoric* itself, in writings by modernists as diverse as H.D., Pound, and Marx. By reading literary texts against Marx's famous passage on the commodity, Davidson demonstrates that the phantasmagoric's frequency in literature has to do with the objectification of the image. The poetic image's mysterious process of commodification makes it part of material culture yet haunted by a specter, just as the earlier magic lantern shows (from whence the modern use of the term derives) were emblematic of the ghost in the machine. For the

latter point, Davidson draws on Terry Castle's fascinating article "Phantasmagoria."

18 I am indebted to some of these studies, and they will be discussed in the following chapter. For further reading on the topic of the present discussion, see John Carlos Rowe's *Literary Culture and U.S. Imperialism*, the introductory chapter of which contains a detailed, interdisciplinary account of the literature on the cultural effects of U.S. imperialism.

19 Hugh Kenner provides a brief but well-informed account of the importance of Douglas to Pound (see *The Pound Era*, esp. 310–17).

20 For the meaning of *nuktos 'agalma*, I have consulted Ruthven, *A Guide to Ezra Pound's "Personae,"* 143.

## 2 Stein's American Allegories

1 When using the words *America* and *American* in this chapter, I am referring to Stein's conceptualization or larger ideological constructs like that of exceptionalism, not the U.S. nation-state itself; the use of *United States* or *U.S.* in other instances is meant to underscore this distinction.

2 In *The Political Unconscious*, Jameson discusses Conrad's use of heroism as a theme, stating that "in the midst of capitalism . . . such a theme must mean something else" (217), and, in his analysis of the novel, the sea and the sea voyage are read as the "absent work place" (the place of labor that would be absent in "high modernist" texts). My reading of *Lord Jim* has a different focus than Jameson's in that my central focus is not the larger one of how this text can be read in the context of Western capitalism but rather how these representational constructions of the non-West and an Englishman's adventures in it function in the cultural narrative of English national identity and the rationalization of its large-scale colonial dominance.

3 In *The Political Unconscious*, Jameson refers to Conrad as an emerging modernist (206) and does not assign his work the status of "high modernism."

4 I am extrapolating from Jenny Sharpe's argument about the shift in English colonial discourse (discussed below) that occurred as a response to the revolts of the late 1850s and the 1860s. This argument is laid out in the introduction to her *Allegories of Empire*. That book makes a strong argument for the centrality of woman and femininity in colonial discourses, in this case by analyzing the role of rape narratives (with a colonial rapist and a British victim) in transformations in nineteenth-century British colonial discourse.

5 In evoking certain anguished questions, Bruno Latour has described modernist (read critical antimodern) temporality in a figure of immobility that vividly recalls that of the *Patna*: "How can we absorb them? The moderns raise the question in anguish. We might have done it; we thought we could do it; we can no longer believe it possible. Like a great ocean liner that slows down and comes to a standstill in the Sargasso Sea, the moderns' time has finally been suspended. But time has nothing to do with it. The connections among beings alone make

time. It was the systematic connection of entities in a coherent whole that constituted the modern flow of time. Now that this laminary flow has become turbulent, we can give up the empty framework of temporality and return to passing time—that is, to beings and their relationships, to the networks that construct reversibility and irreversibility" (*We Have Never Been Modern*, 77). Latour's passage argues for the nontemporal significance of temporality as that of relations and hybrid networks that extend beyond the linear construct that they mediate. Such networks escape the critical appraisal of Conrad's modernism, yet their mediation is silently evoked in the aporia of the questions, equally anguished, that arise out of *Lord Jim*'s narrative plot, which necessitates and disallows any possibility for sociality. In the two chapters following this one, I discuss texts that are not circumscribed by the "empty framework of temporality," but my concerns in this reading lie in understanding the power of the standstill and the end that it seems to indicate and in differentiating the forms that such an "end" takes on in different formations of empire, a consideration that does not come into Latour's account.

6   In "An Image of Africa," Chinua Achebe makes the point that, in *Heart of Darkness*, Africa is presented as a foil for Europe, reduced to the setting of a plot centering on Europeans.

7   In "Home in the Empire, Empire in the Home," George demonstrates the ways in which a protofeminist and nationalist individuality for women first appears in colonial writings on English womanhood and domesticity produced in India. For Armstrong's argument, see the introduction to *Desire and Domestic Fiction*.

8   *Fenhurst, Q.E.D., and Other Early Writings* contains the previously unpublished 1903 draft of the first five chapters of *The Making of Americans* (finished in 1908 but not published until 1925).

9   Zwick, ed., *Anti-Imperialism in the United States: 1898–1935*, http://www.boondocksnet.com/ai/index.html—an interesting Web site on the organized protest against American expansion during this period—contains many useful historical and literary documents.

10  Robert Duncan's 1967 introduction to *Bending the Bow* contains an interesting variation on just such a "field" whose relation to military and economic domination of the Third World has by this time, in this case in light of the Vietnam War, become quite explicit.

11  This formulation of reality as a form of fantasy legitimated as reality for ideological purposes is from Butler's essay "The Force of Fantasy."

12  I return to Isaak's distinction between the presentational and the representational and discuss it in more detail in this chapter's section on *Tender Buttons*.

13  I occasionally use the term *lesbian* in this chapter for convenience since most of the literary criticism on Stein's writing that deals with sexuality does so. However, it may not be the best way to refer to characters in Stein's texts because the identity that it has now come to refer to could not have been a factor in Stein's own sexual formation around the turn of the century. As Judith

Halberstam has argued in *Female Masculinity*, a Foucauldian model of historiography reveals that the lesbian identity that is taken for granted today is not a transhistorical identity: "Within a Foucaultian history of sexuality, 'lesbian' constitutes a term for same-sex desire produced in the mid to late twentieth century within the highly politicized context of the rise of feminism and the development of what Foucault calls a homosexual 'reverse discourse'; if this is so, then 'lesbian' cannot be the transhistorical label for all same-sex activity between women" (51).

14  Sangari's reading is discussed in the introduction, Said's in chapter 1.

15  In *Are Girls Necessary?* Julie Abraham demonstrates how, as "lesbian writing" began to be written about, "the 'lesbian novel' was overidentified with literary realism" (23), thereby causing the extensiveness of lesbian writing to be routinely overlooked: "Prolific writers such as Virginia Woolf, Gertrude Stein, Willa Cather, Amy Lowell, Janet Flanner, H.D., Vita Sackville-West, and so on, who nevertheless did not produce lesbian novels, can be seen as having been silenced only if the lesbian novel is understood as *the* lesbian text. The gap between the multitude of lesbian writers and the comparative paucity of lesbian novels produced by respected or even identifiable writers, then only reinforces a reading of lesbians as silenced. This insistence on the silencing of lesbians either renders invisible most of what I have called lesbian writing, or at least relegates this work to secondary status as unauthentic or opaque—coded" (24). Although it is beyond the scope of this project, Judith Halberstam's point about the historicity of the definition of the term *lesbian* as it is presently used (see n. 13 above) would be helpful in exploring the extent to which what Abraham refers to as the *overidentification* of lesbian writing with realism is premised on the assumption of a transhistorical lesbian identity with unproblematic access to realist representation. This assumption could, e.g., render as "closeted," or even as utterly unrecognizable, other forms of nonnormative characterizations that do not correspond neatly to contemporary understandings of lesbian identity.

16  An interesting parallel to the emergence of modernist literature is the increasing popularity of the new science of psychoanalysis, the need for which arose out of the incipient breakdown of the individual, who, as modernist literary criticism has demonstrated, was increasingly, after each world war, beset with fragmentation. Psychoanalysis can be read as a modernist project to the extent that, through memory and free association, it tries to find amid the fragments a pattern that can restore individuality and identity without forcing those fragments into a reductive wholeness that is no longer experienced as authentic. Because this is impossible, individuality being precisely a reductive wholeness, this goal created an interesting contradiction in psychoanalytic texts, which as early as Freud can be read at times as affirming a normalizing discourse (e.g., demonstrating the perversity of inversion) and at other times as challenging the notion of the normal individual (by positing an innate bisexuality in human nature; see Freud's *Three Essays on the Theory of Sexuality*). More recently, the

most sophisticated psychoanalytic critics (e.g., Jacques Lacan, Luce Irigaray, and Jane Gallop) have had to do away with the notion of individuality altogether and replace it with that of the "split" subject.
17 In "History as Repetition," Jane L. Walker argues that, unlike the characters in realist narratives, who are both "unique individuals and at the same time representatives of social types," Stein's characters are written according to a "typological system" that "emphasizes identities and ignores particularizing differences of social and historical circumstances" (180).
18 My understanding of Stein's complicated use of identity/entity is indebted to the discussion in Davidson, *Ghostlier Demarcations*, 35–63.
19 In "Professing Stein/Stein Professing," Bernstein attempts to rescue Stein from accusations of racism in A. L. Nielson's *Reading Race*; thus, he never acknowledges that Stein's use of Black English Vernacular is itself an act of linguistic colonization.
20 In the introduction to *Reading Race*, Nielson discusses "Melanctha" at some length as the precursor of white modernist texts that contain Negro characters (see 21–28).
21 Isaak writes: "Stein was interested in the presentational rather than the representational in language. . . . Stein's writing derives its meaning from nothing external to the writing, but from her realization of what she presents in, rather than suggests by, her words" ("The Revolutionary Power of a Woman's Laughter," 28).
22 According to "Principle II: The Linear Nature of the Signifier," in chap. 1, "Nature of the Linguistic Sign," of the *Course in General Linguistics*.

## 3 Hsia Yü's "Underground" Poetry

1 Reading Hsia Yü's work for its innovative language "play," scholars have emphasized her mastery of the art of poetic craftsmanship more than her development of a critical poetics or her elaboration of what could be termed an *underground* sensibility. The praise of her craftsmanship is well deserved, as is her reputation as the best living female poet writing in Chinese (although I would argue that these linguistic/cultural and gender qualifications are unnecessary). Over the past two decades, such well-established critics as Chung Ling, Liao Hsien-hao, Li Yuanzhen, and Weng Wen-Xian have brought attention to her work throughout the Chinese-speaking world, and her fame is now spreading into English-speaking contexts through the work of scholars and translators such as Michelle Yeh and Steve Bradbury, among others.
2 Written by John Denver, "Leaving on a Jet Plane" was first recorded by Peter, Paul and Mary in 1967 and released on their *Album 1700*. It was their number one single and was later recorded by John Denver, who included it on his 1974 album *John Denver's Greatest Hits*.
3 This initial, self-published volume is entitled *Beiwang-lu* [Memoranda]. Containing poems dating from 1976 to 1984, *Memoranda* was photocopied and

circulated throughout Taiwan by readers after its appearance in 1986. Ironically, given the plagiarism involved, it was with this early volume that Hsia Yü's reputation as a major poet was first established. Since then, her work has increased in aesthetic complexity and difficulty, especially with the 1995 collection *Moca wuyimingzhuang* [Friction ineffable], which is composed mostly of concise and highly abstract "cutups" from her second volume, *Fuyushu* [Ventriloquy] (1991). Born in Hong Kong and educated in Taiwan, Hsia Yü resided until recently in France, with periodic stays in Taiwan. She has always published out of Taiwan. Her most recent volume, *Salsa* (1999; title in Spanish), contains longer, almost narrative-style poems and has brought a large popular readership and much critical acclaim.

Michelle Yeh has provided translations from Hsia Yü's first two books in her *Anthology of Modern Chinese Poetry*. More recently, Steve Bradbury has completed an entire volume of translations selected from all four books. For those translations and a detailed account of Hsia Yü's literary career, see his *Fusion Kitsch*.

4 For an analysis of an "ambivalent reticence" in Chan's lyrics and videos (also drawing on Liu and Ding's "Reticent Poetics, Queer Politics" [discussed below]), see Fran Martin's "The Perfect Lie."

5 "Chiang Kai-shek proclaimed that 'promotion of civic education must pay special attention to the teaching of 'Chinese History' and 'Chinese Geography.' For it is only through them that the student's patriotic fervor and national pride can really be aroused, that he can be made to realize the fundamental significance of the basic virtues of loyalty . . . a citizen who loves his country more than his own life" (Johnson, "Making Time," 111).

6 This official geography, moreover, directly contradicts the findings of other geographers who understand Taiwan to be part of the "Ring of Fire," which starts in Alaska and runs south, forming Taiwan and other islands in the Pacific (Johnson, "Making Time," 115).

7 The translation of "Leaving on a Jet Plane" is mine. I would like to thank Hsia Yü for her generous suggestions on two drafts of it. I would also like to point out that, as any translator would agree, her poetry is especially difficult to translate, and I take responsibility for the loss of nuance, humor, and music, which I found inevitable if the translation were to remain at all faithful in terms of meaning, and for any remaining mistranslations.

8 Rubinstein points out that the building of a larger, international airport was part of a broad plan for improved communications that was not drawn up until the late 1970s and early 1980s (see his "Taiwan's Socioeconomic Modernization," 373).

9 The off-color setting is quite pronounced in this context: Tao-ming Hans Huang has, in his "State Power, Prostitution, and Sexual Order in Taiwan" (discussed below), demonstrated the strong association in postwar Taiwan of sex work with bars and the accompanying stigma attached to people who go to bars.

10  For a discussion of sublation in domestic fiction, see Spivak, "Three Feminist Readings." Sublation is discussed at greater length later in this chapter.
11  This insight is Teri Silvio's (personal communication, January 10, 2004).
12  As the title "Reticent Poetics, Queer Politics" indicates, the article (discussed below) focuses on queer subjects. I have found it, and other theorizations of queer identity formations, helpful in reading Hsia Yü's poetry even though it is not queer in the strictest sense (in that it is not about same-sex relations) because, in its critique of the institution of marriage and monogamy, it is non-normative with regard to gender and sexuality in its social context.

My understanding of how sexuality is related to epistemological questions of modernity also draws on theoretical work that is not focused on Taiwan or any Chinese-speaking contexts, especially that of Michel Foucault, Judith Butler, Eve Sedgwick, and Judith Halberstam. Their respective elaborations of the ways in which sexuality becomes central to identity formation and knowledge formation in modernity have been most helpful for the present study, including the theorization of gender performativity (Butler), the critique of the paradigm of the formation of sexual identity within psychoanalysis's "repressive hypothesis" (Foucault), the theorization of the limits of ontological and binary epistemological frameworks in accounting for the actual workings of sexuality, including normative sexuality (Sedgwick), and the critique of the condensation mechanisms of Freud's psychoanalysis that create its universalism (Halberstam). In my readings of Hsia Yü's poetry, I am drawing on these theorizations. However, the focus here is the distinct formation of modernity in Taiwan that produces a differently layered epistemology and affective mechanisms with regard to sexuality, within which normative mechanisms rely partly on what in "Reticent Poetics, Queer Politics" Liu and Ding have termed *reticence*. In this sense, my readings may have resonances with Sedgwick's theorization in *Epistemology of the Closet* of a plurality of ignorances and their sexually disciplinary functions and Halberstam's in *Skin Shows* of how Gothic silences and category crises inhabit the heart of realist narrativity.
13  Rosemary George's essay "Calling Kamala Das Queer" has influenced my thinking on the specific problematics of sexual silences in feminist interpretations of women's postcolonial literature. In it George analyzes the functions of the layered silences on same-sex desire in Das's autobiography as this kind of desire is invariably read as a spill-over from hyperactive heterosexual desire or as not sexual at all. For example, with regard to a short account of the autobiographical protagonist's early sexual experiences with another woman, George notes how "we never hear of this girlfriend again—either in the autobiography or in the many critical responses to this text" (744). George also accounts for two types of readings facilitated by this silence: one calling Das a representative "feminine" writer (mostly by male critics) and one that renarrates her sexual adventures as a "feminist" rebellion against patriarchal institutions and oppressions (but not against heterosexuality) (see 757–59 n. 9).
14  I am referring to the concept of *minor literature* defined in the introduction

to *The Nature and Context of Minority Discourse*, ed. Abdul JanMohamed and David Lloyd. Haun Saussy provides an account of the debate over whether Chinese writings are allegorical or simply literal in chap. 1 of *The Problem of a Chinese Aesthetic*. My last point about challenging the assumption of objectivity is following Gayatri Chakravorty Spivak's definition of a critical philosophy (as opposed to a dogmatic one) (see her "More on Power/Knowledge," 25).

15 In her discussion of the feminist politics of Hsia Yü's innovative use of language, Yeh refers to an interview (the same one with which I began this chapter) in which the poet is asked a question about the use of "simulacrum" in her poetry. Yeh interprets Hsia Yü's reply—that the "copy" itself is always in quotation marks and that anything can potentially be put in quotation marks—to mean that "there is no hard and fast line between a 'copy' and an 'original,' and that they are inevitably limited to and defined by the context in which they appear" ("The Feminist Poetic of Hsia Yü," 52). I would agree with Yeh's interpretation of this statement and add that it also disrupts the assignation of a positive value to the original and negativity to the copy, allowing readers to glean the creative and critical aspects of what could otherwise be misrecognized as simply a negative aesthetic (which it also is). As Yeh writes of the highly experimental 1979 "*Lianliankan*," which consists of two vertical rows of unrelated words and a title that instructs the reader to draw lines between the rows connecting individual words into pairs: "The poem makes us reconsider what constitutes poetry and focuses our attention on what takes place in the process of reading" (55). Yeh concludes that this is done in order to "create a language" that not only is "malleable" enough to be appropriate for modern gendered experience but that also "empowers women against patriarchal domination and totalization" (55).

16 For an anthropological study that pays particular attention to changes in women's lives, see Hill Gates's *Chinese Working-Class Lives*. Other analyses of the effects of rapid industrialization and flexible accumulation on the lives and labor of Third World women include Maria Mies's *Patriarchy and Accumulation on a World Scale*, which contains an account of the "housewifization" of femininity in colonized locations; Aiwa Ong's "The Gender and Labor Politics of Postmodernity"; Lisa Rofel's "Rethinking Modernity," which includes an account of the ways in which Chinese women workers subvert spatial discipline; and Swasti Mitter's "What Women Demand of Technology." For an account of the transition from modern to postmodern modes of production and its cultural effects, see David Harvey's *The Condition of Postmodernity*.

17 In *Factory Women in Taiwan*, Lydia Kung has researched the changes in women's forms of work and work relations as an increasing number of women became employed as factory workers in the 1970s, and she concludes that these changes are often experienced ambivalently or as contradictory (rather than necessarily being considered improvements for women in the arenas of social and economic status). Kung demonstrates that, although, when women enter the workforce, their social responsibilities are extended and expanded, this change does not necessarily bring with it a heightened social status or increased authority. She

also demonstrates that the women who constitute these labor forces are not necessarily able to recognize the important fact that their own labor had been a crucial factor in enabling the remarkable economic growth achieved by this period because of the lack of cultural and economic capital attributed to these forms of work.

18  In "Three Feminist Readings," Spivak argues that the Marxist macrostructural model of class conflict within and among nations is, definitionally, a totalizing system that is integrally linked to the microstructures of gender and sexuality, which, in turn, are (equally constitutionally) shifting, multiple, nontotalizable, and "incoherent." She then shows how two novels "dramatize" instances of microstructural relations as "the sort of limit cases that allow us to redefine microstructural exchange" (31). Her readings demonstrate that even those first-person narratives quite accessible to liberal humanist readings can also be mobilized as "a non-expository theory of practice" (24). Her readings of McCullers and Drabble illustrate her description of the difficult task of the Marxist feminist: to trace these linkages without transposing a program for social change derived from a study of macrostructural politics onto the distinct formations of the microstructural (as has been done by many socialist feminists). The latter move would, ultimately, mask the many shifting forms of patriarchal dominance and the equally shifting and multiple demands of normative sexuality when the multiplicity of these forms is precisely what is to be addressed in any feminist project. Spivak's article therefore turns to a discussion of how the fictive narratives of feminist literature (and, to draw on her later "The Politics of Translation," their sometimes experimental and difficult "rhetoric") present limit cases of microstructural exchange. According to Spivak's argument, these limit cases are the "structural irreducibles" that constitute the microstructural relations of gender and sexuality whose "motives come from many different places at once" and whose trajectories cannot be charted by a macrostructural framework, as the microstructural always "straddles the public and private" ("Three Feminist Readings," 20, 24, 16). The latter is a condition that, Spivak argues, the socialist feminist often forgets, and, in this amnesia, feminist practice is sacrificed for a clear, macrostructural theory.

19  For a brief but carefully nuanced reading of some of Hsia Yü's poems, see Li Yuanzhen's "'The Nation' in the Eyes of Taiwan's Women Poets."

20  For this insight, I am indebted to Lisa Rofel and Shih Shu-mei.

21  Bracketed words are my additions (to follow the original diction more closely). My discussion of "Ventriloquy," and especially the layered meaning of *bei zhe*, benefited from conversations with Waiter and Jiazhen Ni.

22  Partly in the interests of recognizing the possibility for organizing queer coalitional work on the basis of difference, in "History, Allegory, Sexuality" Reddy theorizes sexuality as a narrative repository or allegory (in the Benjaminian sense) of overdetermined historical contradiction. In other words, he theorizes an allegorical relation of sexuality (as narrative repository) to the macrostructural contradictions of colonial histories. Reddy focuses on how the charac-

terization in a Hawaiian Filipino queer text by R. Zamora Linmark refuses a representational logic based on equivalence, instead presenting sexual identity as composed of the "belated" and incommensurable sedimented histories of immigration and U.S. racialization in Hawaii.

According to Reddy, then, sexuality functions as a repository of macrostructural contradictions in colonial modernities. In Hsia Yü's poetic dramatizations of sexual and romance themes, this repository is located within (differently formed but also contradictory) microstructural relations. Because the focus is the discontinuity of the microstructural narratives and their role in macrostructural interpellation processes, the microstructural in this poem is presented as the site of the *failed* sublation of the irresolvable contradictions of macrostructural histories.

23 As Spivak writes: "The unsent letters are the fiction of a paradoxically impure signifier that will never be sublated—that is, contradicted and preserved in a higher form—through its contradiction and become a meaning-filled signified because the addressee receives it" ("Three Feminist Readings," 20).

## 4 Pound's Universalism and Cha's Translation

1 *Fenhurst, Q.E.D., and Other Early Writings* and *Lectures in America*, respectively. For details, see the discussion of these texts in chapter 2.
2 In *Siting Translation*, Niranjana demonstrates the importance of translation to critiques of representation in the work of Paul de Man and Jacques Derrida, including the theorization of allegory and *différance*, respectively.
3 I am indebted to Maud Ellman's essay "Ezra Pound" for its analysis of Pound's nondevelopmental concept of history. This essay is discussed below.
4 See Ernest Fenollosa's *The Chinese Written Character as a Medium for Poetry*. In *Ezra Pound's Cathay*, Wai-lim Yip has provided the seminal account of Pound's translations of Chinese poetry. In a similar vein, in "Ukiyo-E," William Tay has provided an account of the influence of Japanese poetry and woodblock carving on the Imagism of Pound's contemporary Amy Lowell. In *Orientalism and Modernism*, Zhaoming Qian has built on Yip's study of Pound's translations with new archival sources, providing a comprehensive account not only of Pound's study of Fenollosa's writings but also of other ways in which Pound's generation was exposed to Oriental cultures through translations and, Qian suggests, somewhat more significantly for Pound owing to his imagistic thinking, popular museum exhibits featuring Oriental art. Qian's research into heretofore unexplored sources provides important information regarding Pound's exposure to such exhibits and his study of the Chinese language.

However, my reading diverges from Qian's argument that Pound was not an Orientalist because he "did not seem to believe in western cultural superiority" (2). Perhaps following Said more closely than Qian does on this point, my reading of Pound's fascination with the Orient does not assume that, once one is positioned as such in relation to the object of one's study, one's status as an Orientalist can be counteracted by a sufficient degree of appreciation for the Oriental culture in question. In fact, it is precisely just such an appreciation of culture that continues to facilitate Orientalist reading modes by positioning the reader as the subject who is able to discern the value of the cultural object. To take one example, in *The Pound Era*, Hugh Kenner sites the passage from canto 74 discussed below that contains the character 顯 [*xian*]. Kenner stresses Pound's technique of using individual components of the character to compose his own poem, presenting this as an instance of the sort of "magnificent misreading" that constitutes Pound's achievement: "The unspotted sun's cord, the tensile light, Erigena: derived from a character in which no one ever had the eyes to discern such wonders before. That was his forte, the magnificent misreading" (459). Kenner's diction attests to the persistence of Orientalist discourse into the later poetic canon and its criticism, as Chinese characters are presented as the site of Pound's discovery of new wonders.

5 William Appleby Williams explains how the Open Door policy resolved the heated debate begun in the 1890s over expansionism by providing the markets that the expansionists wanted without establishing formal colonies. In "Imperial Anticolonialism," he terms this strategy *imperial anticolonialism*.

6 Pound's radio show in Italy, imprisonment at Pisa for treason, and confinement at St. Elizabeth's constitute the infamous legend of his fascism. It cannot be recounted without political didacticism. I do not aim to defend Pound's fascism, but I do want to point out that the legend's didacticism places the burden of blame on Pound's individual choices and "errors," as if, to become a fascist, one had to be antipatriotic. It detracts from inquiry into the structure of U.S. society and thought, inquiry that, if undertaken, would suggest that Pound might not have discovered all the logics of fascism in Italy. On the contrary, the abiding appeal of the hierarchical society he admired so much in "Kung" stemmed from the circumstances of his own background, issuing from the structure of late-nineteenth-century U.S. society's racial organization and troubled obsession with exclusion and purity.

7 Pound worked on the *Pisan Cantos* while imprisoned in Pisa for treason after World War II, hence their title (Pound, *The Cantos of Ezra Pound*, 428–429).

8 I have consulted Carroll F. Terrell's *A Companion to the Cantos of Ezra Pound* on Pound's understanding and use of the references in these lines.

9 Michael Davidson has noted that Chinese was increasingly important "as a language whose structure and origin were 'foreign' to Pound in ways that Western languages were not. In a sense, then, Chinese was Pound's first 'foreign' language, and its otherness became a part of the poem's concern" (*Ghostlier Demarcations*, 102). In this discussion, Davidson also states that Chinese became less important "as a method of composition" (102) as its foreignness became more significant; I would argue that, while the latter grows out of the former, it does not necessarily replace it altogether. Rather, the two seem to be mutually reinforcing, especially if we consider the importance of the foreignness of the

ideogram itself in its insertion into the text as what I am terming a *modernist translation*, which is a mode of composition as well.

10   In *The Lure of the Modern*, Shu-mei Shih makes a fascinating point about the distinct formation of modernism's universalist representational strategies vis-à-vis China in poetry as opposed to narrative: "Western modernism's two modes of using 'China'—orientalizing it and appropriating its cultural material—roughly follow the genre division of narrative and poetry. Orientalism most commonly manifests itself in narrative containment of the Other, while formal appropriation manifests itself in poetic grafting. Narrative requires China as a setting and therefore involves Chinese characters and scenes, but poetry can simply lift fragments out of the Chinese context; in either case, 'China' as a historical and cultural entity disappears" (9).

11   I am thinking of Pound's lines from canto 110, one of the last, that read: "From time's wreckage shored, / these fragments shored against ruin" (*The Cantos of Ezra Pound*, 781). These lines rework one of Eliot's lines from *The Wasteland* (famously edited by Pound): "These fragments I have shored against my ruins" (line 431).

12   For example, in "The 'Liberatory Voice' of Theresa Hak Kyung Cha's *Dictee*," L. Hyun Yi Kang describes how, during her first reading of the novel, she felt that, for another Korean immigrant woman reader, the text should have been more accessible than it was. She then describes how it became clear that what seemed to be its "slipperiness" was an engagement with "the very notions of language" that are central to her own work (73–74).

13   In *The New Imperialism* (see esp. 204–27), V. G. Keirnan defines *neocolonialism* as indirect control of local economies in postcolonial nations that leads to political manipulation, often accompanied by military presence or funding. Keirnan then examines the case of Korea, arguing that, if left alone, Korea would have rather smoothly transitioned into unified government by the North. Taiwan is also cited as a particularly successful instance of U.S. neocolonial strategy (see 204–27, esp. 223–24).

14   The final chapter of *Dictee* is prefaced as "Tenth, a circle within a circle, a series of concentric circles" (175), concentric circles being circles with a shared center. The final lines of the novel extend this metaphor to the movement of sound waves: ". . . to break the stillness as the bells fall peal follow the sound of ropes holding weight scraping on wood to break stillness bells fall a peal to sky" (179).

15   "Pound contrasts the *idea* which petrifies history to the image in which history is stored. Images and monuments transport the past into the present, and thus make history possible at all: for history is not the past as such, but the force that sweeps the past into the present 'in ripples and spirals eddying out from us and from our own time'" (Maud Ellman, "Ezra Pound," 247).

16   This distinction is significant to the extent that, as Spivak has put it, microstructures are generated "from many sources at once," sources that are very difficult

to trace as they "straddle the public and private" ("Three Feminist Readings," 15).

17  In addition to her reading of overdetermination, Lowe addresses the question of the different formation of gendered interpellation even within nationalism partly through the issue of alterity. Lowe argues that *Dictee* exposes the ways in which the internal contradictions of nationalist interpellation processes can produce alterity rather than identity as the nation both requires and "expels" female subjects, suggesting that, "in addition to the strategic and necessary attacks on the prevailing form of domination in the terms of that domination, it may also be interventions from standpoints of alterity to the structure in dominance which enable the displacement of that dominance" ("Unfaithful to the Original," 57). If we bring Lowe's reconsideration of alterity to the macrostructural hailings of nationalism into a discussion of what Spivak terms *microstructures* (perhaps what Lowe identifies as the densely layered interpellative apparatuses of postcoloniality for gendered subjects), we are alerted to the possibility of positions of alterity to these microstructural interpellation processes as well. The subject of *Dictee*, however, does not take up a position of alterity to normative sexuality, so microstructural alterity cannot be easily "identified" in the novel.

18  I am drawing on Chandan Reddy's discussion, in "Homes, Houses, Non-Identity," of this kind of nonequivalence and its cultural expression.

# Works Cited

Abraham, Julie. *Are Girls Necessary? Lesbian Writing and Modern Histories.* New York: Routledge, 1996.
Achebe, Chinua. "An Image of Africa: Racism in Conrad's *Heart of Darkness*" (1977). Reprinted in *"Heart of Darkness": An Authoritative Text, Background and Sources, Criticism* (3rd ed.), ed. Robert Kimbrough, 251–61. London: Norton, 1988.
Alarcón, Norma, and Elaine H. Kim, eds. *Writing Self, Writing Nation: A Collection of Essays on "Dictee" by Theresa Hak Kyung Cha.* Berkeley: Third Woman, 1994.
Althusser, Louis. "Ideology and Ideological State Apparatuses: Notes towards an Investigation." 1970. In *Lenin and Philosophy, and Other Essays*, trans. Ben Brewster, 127–86. New York: Monthly Review Press, 1971.
Anderson, Benedict. *Imagined Communities: Reflections on the Origin and Spread of Nationalism.* 1983. Rev. ed., London: Verso, 1991.
Armstrong, Nancy. *Desire and Domestic Fiction: A Political History of the Novel.* Oxford: Oxford University Press, 1987.
Arnold, Matthew. *Culture and Anarchy.* 1869. Edited by J. Dover Wilson. Cambridge: Cambridge University Press, 1932.
Bakhtin, Mikhail. *The Dialogic Imagination: Four Essays in Criticism.* 1973. Edited by Michael Holquist. Translated by Caryl Emerson and Michael Holquist. Austin: University of Texas Press, 1981.
Benjamin, Walter. "Theses on the Philosophy of History." 1955. In *Illuminations*, ed. Hannah Arendt, trans. Harry Zohn, 253–64. New York: Harcourt, Brace and World, 1968; reprint, New York: Schocken, 1985.
———. *The Origin of German Tragic Drama.* 1963. Translated by John Osborne. 1977. Reprint, London: Verso, 1990.
Benstock, Shari. *Women of the Left Bank: Paris, 1900–1940.* Austin: University of Texas Press, 1986.
Berman, Marshall. *All That Is Solid Melts into Air: The Experience of Modernity.* New York: Simon and Schuster, 1982.
Bernstein, Charles. "Professing Stein/Stein Professing." *Poetics Journal* 9 (June 1991): 44–50.
Bhabha, Homi. *Nation and Narration.* London: Routledge, 1990.
———. *The Location of Culture.* London: Routledge, 1994.
Bradbury, Steve. "Through the Open Door: American Translation of Chinese Poetry and the Translations of American Empire." Ph.D. diss., English Department, University of Hawaii, 1997.
———, trans. *Fusion Kitsch: Poems from the Chinese of Hsia Yü.* Boston: Zephyr, 2001.
Butler, Judith. "The Force of Fantasy: Feminism, Mapplethorpe, and Discursive Ex-

cess." *Differences: A Journal of Feminist Cultural Studies* 2.2 (summer 1990): 105–25.

———. *Gender Trouble: Feminism and the Subversion of Identity.* New York: Routledge, 1990.

Calinescu, Matai. *Five Faces of Modernity: Modernism, Avant-Garde, Decadence, Kitsch, and Postmodernism.* Durham: Duke University Press, 1987.

Canclini, Nestor Garcia. *Hybrid Cultures: Strategies for Entering and Leaving Modernity.* 1990. Translated by Christopher L. Chiappari and Sylvia L. Lopez. Minneapolis: University of Minnesota Press, 1995.

Castle, Terry. "Phantasmagoria: Spectral Technology and the Metaphorics of Modern Reverie." *Critical Inquiry* 15.1 (autumn 1988): 26–61.

Cha, Theresa Hak Kyung. *Dictee.* New York: Tanam, 1982.

Chakrabarty, Dipesh. "Postcoloniality and the Artifice of History: Who Speaks for the Indian Pasts?" *Representations* 37 (winter 1992): 1–26.

Chang, Sung-sheng Yvonne. *Modernism and the Nativist Resistance: Contemporary Chinese Fiction from Taiwan.* Durham: Duke University Press, 1993.

Chao, Antonia. "Embodying the Invisible: Body Politics in Constructing Contemporary Taiwanese Lesbian Identities." Ph.D. diss., Department of Anthropology, Cornell University, 1996.

———. "U.S. Space Shuttle Going to the Moon: Global Metaphors and Local Strategies in Building Taiwan's Lesbian Identities." Paper presented at the Second International Conference for the Study of Sexuality, Culture, and Society, Department of Sociology, Manchester Metropolitan University, July 1999.

Chen, Kuan-hsing. "The Decolonization Question." In *Trajectories: Inter-Asia Cultural Studies*, ed. Kuan-hsing Chen, 1–53. London: Routledge, 1998.

———. "Missile Internationalism." In *Orientations: Mapping Studies in the Asian Diaspora*, ed. Kandice Chuh and Karen Shimakawa, 172–86. Durham: Duke University Press, 2001.

Chi, Pang-yuan, John J. Deeney, Ho Hsin, Wu Hsi-chen, and Yü Kwang-chung, eds. *An Anthology of Contemporary Chinese Literature.* Vol. 1. Taipei: National Institute for Compilation and Translation, 1975.

Ching, Leo T. S. *Becoming "Japanese": Colonial Taiwan and the Politics of Identity Formation.* Berkeley and Los Angeles: University of California Press, 2001.

Choi, Chungmoo. "The Discourse of Decolonization and Popular Memory." *Positions* 1.1 (spring 1993): 77–102.

Chow, Rey. *Writing Diaspora: Tactics of Intervention in Contemporary Cultural Studies.* Bloomington: Indiana University Press, 1993.

Conrad, Joseph. *Lord Jim.* 1899. New York: Signet/Penguin, 1961.

Cumings, Bruce. *Parallax Visions: Making Sense of American–East Asian Relations at the End of the Century.* Durham: Duke University Press, 1999.

Davidson, Michael. *Ghostlier Demarcations: Modern Poetry and the Material World.* Berkeley and Los Angeles: University of California Press, 1997.

Dearborn, Mary V. *Pocahontas's Daughters: Gender and Ethnicity in American Culture.* New York: Oxford University Press, 1986.

Deleuze, Gilles, and Félix Guattari. "What Is a Minor Literature?" In *Kafka: Toward a Minor Literature* (1975), trans. Dana Polan, 16–27. Minneapolis: University of Minnesota Press, 1986.

de Man, Paul. *Blindness and Insight: Essays in the Rhetoric of Contemporary Criticism.* Minneapolis: University of Minnesota, 1983.

Ding, Naifei. "Feminist Knots: Sex and Domestic Work in the Shadow of the Bondmaid-Concubine." *Inter-Asia Cultural Studies* 3.3 (2002): 449–67.

H.D. [Doolittle, Hilda]. *End to Torment.* New York: New Directions, 1979.

———. *HERmione.* New York: New Directions, 1981.

———. *Bid Me to Live.* Redding Ridge: Black Swan, 1983.

———. *Selected Poems.* Edited by Louis L. Martz. New York: New Directions, 1988.

DuBois, Page. *Torture and Truth.* New York: Routledge, 1991.

Duncan, Robert. *Bending the Bow.* New York: New Directions, 1968.

Ellman, Maud. "Ezra Pound: The Erasure of History." In *Poststructuralism and the Question of History*, ed. Derek Attridge et al., 244–62. Cambridge: Cambridge University Press, 1987.

Fabian, Johannes. *Time and the Other: How Anthropology Makes Its Object.* New York: Columbia University Press, 1983.

Fenollosa, Ernest. *The Chinese Written Character as a Medium for Poetry.* 1920. San Francisco: City Lights, 1936. Reprint, San Francisco: City Lights, 1991. The essay first appeared in the London journal *Instigations*.

Foucault, Michel. *The History of Sexuality.* Vol. 1, *An Introduction.* 1978. Translated by Robert Hurley. Reprint, New York: Vintage, 1990.

Freeman, Elizabeth. "Queer Syntactic Strategy, Body Performance, and the Dialect of Lesbian Couplehood in Gertrude Stein." English Department, University of California, Davis, 1995. Typescript.

Freud, Sigmund. *Three Essays on the Theory of Sexuality.* 1905. Translated by James Strachey. New York: Basic, 1975.

———. "Mourning and Melancholia." 1917. In *A General Selection of the Work of Sigmund Freud*, ed. John Rickman, 124–40. New York: Anchor/Doubleday, 1989.

Gates, Hill. *Chinese Working-Class Lives: Getting by in Taiwan.* Ithaca: Cornell University Press, 1987.

George, Rosemary Marangoly. "Home in the Empire, Empire in the Home." *Cultural Critique* 26 (winter 1993–94): 95–127.

———. "Calling Kamala Das Queer: Rereading 'My Story.'" *Feminist Studies* 26.3 (fall 2000): 731–63.

———. "Recycling: Long Routes to and from Domestic Fixes." In *Burning Down the House: Recycling Domesticity*, ed. Rosemary Marangoly George, 1–20. Boulder: Westview, 1998.

Gilroy, Paul. *The Black Atlantic: Modernity and Double Consciousness.* Cambridge: Harvard University Press, 1993.

Gopinath, Gayatri. "'Bombay, U.K., Yuba City': Bhangra Music and the Engendering of Diaspora." *Diaspora* 4.3 (1995): 303–21.

Halberstam, Judith. *Skin Shows: Gothic Horror and the Technology of Monsters*. Durham: Duke University Press, 1995.
———. *Female Masculinity*. Durham: Duke University Press, 1996.
Halberstam, Judith, and Ira Livingston, eds. *Posthuman Bodies*. Bloomington: Indiana University Press, 1995.
Harvey, David. *The Condition of Postmodernity*. Oxford: Blackwell, 1989.
Hawkins, Susan E. "Sneak Previews: Stein's Syntax in *Tender Buttons*." In *Gertrude Stein and the Making of Literature*, ed. Shirley Neuman and Ira B. Nadel, 119–23. Boston: Northeastern University Press, 1988.
Huang, Tao-ming Hans. "State Power, Prostitution, and Sexual Order in Taiwan: Towards a Genealogical Critique of 'Virtuous Custom.'" *Inter-Asia Cultural Studies* 5.2 (2004): 237–59.
Isaak, Jo-Anna. "The Revolutionary Power of a Woman's Laughter." In *Gertrude Stein Advanced: An Anthology of Criticism*, ed. Richard Kostelanetz, 24–50. Jefferson: MacFarland, 1990.
James, William. *The Writings of William James: A Comprehensive Edition*. Edited by John J. McDermott. Chicago: University of Chicago Press, 1977.
Jameson, Fredric. *The Political Unconscious: Narrative as a Socially Symbolic Act*. Ithaca: Cornell University Press, 1981.
———. "Modernism and Imperialism." In *Nationalism, Colonialism, and Literature*, by Terry Eagleton, Fredric Jameson, and Edward Said, 43–66. Minneapolis: University of Minnesota Press, 1990.
JanMohamed, Abdul R., and David Lloyd. "Introduction: Minority Discourse—What Is to Be Done?" In *The Nature and Context of Minority Discourse*, ed. Abdul R. JanMohamed and David Lloyd, 1–16. New York: Oxford University Press, 1990.
Johnson, Marshall. "Making Time: Historic Preservation and the Space of Nationality." In *New Asian Marxisms*, ed. Tani E. Barlow, 105–71. Durham: Duke University Press, 2002.
Kang, L. Hyun Yi. "The 'Liberatory Voice' of Theresa Hak Kyung Cha's *Dictee*." In *Writing Self, Writing Nation: A Collection of Essays on "Dictee" by Theresa Hak Kyung Cha*, ed. Norma Alarcón and Elaine H. Kim, 73–99. Berkeley: Third Woman, 1994.
Kaplan, Amy. "Left Alone with America." In *Cultures of United States Imperialism*, ed. Amy Kaplan, 3–21. Durham: Duke University Press, 1993.
Keirnan, V. G. *The New Imperialism: From White Settlement to World Hegemony*. London: Zed, 1978.
Kenner, Hugh. *The Pound Era*. Berkeley: University of California Press, 1974.
Kim, Elaine H. "Poised on the In-Between: A Korean American's Reflections on Theresa Hak Kyung Cha's *Dictee*." In *Writing Self, Writing Nation: A Collection of Essays on "Dictee" by Theresa Hak Kyung Cha*, ed. Norma Alarcón and Elaine H. Kim, 3–30. Berkeley: Third Woman, 1994.
Kung, Lydia. *Factory Women in Taiwan*. Ann Arbor: University of Michigan Research Press, 1983.

Latour, Bruno. *We Have Never Been Modern*. 1991. Translated by Catherine Porter. Cambridge: Harvard University Press, 1993.

Lee, Leo Ou-fan. "'Modernism' and 'Romanticism' in Taiwan Literature." In *Chinese Fiction from Taiwan: Critical Perspectives*, ed. Jeannette L. Faurot, 6–30. Bloomington: Indiana University Press, 1980.

Lefebvre, Henri. *The Production of Space*. 1974. Translated by Donald Nicholson-Smith. Oxford: Blackwell, 1991.

Liao, Chaoyang. "Borrowed Modernity: History and the Subject in *A Borrowed Life*." *Boundary 2* 24.3 (1997): 225–45.

Liao, Ping-hui. "Rewriting Taiwanese National History: The February 28 Incident as Spectacle." *Public Culture* 5.1 (winter 1993): 281–96.

Liao, Sebastian Hsien-hao. "Nationalism at the Crossroads: The Last Fin-de-Siècle and Contemporary Taiwan." Paper presented at the eighth quadrennial International Conference on Comparative Literature in the ROC, Taipei, August 1999.

Lin, Julia. *Essays on Contemporary Chinese Poetry*. Athens: Ohio University Press, 1985.

Liu, Jen-peng, and Naifei Ding. "Reticent Poetics, Queer Politics." *Inter-Asia Cultural Studies* 6.1 (February 2005): 30–55.

Lloyd, David. "Genet's Genealogy: European Minorities and the Ends of the Canon." In *The Nature and Context of Minority Discourse*, ed. Abdul R. JanMohamed and David Lloyd, 369–93. New York: Oxford University Press, 1990.

Lowe, Lisa. "On the Location of Culture." Literature Department, University of California, San Diego, 1994. Typescript.

———. "Unfaithful to the Original: The Subject of *Dictee*." In *Writing Self, Writing Nation: A Collection of Essays on "Dictee" by Theresa Hak Kyung Cha*, ed. Norma Alarcón and Elaine H. Kim, 35–69. Berkeley: Third Woman, 1994.

———. "Canon, Institutionalization, Identity: Contradictions for Asian American Studies." In *The Ethnic Canon: Histories, Institutions, and Interventions*, ed. David Palumbo-Liu, 48–68. Minneapolis: University of Minnesota Press, 1995.

———. "Decolonization, Displacement, Disidentification: Asian American 'Novels' and the Question of History." In *Cultural Institutions of the Novel*, ed. Deidre Lynch and William Warner, 96–128. Durham: Duke University Press, 1996.

———. *Immigrant Acts: On Asian American Cultural Politics*. Durham: Duke University Press, 1996.

Martin, Fran. "The Perfect Lie: Sandee Chan and Lesbian Representability in Mandarin Pop Music." *Inter-Asia Cultural Studies* 4.2 (2003): 264–80.

McClintock, Anne. "The Angel of Progress: Pitfalls of the Term 'Post-Colonialism.'" *Social Text* 31–32 (1992): 84–98. Reprinted in *Colonial Discourse/Postcolonial Theory: A Reader* (The Essex Symposia: Literature, Politics, Theory), ed. Francis Barker, Peter Hulme, and Margaret Iversen, 291–304. Manchester: Manchester University Press, 1994.

Mies, Maria. *Patriarchy and Accumulation on a World Scale: Women in the International Division of Labour*. London: Zed, 1986.

Mitter, Swasti. "What Women Demand of Technology." *New Left Review* 205 (1994): 100–110.

Miyake, Akiko. *Ezra Pound and the Mysteries of Love: A Plan for the Cantos*. Durham: Duke University Press, 1991.

Miyoshi, Masao. "A Borderless World? From Colonialism to Transnationalism and the Decline of the Nation-State." *Critical Inquiry* 19.4 (summer 1993): 726–51.

Nielson, A. L. *Reading Race: White American Poets and the Racial Discourse in the Twentieth Century*. Athens: University of Georgia Press, 1988.

Niranjana, Tejaswini. *Siting Translation: History, Poststructuralism, and the Colonial Context*. Berkeley and Los Angeles: University of California Press, 1992.

North, Michael. *The Dialect of Modernism: Race, Language, and Twentieth-Century Literature*. New York: Oxford University Press, 1994.

Omi, Michael, and Howard Winant. *Racial Formation in the United States: From the 1960s to the 1990s*. 1986. 2nd ed. New York: Routledge, 1994.

Ong, Aihwa. "The Gender and Labor Politics of Postmodernity." *Annual Review of Anthropology* 20 (1991): 270–309.

Pai, Ch'iu. *Selflove*. Taipei: Li Poetry Society Press, 1990.

Phillips, Steven. "Between Assimilation and Independence: Taiwanese Political Aspirations under National Chinese Rule, 1945–1948." In *Taiwan: A New History*, ed. Murray A. Rubinstein, 275–319. Armonk: A. E. Sharpe, 1999.

Pound, Ezra. *The Spirit of Romance*. 1910. Reprint, New York: New Directions, 1968.

———. "A List of Books." *Little Review* 4.11 (March 1918): 56–58. Excerpt reprinted in *The Gender of Modernism*, ed. Bonnie Kime Scott, 365–67. Bloomington: Indiana University Press, 1990.

———. *Literary Essays*. 1918. New York: New Directions, 1968; reprint, Westport: Greenwood, 1979.

———. "Hugh Selwyn Mauberley." In *Personae*, rev. ed., prepared by Lea Baechler and A. Walton Litz, 183–202. New York: New Directions, 1990.

———. *Personae*. 1926. Rev. ed., prepared by Lea Baechler and A. Walton Litz, New York: New Directions, 1990.

———. *The ABC of Reading*. 1934. New York: New Directions, 1987; reprint, New York: New Directions, 1987.

———. *Guide to Kulchur*. 1938. Reprint, New York: New Directions, 1970.

———. *The Cantos of Ezra Pound*. New York: New Directions, 1970; reprint, New York: New Directions, 1986.

Prakash, Gyan. "Writing Post-Orientalist Histories of the Third World." *Comparative Studies in Society and History* 32.2 (1990): 383–408.

Qian, Zhaoming. *Orientalism and Modernism: The Legacy of China in Pound and Williams*. Durham: Duke University Press, 1995.

Quinones, Ricardo J. *Mapping Literary Modernism: Time and Development*. Princeton: Princeton University Press, 1985.

Raphael, Vincente. "White Love: Surveillance and National Resistance in the U.S.

Colonization of the Philippines." In *Cultures of United States Imperialism*, ed. Amy Kaplan and Donald Pease, 185–218. Durham: Duke University Press, 1993.

Reddy, Chandan C. "History, Allegory, Sexuality: The Minors of Linmark's *Rolling the R's*." Paper presented at the annual meeting of the American Studies Association, November 1996.

———. "Homes, Houses, Non-Identity: *Paris Is Burning*." In *Burning Down the House: Recycling Domesticity*, ed. Rosemary Marangoly George, 355–79. Boulder: Westview, 1998.

———. "The Migrating Present: Alienage, Sexuality, and the Spaces of Modernity." Ph.D. diss., English Department, Columbia University, 2004.

Rofel, Lisa. "Rethinking Modernity: Space and Factory Discipline in China." *Cultural Anthropology* 7.1 (February 1992): 93–114.

Rowe, John Carlos. *Literary Culture and U.S. Imperialism: From the Revolution to World War II*. Oxford: Oxford University Press, 2000.

Rubinstein, Murray A. "Taiwan's Socioeconomic Modernization, 1971–1996." In *Taiwan: A New History*, ed. Murray A. Rubinstein, 366–402. Armonk: A. E. Sharpe, 1999.

Ruthven, K. K. *A Guide to Ezra Pound's "Personae" (1926)*. Berkeley: University of California Press, 1969.

Said, Edward. *Orientalism*. New York: Vintage, 1978.

———. *Culture and Imperialism*. New York: Vintage, 1994.

Sakai, Naoki. "The Dislocation of the West and the Status of the Humanities." In "Specters of the West and Politics of Translation," ed. Naoki Sakai and Yukiko Hanawa. Special issue, *Traces: A Multilingual Journal of Cultural Theory and Translation* 1 (2001): 71–94. Ordering information available at http://www.arts.cornell.edu/traces/index.htm.

Sangari, Kumkum. "The Politics of the Possible." In *The Nature and Context of Minority Discourse*, ed. Abdul R. JanMohamed and David Lloyd, 216–45. New York: Oxford University Press, 1990.

Saussy, Haun. *The Problem of a Chinese Aesthetic*. Stanford: Stanford University Press, 1993.

Sedgwick, Eve Kosofsky. *Epistemology of the Closet*. Berkeley and Los Angeles: University of California Press, 1990.

———. *Tendencies*. Durham: Duke University Press, 1993.

Shang Ch'in. *The Frozen Torch*. Translated by N. G. D. Malmqvist. London: Wellsweep, 1992.

Sharpe, Jenny. *Allegories of Empire: The Figure of Woman in the Colonial Text*. Minneapolis: University of Minnesota Press, 1993.

Shih, Shu-mei. *The Lure of the Modern: Writing Cultural Modernism in Semicolonial China*. Berkeley and Los Angeles: University of California Press, 2001.

Silverberg, Miriam. *Changing Song: The Marxist Manifestos of Nakano Shigeharu*. Princeton: Princeton University Press, 1990.

Solomon, Jon. "Taiwan Incorporated: A Survey of Biopolitics in the Sovereign Police's Pacific Theater of Operations." In *Impacts of Modernities* (Traces: A Multilingual Series of Cultural Theory and Translation, vol. 3), ed. Thomas Lamarre and Kang Nae-Hui, 229–54. Hong Kong: Hong Kong University Press, 2004. Ordering information available at http://www.arts.cornell.edu/traces/index.htm.

Sommer, Doris. "Love and Country in Latin America: An Allegorical Speculation." *Cultural Critique* 16 (fall 1990): 109–28.

Spence, Jonathan. *The Search for Modern China*. New York: Norton, 1990.

Spivak, Gayatri Chakravorty. "Three Feminist Readings: McCullers, Drabble, Habermas." *Union Seminary Quarterly Review* 35.1–2 (fall–winter 1979–80): 15–34.

———. *In Other Worlds: Essays in Cultural Politics*. 1987. Reprint, New York: Routledge, 1988.

———. "Thinking Academic Freedom in Gendered Post-Coloniality." T.B. Davie Academic Freedom Lecture, University of Capetown, August 1992.

———. "Woman in Difference: Mahasweta Devi's *Douloti the Beautiful*." In *Nationalisms and Sexualities*, ed. Andrew Parker, Mary Russo, Doris Sommer, and Patricia Yaeger, 96–117. New York: Routledge, 1992.

———. "More on Power/Knowledge." In *Outside in the Teaching Machine*, 25–51. New York: Routledge, 1993.

———. "The Politics of Translation." In *Outside in the Teaching Machine*, 179–200. New York: Routledge, 1993.

Stein, Gertrude. "Composition and Explanation." 1926. In *Selected Writings of Gertrude Stein*, ed. Carl Van Vechten, 515–23. New York: Vintage, 1990.

———. *The Making of Americans*. 1925. Normal: Dalkey Archive, 1995.

———. *Lectures in America*. Boston: Beacon, 1935.

———. *The Geographical History of America; or, The Relation of Human Nature to the Human Mind*. 1936. Reprint, with a new introduction, New York: Vintage, 1973.

———. *Fenhurst, Q.E.D., and Other Early Writings*. 1973. Reprint, New York: Liveright, 1983. Q.E.D. was originally published in 1950 as *Things as They Are*.

———. *Tender Buttons*. n.d. Reprint, Los Angeles: Sun and Moon, 1914.

Stimpson, Catherine. "The Mind, the Body, and Gertrude Stein." *Critical Inquiry* 3.3 (spring 1977): 491–506.

Tay, William. "Ukiyo-E: Waka, Haiku, and Amy Lowell." *American Studies* (美國研究) [Meiguo yenjiu] (Taipei) 5.3–4 (December 1975): 55–72.

Terrell, Carroll F. *A Companion to the Cantos of Ezra Pound*. 2 vols. Berkeley and Los Angeles: University of California Press, 1984.

Tsai, Ying-chun. "The Poetics of Reticence." Paper delivered at the second International Crossroads Conference in Cultural Studies, Tampere, Finland, July 1997.

Wald, Priscilla. *Constituting Americans: Cultural Anxiety and Narrative Form*. Durham: Duke University Press, 1995.

Walker, Jane L. "History as Repetition: 'The Making of Americans.'" In *Gertrude Stein*, ed. Harold Bloom, 177–99. New York: Chelsea House, 1986.

Wang, Jing. "Taiwan Hsiang-tu Literature: Perspectives in the Evolution of a Literary Movement." *Chinese Fiction from Taiwan: Critical Perspectives*, ed. Jeannette L. Faurot, 43–70. Bloomington: Indiana University Press, 1980.

Wang, Peter Chen-main. "A Bastion Created, a Regime Reformed, an Economy

Reengineered." In *Taiwan: A New History*, ed. Murray A. Rubinstein, 320–38. Armonk: A. E. Sharpe, 1999.

Williams, Raymond. *The Politics of Modernism: Against the New Conformists*. Edited by Tony Pinkney. London: Verso, 1989.

Williams, William Appleman. "Imperial Anticolonialism." 1959. In *A William Appleman Williams Reader: Selections from His Major Historical Writings*, ed. Henry W. Berger, 116–32. Chicago: Ivan R. Dee, 1992.

———. *Empire as a Way of Life*. New York: Oxford University Press, 1980.

———. *A William Appleman Williams Reader: Selections from His Major Historical Writings*. Edited by Henry W. Berger. Chicago: Ivan R. Dee, 1992.

Wilson, Rob. *The American Sublime: The Genealogy of a Poetic Genre*. Madison: University of Wisconsin Press, 1991.

Woolf, Virginia. *The Voyage Out*. 1915. Set from the 1st ed., with a new introduction by Phyllis Rose, London: Hogarth, 1957.

———. *Orlando*. 1928. Reprint, New York: Harcourt Brace Jovanovich, 1956.

Yeh, Michelle, ed. and trans. *Anthology of Modern Chinese Poetry*. New Haven: Yale University Press, 1992.

———. "The Feminist Poetic of Hsia Yü." *Modern Chinese Literature* 7.1 (spring 1993): 33–60.

Yip, Wai-lim. *Ezra Pound's Cathay*. Princeton: Princeton University Press, 1969.

———. *Lyrics from Shelters: Modern Chinese Poetry, 1930–1950*. New York: Garland, 1992.

———. "Language Strategies and Historical Relevance in the Poetry of 1930–1950." In *Lyrics from Shelters: Modern Chinese Poetry, 1930–1950*, 15–41. New York: Garland, 1992.

———. "Displacements: Between Landscapes." Literature Department, University of California, San Diego, n.d. Typescript.

Zinn, Howard. *A People's History of the United States*. 1980. Reprint, New York: HarperPerennial, 1990.

Zwick, Jim, ed. *Anti-Imperialism in the United States: 1898–1935*. 1995. http://www.boondocksnet.com/ai/index.html.

## Texts in Chinese

In romanizing the names of the Chinese publishers listed here, I have used the standard Pinyin. In romanizing the names of individual authors, I have also used Pinyin, except where the writers themselves have published in English using a different system, in which case I have employed that system.

Anonymous. "假台灣人: 台灣的第五大族群" (Jia Taiwanren: Taiwan de diwudazuqun) [Fake Taiwanese people: Taiwan's fifth ethnic group]. *Daoyu bianyuan* [Isle margin] (Taipei and Hsinchu) 2.8 (1993): 35–46.

Chi Pang-yuan, Li Da-san, Ho Hsin, Wu Hsi-chen, and Yü Kwang-chung, eds. 中國現代文學選集 *Zhongguo xiandai wenxue xuanji* [An anthology of Chinese modern literature]. Vol. 1. Taipei: Aoya, 1983.

Chou Zhao-ming [周昭明]. "別解: 謎, 表意文字, 龐德的詩章" (Biejie: Mi, biaoyi-wenzi, pangde de shizhang) [The other solution: Riddles, ideograms, and Pound's *Cantos*]. In 第五屆美國文學與思想研討會論文選集: 文學論 (Diwujie meiguo wenxue yu sixiang yantaohuei lunwenxüanji: Wenxuelun) [Papers from the fifth Conference on American Literature and Thought: On literature], ed. Ji Yuan-wen 紀元文, 229–54. Taipei: Zhongyang yianjiuyuan Oumeisuo [Institute of Euro-American Studies, Academia Sinica], 1997.

Chung Ling [鍾玲]. 現代中國謬司: 台灣女詩人作品析論 (Xiandai zhongguo miusi: Taiwan nü shiren zuopin xilun) [Modern Chinese muses: An analysis of the works of Taiwan women poets]. Taipei: Lianjing Press, 1989.

Hsia Yü [夏宇]. 備忘錄 (Beiwang-lu) [Memoranda]. Taipei, 1986.

———. 腹語術 (Fuyushu) [Ventriloquy]. Taipei: Xiandaishi jikanshe [Modern Poetry Quarterly Press], 1991.

———. 摩擦無以名狀 (Moca wuyimingzhuang) [Friction ineffable]. Taipei: Xiandaishi jikanshe [Modern Poetry Quarterly Press], 1995.

———. *Salsa*. Taipei: Tang Shan Press, 2000. Original title in Spanish.

Ko Ching-ming [柯慶明]. "六十年代現代主義文學" (Liushiniandai xiandaizhuyi wenxue?) [1960s modernist literature?]. In 四十年來中國文學 (Sishinianlai zhongguo wenxue) [Chinese literature for the past forty years], 85–146. Taipei: Lianhewenxue Press, 1995.

Li Yuanzhen [李元貞]. "台灣女詩人眼中的 '國家'" (Taiwan nushiren yanzhongde "guojia") ["The nation" in the eyes of Taiwan's women poets]. *Daoyubianyuan* [Isle margin] (Taipei and Hsinchu) 2.9 (1993): 18–22.

Liao Hsien-hao [廖咸浩]. "物質主義的叛變: 從文學史, 女性化, 後現代之脈絡看夏宇的陰性詩" (Wuzhizhuyi de panbian: Cong wenxueshi, nuxinghua, houxiandai zhi mailuo kan Xia-yu de yinxingshi) [Materialism's mutiny: Looking at Hsia Yü's "feminine poetry" from the models of literary history, feminization, and postmodernism]. In 當代台灣女性文學論 (Dangdai Taiwan nuxing wenxue lun) [On contemporary women's literature in Taiwan], ed. 鄭明俐 [Zheng Ming-li], 236–76. Taipei: Shibaowenhua [China Times Press], 1993.

Liu Jen-peng [劉人鵬] and Ding Naifei [丁乃非]. 罔兩問景: 含蓄美學與酷兒政略 (Wangliang wen ying: Hanxu meixue yu kuer zhenglue) [Reticent poetics, queer politics]. In 酷兒理論與政治 (Kuer lilun yu zhengzhi) [Queer theory and politics], a special issue of 性/別研究 (Xing/bie yanjiu) [Working papers in gender/sexuality studies], nos. 3–4 (September 1998): 109–55.

Weng Wen Hsian [翁文嫻]. "'興'之涵義在現代詩創作上的思考" (*Xing* zhi hanyi zai xiandaishi chuangzuo shang de sikao) [A consideration of the implications of *xing* in the creation of modern poetry]. 台灣詩學季刊 (Taiwan shixue jikan) [Taiwan poetry quarterly] 7 (June 1994): 111–28.

# Index

Abraham, Julie, 76, 161 n.15
Achebe, Chinua, 160 n.6
Alarcón, Norma, 127
*Allegories of Empire* (Sharp), 47–48, 159 n.4
Allegory, 34, 115, 118, 120; and subjectivity, 155 n.15. *See also* Benjamin, Walter: and allegory; Nondevelopmental form: as allegory
"Allegory and Trauerspiel" (Benjamin), 131–133
*All That Is Solid Melts into Air* (Berman), 156 n.1
Althusser, Louis, 155–56 n.16
Anderson, Benedict, 114
"Angel of Progress, The" (McClintock), 154, n.7
*Anthology of Modern Chinese Poetry* (Yeh), 162–163 n.3
*Are Girls Necessary?* (Abraham), 76, 161 n.15
Armstrong, Nancy, 53, 160 n.7
Arnold, Matthew, 64
Asian American and immigrant cultural production. *See* Cultural production, of Asian Americans and immigrants

Bakhtin, Mikhail, 23, 156 n.1
"Bastion Created, A" (Wang), 157 n.8
*Becoming Japanese* (Ching), 158 n.15
*Beloved* (Morrison), 6
*Bending the Bow* (Duncan), 160 n.10
Benjamin, Walter, 121, 136; and allegory, 10, 14–15, 77–79, 131–133, 166–167 n.22
Berman, Marshall, 156 n.1
Bernstein, Charles, 67, 162 n.19

"Between Assimilation and Independence" (Phillips), 87
Bhabha, Homi, 10, 25, 157 n.7
*Black Atlantic, The* (Gilroy), 6
"Borderless World?, A" (Miyoshi), 25
"Borrowed Modernity" (Liao), 155 n.11
Bradbury, Steve, 104, 154 n.10, 162 n.1, 162–163 n.3
Butler, Judith, 56–58, 160 n.11, 164 n.12

Calinescu, Matei, 153 n.1, 153 n.5
"Calling Kamala Das Queer" (George), 164 n.13
Canclini, Néstor García, 7
Canonical function, 5–6; of modernism, 7–8, 16–17, 19, 33–43, 45, 55, 66, 73, 81, 112, 114, 128, 146, 149–152. *See also* Minor literature: vs. canonical function; Modernism: and universalism
*Cantos* (Pound), 19, 119–120, 123–127, 168 n.7, 169 n.11
Cha, Theresa Hak Kyung, 6, 9, 18–19, 81, 113, 118, 127–147, 151, 155–156 n.16
Chakrabarty, Dipesh, 114
Chan, Natalia, 106
Chan, Sandee, 83, 163 n.4
Chang, Yvonne, 158 n.13
*Changing Song* (Silverberg), 156–157 n.1
Chen, Kuan-hsing, 11, 13, 21, 26, 29, 89, 154 n.9
China, 26–28, 122, 165 n.16; as "mainland" for Taiwan, 23, 28, 30, 31; modernism of, 25, 157 n.6. *See also* Modernism: Western representations of China in

*Chinese Working Class Lives* (Gates), 157–158 n.12, 165 n.16
*Chinese Written Character as a Medium for Poetry, The* (Fenollosa), 167 n.3
Ching, Leo, 158 n.15
Chou, Zhao-ming, 119–120
Chronotope, 23–24, 156–157 n.1
Chung, Ling, 103, 162 n.1
Cold War, 3–4, 13, 26, 90–91, 96, 116, 130, 134, 151–152
Colonialism, internal, 7, 153 n.3
*Companion to the Cantos of Ezra Pound, A* (Terrell), 168 n.8
Comparative modernisms (or critical comparativism), 3–5, 6, 9, 11, 16–17, 19, 21–43, 46, 113–147, 149–150, 154 n.8
*Condition of Postmodernity, The* (Harvey), 153 n.1, 165 n.16
Conrad, Joseph, 17, 45–52, 54–55, 60, 153 n.1, 159 nn.2–3, 159–160 nn.5–6
"Consideration of the Implications of *Xing*, A" (Weng), 100, 157 n.6
*Constituting Americans* (Wald), 76–77
*Course in General Linguistics* (Saussure), 162 n.22
Cultural production, of Asian Americans and immigrants, 2, 3, 6, 19, 127, 134, 155–156 n.16, 169 n.12
*Culture and Anarchy* (Arnold), 64
*Culture and Imperialism* (Said), 35–36
Cumings, Bruce, 4, 26, 30–31, 33, 114, 157–158 n.12

Davidson, Michael, 153 n.1, 158 n.17, 162 n.18, 168–169 n.9
Dearborn, Mary, 62–63
"Decolonization Problem, The" (Chen), 11, 89, 154 n.9
Deleuze, Gilles, 5
De Man, Paul, 121, 167 n.2
Derrida, Jacques, 121, 167 n.2
*Desire and Domestic Fiction* (Armstrong), 160 n.7

*Dictee* (Cha), 16, 19, 155–156 n.16, 113–118, 127–147, 169 n.14, 170 n.17
Ding, Naifei, 94–95, 97–99, 105, 163 n.4
"Dislocation of the West, The" (Sakai), 154 n.9
Doolittle, Hilda (H.D.), 33, 158 n.16, 158 n.17
Du Bois, W. E. B., 6
Duncan, Robert, 160 n.10

East/West binary, 11–13, 29, 120, 126, 154 nn.8–9
Eliot, T. S., 169 n.11
Ellman, Maud, 125, 144, 167 n.3, 169 n.15
*Epistemology of the Closet* (Sedgwick), 164 n.12
"Ezra Pound" (Ellman), 125, 169 n.15
*Ezra Pound and the Mysteries of Love* (Miyake), 119
*Ezra Pound's Cathay* (Yip), 167 n.3

*Factory Women in Taiwan* (Kung), 165–166 n.17
"Fake Taiwanese People" (anonymous), 157 n.10
February Twenty-eighth Incident, 28
*Female Masculinity* (Halberstam), 160–161 n.13
"Feminist Knots" (Ding), 97
"Feminist Poetic of Hsia Yü, The" (Yeh), 81, 100–101, 103, 153 n.2, 165 n.15
*Fenhurst* (Stein), 54, 160 n.8, 167 n.1
Fenollosa, Ernest, 119, 126, 167 n.3
*Five Faces of Modernity* (Calinescu), 153 n.1, 153 n.5
"Force of Fantasy, The" (Butler), 160 n.10
Foucault, Michel, 121, 164 n.12
Fragmentation. See Modernism: formal qualities of
Freeman, Elizabeth, 68–69
Freud, Sigmund, 161–162 n.16

*Friction Ineffable* (Hsia Yü), 105, 162–163 n.3
*Frozen Torch, The* (Shang Ching), 157 n.4.
*Fusion Kitsch* (Bradbury), 104, 162–163 n.3

Gates, Hill, 157–158 n.12, 165 n.16
"Gender and Labor Politics of Postmodernity, The" (Ong), 165 n.16
"Genet's Genealogy" (Lloyd), 5
*Geographical History of America, The* (Stein), 1, 18, 54, 64, 73–79
George, Rosemary, 53, 72, 160 n.7, 164 n.13
*Ghostlier Demarcations* (Davidson), 153 n.1, 158 n.17, 162 n.18, 168–169 n.9
Gilroy, Paul, 6
Guattari, Félix, 5
*Guide to Ezra Pound's "Personae," A* (Ruthven), 158 n.20
*Guide to Kulchur* (Pound), 35, 37–38, 119, 132

Halberstam, Judith, 154 n.6, 160–161 n.13, 161 n.15, 164 n.12
Hall, Stuart, 134
Harvey, David, 153 n.1, 165 n.16
Hawkins, Susan E., 68–69, 70
H.D. *See* Doolittle, Hilda
"History, Allegory, Sexuality" (Reddy), 106, 166–167 n.22
"History as Repetition" (Walker), 162 n.17
"Home in the Empire, Empire in the Home" (George), 160 n.7
"Homes, Houses, Non-Identity" (Reddy), 155 n.14, 170 n.18
*Hsiang-t'u* literature, 29, 89, 158 n.13
Hsia Yü, 6, 8–9, 15, 18, 80–112, 115, 151, 153 n.1, 162–163 n.3, 163 n.7, 164 n.12, 165 n.15, 166 n.19, 166–167 n.22
"Hsilo Bridge" (Yü Kwang-chung), 16–17, 21–26, 34

Huang, Tao-ming Hans, 96–98, 163 n.9
"Hugh Selwyn Mauberley" (Pound), 16–17, 21, 34–43, 44, 119–120, 151
Huters, Theodore, 155 n.12
Hybridity, 4, 6–8, 89–90, 131, 153 n.4; as hybrid cultures, 7

Ideogramic method, 19, 124–127, 143–144
"Ideology and Ideological State Apparatuses" (Althusser), 155–156 n.16
"Image of Africa, An" (Achebe), 160 n.6
*Immigrant Acts* (Lowe), 33, 111, 155–156 n.16
Imperial anticolonialism, 7, 153 n.3, 168 n.5
Imperialism, 4, 141, 153 n.3; models of, 7, 63–64. *See also* Modernism: and U.S. imperialism; United States: neocolonialism
*In Other Worlds* (Spivak), 149, 155 n.15
Internal colonialism, 7, 153 n.3
Isaak, Jo Anna, 56, 70, 160 n.10, 162 n.21

James, William, 76
Jameson, Fredric, 3, 17, 46–47, 51, 53–54, 58, 64–66, 76, 153 n.1, 159 nn.2–3
JanMohamed, Abdul, 5–6, 164–165 n.14
Johnson, Marshall, 28, 30, 84–85, 93, 163 nn.5–6

Kang, L. Hyun Yi, 169 n.12
Keirnan, V.G., 31, 155 n.13
Kenner, Hugh, 119, 158 n.19, 168 n.4
Kim, Elaine H., 127
KMT (Kuomintang), 7, 13, 24, 27–29, 31, 84, 157 n.3
Ko, Ching-ming, 157 n.6, 158 n.14
Korea, 114–116, 127–129, 134, 136, 139–140, 142, 169 n.13
Kung, Lydia, 165–166 n.17

"Language Strategies" (Yip), 25

Latour, Bruno, 8, 13, 126, 153 n.4, 159–160 n.5
"Leaving on a Jet Plane" (Chan), 83
"Leaving on a Jet Plane" (Hsia Yü), 80, 83–94, 102, 106, 163 n.7
*Lectures in America* (Stein), 17, 54–55, 63–67, 69–70, 74, 77, 167 n.1
Li, Yuanzhen, 81, 95, 162 n.1, 166 n.19
"*Lianliankan*" (Hsia Yü), 165 n.15
Liao, Chaoyang, 155 n.11
Liao, Ping-hui, 157 n.12
Liao, Sebastian Hsien-hao, 103, 158 n.13, 162 n.1
"Liberatory Voice of Thersa Hak Kyung Cha's *Dictee*, The" (Kang), 169 n.12
*Literary Culture and U.S. Imperialism* (Rowe), 158 n.18
*Literary Essays* (Pound), 158 n.16
Liu, Jen-peng, 94–95, 97–99, 105, 163 n.4
Lloyd, David, 5–6, 164–165 n.14
*Location of Culture, The* (Bhabha), 10, 157 n.7
*Lord Jim* (Conrad), 17, 45–54, 159 n.2, 159–160 n.5
"Love and Country in Latin America" (Sommer), 97
Lowe, Lisa, 33, 111, 127–128, 134, 136, 155–156 n.16, 170 n.17
Lowell, Amy, 167 n.3
*Lure of the Modern, The* (Shih), 169 n.10

*Making of Americans, The* (Stein), 54, 57, 60–63, 74, 76–77, 160 n.8
"Making Sentences" (Hsia Yü), 106–112
"Making Time" (Johnson), 28, 30, 84–85, 163 nn.5–6
*Mapping Literary Modernism* (Quinones), 153 n.1, 153 n.4
Martin, Fran, 163 n.4
"Materialism's Mutiny" (Liao), 103
McClintock, Anne, 154 n.7
"Me and My Unicorn" (Hsia Yü), 105

"Melanctha" (Stein), 57, 67–68, 162 n.20
*Memoranda* (Hsia Yü), 106, 111, 162–163 n.3
Mies, Maria, 165 n.16
"Migrating Present, The" (Reddy), 155 n.14
"Mind, the Body and Gertrude Stein, The" (Stimpson), 57
Minority discourse. *See* Minor literature: definition of
Minor literature: vs. canonical function, 5–6, 9, 16, 21–43, 45, 128, 133–135, 138, 143–144, 146, 149–152, 155 n.15; definition of, 5–6, 164–165 n.14; as minor modernism, 4–5, 8–9, 14, 16–19, 21–26, 95, 100, 150, 153 n.4; vs. normative sexuality, 95–112
"Missile Internationalism" (Chen), 13, 21, 26, 29, 89
Mitter, Swati, 165 n.16
Miyake, Akiko, 119
Miyoshi, Masao, 26
*Modern Chinese Muses* (Chung), 103
Modernism: and countermodernism, 135, 143, 144; as criticism of modernity, 1–5, 7–9, 14, 17, 34, 35, 38, 41, 52, 82, 120, 135, 149–150, 159–160 n.5; cultural politics of, 1–19, 26, 33, 60, 82, 148–152, 153 n.4; differences between U.S. and British forms, 3, 17–18, 26, 33, 35–38, 41–42, 44–56, 63–66, 121–123, 159–160 n.5; formal qualities of, 1–18 passim, 21, 24–26, 33, 35–37, 46–48, 51, 81, 94–95, 99, 130–131, 143–144, 158 n.16; and history, 2–4, 7–19, 23, 25–26, 33–39, 41, 45–48, 52, 54–55, 58–60, 63, 72–74, 78–79, 82, 84, 100, 102, 114–120, 127–136, 139–143, 147, 162 n.17; and modernity, 1–19, 21–43, 46, 52, 54, 58, 72–74, 81–94, 97, 101–102, 106, 115, 145–146, 151–152; and postmodernism, 57, 59, 99–101, 154 n.6; as Pound's historiography,

113–114, 118–127; and progress, 1–5, 8–11, 15–17, 25, 34, 36–37, 45–46, 52, 55–56, 59, 62–63, 72–73, 75, 78, 106, 109, 129, 139–140, 153 n.1; and realism, 2, 4, 16–17, 47, 61, 65, 76, 102, 135, 140–142, 144–146, 157 n.6, 161 n.15, 162 n.17; representational crisis of, 2–3, 34, 55, 59; and subjectivity, 2–4, 9, 12, 38, 41, 48, 53, 81, 89, 105–106, 155 n.15; as subversive, 3–4, 7–8, 59, 163 n.4; and temporal disjuncture, 9, 13, 24, 40, 48–49, 111, 148, 151; and universalism, 4–5, 8, 14, 16–17, 19, 21, 37, 43, 51–52, 63, 72, 111, 113–114, 118, 120, 123, 125–126, 143–144, 149, 169 n.10; and U.S. imperialism, 3–19, 21, 25–26, 33– 47, 53–79, 120, 122–127; Western representations of China in, 12, 122–124, 126, 154 n.8, 154–155 n.10, 167–168 n.4, 169 n.10; as Western self-definition, 8, 11, 42, 81, 150. *See also* Minor literature: as modernism; Nondevelopmental form; Taiwan: modernism of

"Modernism and Imperialism" (Jameson), 46–47, 51, 53–54, 76

*Modernism and the Nativist Resistance* (Chang), 158 n.13

"More on Power/Knowledge" (Spivak), 164–165 n.14

*Nationalism at the Crossroads* (Liao), 158 n.13

"Nation in the Eyes of Taiwan's Woman Poets, The" (Li), 81, 95, 166 n.19

*Nature and Context of Minority Discourse, The* (JanMohamed and Lloyd), 5–6, 164–165 n.14

Neocolonialism, 4, 13–14, 16, 18–19, 21, 26, 30, 34, 97, 98, 116, 130, 134, 139–140, 146, 150–152, 155 n.13, 169 n.13; knowledge formations of, 81–94; neocolonial modernities defined, 7

*New Imperialism, The* (Keirnan), 155 n.13, 169 n.13

Ni, Jiazhen, 166 n.21

Nielson, A. L., 67–68, 162 nn.19–20

"1960s Modernist Literature?" (Ko), 157 n.6

Niranjana, Tejaswini, 6; 19, 118, 120–122, 130–133, 136, 167 n.2

Nondevelopmental form, 4–7, 64–66, 73, 128, 138; as allegory, 10, 14–16, 18–19, 25–26, 36, 73–79, 106–112, 117–119, 127, 131–133, 135–136, 141–144, 155–156 n.16; as hesitation, 51–52, 76; and minority discourse, 5; as new universalism, 8–9, 14, 16–18, 37, 41, 45, 52, 125–126, 135, 143–144, 151. *See also* Modernism: formal qualities of

Omi, Micheal, 153 n.3

Ong, Aiwa, 165 n.16

*Orientalism and Modernism* (Qian), 122, 167–168 n.4

*Origin of German Tragic Drama, The* (Benjamin), 14, 77–78, 130–133

*Orlando* (Woolf), 158 n.16

"Other Solution, The" (Chou), 119

*Parallax Visions* (Cumings), 4, 26, 30–31, 33, 114, 157–158 n.12

*Patriarchy and Accumulation on a World Scale* (Mies), 165 n.16

*People's History of the United States, A* (Zinn), 32

"Perfect Lie, The" (Martin), 163 n.4

*Personae* (Pound), 124

Phillips, Steven, 87

*Pocahontas's Daughters* (Dearborn), 62–63

"Poetics of Reticence, The" (Tsai), 98–99

Poetry, 15–16, 24, 26, 33–37, 41, 60, 89, 94–95, 99–103, 124, 148–149; as Chinese poetics 25, 95, 98, 100, 103,

Poetry (*continued*)
    164–165 n.14; formal elements defined, 15–16
"Poised on the In-Between" (Kim), 127
*Political Unconscious, The* (Jameson), 47, 153 n.1, 159 nn.2–3
*Politics of Modernism, The* (Williams), 153 n.1
"Politics of the Possible, The" (Sangari), 10–13, 58–60
"Politics of Translation, The" (Spivak), 136, 166 n.18
Postcolonial modernities, 10–11, 13, 164 n.13
Pound, Ezra, 8–9, 16–17, 18–19, 21, 33, 81, 113–114, 118–120, 122–127, 132–134, 143–144, 150–151, 154–155 n.10, 158 nn.16–17, 167–168 nn.3–4, 168–169 nn.6–9, 169 n.11, 169 n.15
*Pound Era, The* (Kenner), 119, 158 n.19, 168 n.4
*Problem of a Chinese Aesthetic, The* (Saussy), 100, 164–165 n.14
"Professing Stein/Stein Professing" (Bernstein), 67, 162 n.19

*Q.E.D.* (Stein), 57
Qian, Zhaoming, 122, 167–168 n.4
"Queer Syntactic Strategy" (Freeman), 68–69
Quinones, Ricardo J., 153 n.1, 153 n.4

*Racial Formation in the United States* (Omi and Winant) 153 n.3
*Reading Race* (Nielson), 67–68, 162 nn.19–20
"Recycling" (George), 72
Reddy, Chandan, 15, 106, 155 n.14, 166–167 n.22, 170 n.18
"Renaissance, The" (Pound), 113
"Rethinking Modernity" (Rofel), 165 n.16

"Reticent Poetics, Queer Politics" (Liu and Ding), 94–95, 97–99, 163 n.4, 164 n.12
"Retrospect, A" (Pound), 158 n.16
"Revolutionary Power of a Woman's Laughter, The" (Isaak), 56, 162 n.21
"Rewriting National Taiwanese History" (Liao), 157 n.12
Rofel, Lisa, 165 n.16, 166 n.20
Rowe, John Carlos, 159 n.18
Rubinstein, Murray A., 88, 163 n.8
Ruthven, K. K., 158 n.20

Said, Edward, 4, 35–36, 41, 46–47, 57, 161 n.14, 167–168 n.4
Sakai, Naoki, 154 n.9
*Salsa* (Hsia Yü), 94, 162–163 n.3
Sangari, Kumkum, 10–13, 47, 58–60, 161 n.14
Saussure, Ferdinand de, 77
Saussy, Haun, 100, 164–165 n.14
*Search for Modern China, The* (Spence), 27, 157 n.9
Sedgwick, Eve Kosofsky, 164 n.12
Sexuality: and bar stigma in Taiwan, 163 n.9; as challenge to heterosexual matrix, 56–57, 69; changing understandings of, in modernism, 2; and critique of gender norms, 70–73, 103, 115, 128, 146–147; as excluded absence in modernism, 58–59; as Freeman's erotic syntax, 68–69; Freud's ambivalence on, 161–162 n.16; and historical specificity of lesbian identity, 160–161 n.13; lesbian writing of, 161 n.15; and Marxism, 166 n.18; new representational possibilities for, 18, 70, 95, 99; nonnormative or alterior knowledge formations of, 6, 12, 13–15, 81, 91, 105–112, 155 n.14, 170 n.17; queer theorizations of, 164 nn.12–13; and the quotidian, 81, 83, 85, 151; as Reddy's allegorical repository, 15,

166–167 n.22; and reticence, 94–112; state regulation of, 96–97; Stein's allegorical histories of, 46, 73–79, 115; and universalism, 115, 128, 134–139, 142, 147
Shang Ching, 157 n.4
Sharp, Jenny, 47–48, 159 n.4
Shih, Shumei, 166 n.20, 169 n.10
Silverberg, Miriam, 15–157 n.1
*Siting Translation* (Niranjana), 120–122, 167 n.2
*Skin Shows* (Halberstam), 164 n.12
*Sneak Previews* (Hawkins), 68–69, 70
Solomon, Jon, 157 n.8
Sommer, Doris, 97
Spence, Jonathan, 27, 157 n.9
*Spirit of Romance, The* (Pound), 123
Spivak, Gayatri Chakravorty, 102–103, 134, 136, 149, 155 n.15, 164 n.10, 164–165 n.14, 166 n.18, 167 n.23, 169–170 n.16, 170 n.17
"State Power, Prostitution, and Sexual Order in Taiwan" (Huang), 96–97, 163 n.9
Stein, Gertrude, 1, 8, 9; 17–19, 33, 35, 44–46, 53–79, 81, 95, 115–116, 120
Stimpson, Catherine, 57
Sublation, 16, 18, 25, 34, 81, 85, 88, 106, 109, 111–112, 144, 155–156 n.16, 164 n.10, 166–167 nn.22–23

Taiwan, 5–6; history of, 26–28, 155 n.13, 157–158 n.12, 165–166 n.17; Japanese occupation of, 13, 27, 29–31, 84; modernism of, 2–4, 12, 150, 158 n.13.; modernity of, 7, 13, 18–19, 21–31, 81–94, 96–97, 101, 164 n.12, 169 n.13; question of national identity in, 82–84, 101–102, 109, 163 n.5. *See also* KMT; Neocolonialism: knowledge formations of
"Taiwan Incorporated" (Solomon), 157 n.8

"Taiwan's Socioeconomic Modernization" (Rubinstein), 88, 163 n.8
"Task of the Translator, The" (Benjamin), 121, 136
Tay, William, 167 n.3
*Tender Buttons* (Stein), 18, 54, 57, 60, 66–73, 77
Terrell, Carroll F., 168 n.8
*Three Essays on the Theory of Sexuality* (Freud), 161–162 n.16
"Three Feminist Readings" (Spivak), 102–103, 164 n.10, 166 n.18, 167 n.23, 169–170 n.16
"Through the Open Door" (Bradbury), 154–155 n.10
Time lag, 10
Translation, 12, 13–14 (defined), 119; as colonial discourse, 120–122, 13–131; as interventionary, 6, 19, 114, 116, 118 (defined), 128–138, 142, 145, 147; as modernist or ideogramic universalism, 19, 114, 119–120, 124–127, 168–169 n.9; and subjectivity, 128, 137–138
Tsai, Ying-chun, 98–99

"Ukiyo-E" (Tay), 167 n.3
"Unfaithful to the Original" (Lowe), 127–128, 134, 136, 170 n.17
United States: as foreign "mainland" for Taiwan, 23; imperialism and culture of, 3–6, 9, 13–14, 16–19, 33–47, 51, 54–79 passim, 83, 85, 88–90, 114–116, 118–119, 122–127, 150, 158 n.18; imperialism in Asia, 4, 13–14, 16, 26, 30–33, 55, 96–97, 116, 129–130, 139, 146, 151, 166–167 n.22, 169 n.13; neocolonialism vs. British colonialism, 3, 6, 17–18, 26, 32–33, 41–42, 44–47, 63–66, 116, 121–122; as synonymous with the West, 29, 85, 89. *See also* Modernism: differences between U.S. and British forms; Modernism: and U.S. imperialism

*Ventriloquy* (Hsia Yü), 80–81, 102–106, 162–163 n.3, 165 n.15, 166 n.21
*Voyage Out, The* (Woolf), 53

Wald, Priscilla, 75–77
Walker, Jane, 162 n.17
Wang, Peter Chen-main, 157 n.8
*Wasteland, The* (Eliot), 169 n.11
*We Have Never Been Modern* (Latour), 126, 153 n.4, 159–160 n.5
Weng Wen Hsian, 100, 157 n.6, 162 n.1
"What Is a Minor Literature" (Deleuze and Guattari), 5
"What Women Demand of Technology" (Mitter), 165 n.16

Williams, William Appleman, 31, 153 n.3, 168 n.5
Williams, Raymond, 153 n.1
Winant, Howard, 153 n.3
Wright, Richard, 6
*Writing Self, Writing Nation*, 127
*Writings of William James, The*, 76
Woolf, Virginia, 53, 158 n.16

Yeh, Michelle, 81, 100–101, 103, 153 n.2, 162–163 nn.1–2, 165 n.15
Yip, Wai-lim, 25, 157 n.5, 167 n.3
Yü, Kwang-chung, 16–17; 21–26, 150–151

Zinn, Howard, 31, 32

Chapter 2 first appeared as "Modernism and Domesticity: From Conrad's Eastern Road to Stein's Empty Spaces in the Home," in *Burning Down the House: Recycling Domesticity* (Politics and Culture Book Series, vol. 7), ed. Rosemary Marangoly George (Boulder: HarperCollins/Westview Press, 1998). Reprinted by permission of Westview Press, a member of Perseus Books, L.L.C.

A portion of chapter 4 first appeared in "'For the Other Overlapping Time': Sexuality and the Allegorical Temporalities of Translation in *Dictee*," trans. Chen Ting (into Chinese), in *Remapping the Territory of Literary Studies: Perspectives on Foreign Literatures from Taiwan*, ed. Pin-chia Feng (Hsinchu: National Chiao Tung University Press, 1999). Reprinted by permission.

Amie Elizabeth Parry is an associate professor in the English Department at National Central University in Taiwan.

*Library of Congress Cataloging-in-Publication Data*

Parry, Amie Elizabeth
Interventions into modernist cultures : poetry from beyond the empty screen / Amie Elizabeth Parry.
p. cm. — (Perverse modernities)
Includes bibliographical references and index.
   ISBN-13: 978-0-8223-3803-1 (acid-free paper)
   ISBN-13: 978-0-8223-3818-5 (pbk. : acid-free paper)
1. American poetry—20th century—History and criticism.
2. Chinese poetry—Taiwan—History and criticism. 3. Pound, Ezra, 1885–1972—Criticism and interpretation. 4. Stein, Gertrude, 1874–1946—Criticism and interpretation. 5. Yu, Guangzhong, 1928—Criticism and interpretation. 6. Xia, Yu, 1956—Criticism and interpretation. 7. Literature, Comparative—American and Chinese. 8. Literature, Comparative—Chinese and American. 9. Modernism (Literature)—United States. 10. Modernism (Literature)—Taiwan. I. Title.
PS310.M57P36 2007
811'.5409—dc22   2006032813

www.ingramcontent.com/pod-product-compliance
Lightning Source LLC
Chambersburg PA
CBHW051542230426
43669CB00015B/2688